General Principles of Business Law

GW00497276

General Principles
of
Business Law

Questions and Answers

B.S.Grewal – B.A., LL.M., F.A.B.E., of Inner Temple, Barrister,
Chief Examiner of the Association of Business Executives

J.D.DeFreitas – LL.M., M.A., F.A.B.E., Solicitor,
Examiner in Business Law to the Association
of Business Executives

Castlevale, London

First published by Castlevale Ltd, 1980
Second Edition, 1984
Third Edition, 1992

Castlevale Ltd
William House
14 Worple Road
Wimbledon
London SW19
081–879 1973

ISBN 0 907235 06 9

Typesetting by Capital Impressions, London
Printed in Great Britain by BPCC Wheatons Ltd, Exeter

Contents

To my parents Ajit and Rattan Grewal

Preface to the Third Edition

Once again, this edition has been substantially rewritten and updated, on the basis of comment received from tutors and students who have used the 'Green Book' over the years. The authors have taken this opportunity of revising the text in the light of cases like Williams v. Roffey Bros. and Nicholls (1990) and Caparo Industries plc v. Dickman and Other (1990). In response to the changes in the syllabus of I.C.S.A. this edition covers the areas relating to intellectual property and the Consumer Protection Act 1987. Chapter 10 has been rearranged and substantially rewritten. Technical questions relating to Trust Accounts and Bankruptcy have been excluded. This edition has taken into account the changes in the law in the syllabuses of the various professional bodies.

We are grateful to the following examining bodies for permission to reproduce questions from their past examination papers:

Chartered Association of Certified Accountants
Chartered Institute of Management Accountants
Institute of Chartered Secretaries and Administrators
Association of Business Accountants
Chartered Institute of Bankers
Association of Accounting Technicians

We trust that all students of Law will find this work a valuable guide.

Temple Chambers   *B.Grewal*
Temple Avenue   *January 1992*
London EC4Y 0HP

Examination Technique

We know from experience that most students work very hard, but that very many fail to do justice to themselves in the examination. We firmly believe that this is because many do not know what is expected of them, and are not familiar with the technique of writing specific answers in response to specific questions.

GENERAL
Students should bear the following general points in mind:
1. Read the instructions in the question paper carefully. Do not assume they are the same as last year's.
2. Read **all** the questions carefully before starting to write the answers. Do not worry if your mind goes completely blank when you first read them. You might even feel that you cannot answer a single question. Re-read the questions, and you will be pleasantly surprised to discover that there are some you can answer. Once you start writing you will recall things you learnt a long time ago, which were stored somewhere in the deep recesses of your memory.
3. Do your easiest question first, but not before you have read the others. To start by answering your easiest question calms your nerves, and gives you all-important confidence.
4. You **must** budget your time and allocate almost equal time to each question. However, it is not unusual to spend a little more time on your first answer. You will find that your writing speed improves with time. You should allow yourself ten or fifteen minutes to spare at the end for a final check-up on all answers.
5. Plan your answers in rough outline before you begin writing. Write down all the points you wish to discuss, and the names of relevant cases. As soon as you think of another point, write it down before it escapes your memory. It is perfectly reasonable to make rough notes on your examination script. You need not be anxious about the examiner's noticing your rough sketch. In our experience, it creates a favourable impression on the examiner; it is a sign of an orderly mind.
6. Do not answer a question any part of which you do not understand.
7. Answer the question asked, and not the one you hoped to find. It is a mistake to assume that the mention of a topic in

the question is an invitation for you to write everything you know about that and other related subjects. You must answer the question asked, and no other. Pages of irrelevant material are a waste of your valuable time, earn no marks, and may annoy the examiner.

8. Remember that the examiner has prepared a marking scheme allocating marks to different parts of the question. It is essential that you answer all the questions you are required to answer. You must not spend a disproportionate amount of time on any question or part of it. You must answer all parts of the question even if it is in note form. Remember – no answer, no marks!

9. It is in your interest to get the examiner on your side. It should not come as a surprise to you that examination scripts are marked under pressure and in a hurry. Examiners have to meet the deadline set by the examining bodies. Try to help the examiner by writing neatly. Make use of headings and sub-headings, and underline important parts of your answer. Examiners hate dull-looking unbroken long essays.

10. Start each answer on a new page, and always leave some space at the end of each answer. You might wish to add to your answer at a later stage.

11. We know that it is easier said than done, but if at all possible check over answers at the end. You may have missed out the important negative which is vital to your answer.

12. Don't leave the examination room before the end of the examination. Even if you are unable to think of anything else to write, stay there. Your subconscious mind might retrieve some valuable information.

USE OF CASES

Do not be over-anxious about the number of cases you will have to encounter and remember. They are intended to illustrate the legal principles stated, and are not meant to be committed to memory in their entirety. As a rule it is sufficient to cite one case to support a legal point.

Of course it looks better if you can remember the names of the cases, but it is not essential to remember all of them. You are expected to remember names of only important and well-known ones. If your memory is not good, don't despair. It is sufficient to say 'in a well-known case'; if you know it, it must be well known. The examiner is interested in finding out whether you understand the principle established in a particular case, and does not expect you to relate the facts of the case in great detail. Resist the temptation to retell the 'story' in your own humorous and irresistible style, even if your tutor does so in class; the examiner has heard it before. However, you must give sufficient facts to make sure of the decision.

It is of very little use to put the name of a case in brackets at the end of a paragraph without comment. We are aware that some text book writers do not set a good example.

It is permissible to invent hypothetical cases to illustrate your point as long as you make it clear that they are your own invention. Do not pretend that they are facts of some recent fictitious case.

ALWAYS UNDERLINE CASE-NAMES AND REFERENCES TO STATUTES.

ANSWERING PROBLEM QUESTIONS

This type of question is meant to test your ability to apply basic legal principles to factual situations. Many candidates fail because they do not display their knowledge sufficiently, and leave too much unsaid.

You should identify the legal points involved, explain the relevant principles, apply them to a given set of facts and come to a conclusion. You must come to a conclusion; but it need not be a definite one. It is permissible to suggest alternatives, and make reasonable assumptions about additional facts or other information. Many problems are deliberately set with scope for agreement on both sides.

Remember it is the reasoning that earns marks, not a good guess at the right conclusion. The examiner wishes to see your reasoning set out in the script. You earn good marks even if you reach the 'wrong' conclusion, i.e., different from that of the examiner.

If you are asked to advise one of the parties, there is no need to write a personal letter with all the necessary details. You should do it in the form of a note or memorandum concluding "John Smith is advised...", or "It is submitted John Smith is unlikely to succeed...". Clever answers like "John Smith is advised to consult his solicitors" should be avoided. You should concentrate on giving legal advice. Extra-legal advice regarding an individual's moral obligations, etc. should be avoided. Answers based on common sense are unlikely to earn many marks. The examiner expects legal advice, supported by legal authority.

Firm grip of the facts is essential. If the facts are complicated, you may draw diagrams (which you can cross out afterwards) to understand the problem exactly.

Students must accept facts given. It is not very clever to criticise the examiner by suggesting or implying that the facts are insufficient, or that the question could have been better drafted. Similarly, it is not desirable to sound patronising by saying "It is a good question", etc.

Chapter 1

Sources of Law

QUESTION 1 What is meant by:
(a) European Community Law; and
(b) a Code of Practice?
Explain in both cases the extent to which these are sources of English Law.

I.C.M.A. 1980

ANSWER (a) The United Kingdom became part of the European Community on the 1st of January 1973 after signing the Treaty of Accession in 1972. As it is a cardinal principle of the British Constitution that no treaty can bind the country unless an Enabling Act is passed by Parliament, the European Communities Act 1972 was passed and placed in the Statute Book. This Act provided for the immediate incorporation of Community Law in the English legal system.

European Law is made up of Primary Law and Secondary Law. Primary Law is the law contained in the three Community Treaties, namely the Treaty of Paris 1951 and the two treaties of Rome 1957. Secondary Law is the law made by the Council of Ministers. The power to make Secondary Law is derived from Article 189 of the E.E.C. Treaty and it may take the form of a Regulation, Decision or a Directive.

A Regulation is similar to an Act of Parliament in that it is self-executing and it applies to all member states in the Common Market. A Regulation normally covers matters to do with the freedom of movement amongst member states of workers, goods, capital and business.

A Decision also has direct effect in a national legal system but it differs from a Regulation in that while the latter is of general application, the former applies within the particular state to which it is addressed. A Decision is generally of an administrative nature, implementing Community Law by either granting exemption to a member state or by imposing fines for non-compliance. It may cover matters relating to common agricultural policy or common transport.

A Directive is an instrument requiring a stated objective to be achieved but it leaves the means by which this is to be done for each state to decide. An example of a Directive is the 1968

Directive on company capacity which was enacted in the United Kingdom by section 9 of the European Communities Act 1972.

The European Court of Justice hears dispute as to the application and interpretation of E.E.C. Law, but its decision only forms a persuasive rather than a binding precedent in the U.K.

(b) A Code of Practice is similar to delegated legislation in that the power to issue a Code is conferred by statute on a specified body. For example, the Advisory, Conciliation and Arbitration Service (ACAS) is given power under the Employment Protection (Consolidation) Act 1978 to issue Codes of Practice containing 'such practical guidance as the Service thinks fit for the purpose of promoting the improvement of industrial relations'. Similarly, the Health and Safety Commission is empowered under the Health and Safety at Work Act 1974 S.16 to issue Codes to promote health and safety. A Code of Practice is not, however, legally binding. Nevertheless, it is admissible evidence in legal proceedings and although judges are not legally bound to agree with a particular Code, they must at least take it into account before reaching a decision. In criminal proceedings a breach of a Code may be *prima facie* evidence of contravention of the provisions of the Act to which the Code relates (see S.17 Health and Safety at Work Act 1974).

QUESTION 2 Explain and discuss the principles adopted by the court in the interpretation of statutes.

A.C.C.A. 1982

ANSWER The meaning of a statute is seldom absolutely clear and as judges must follow the law, the courts have had to develop certain rules of construction to ascertain the true intention of Parliament. The main rules of interpretation are:

(a) **The Literal Rule.** This rule states that the words of a statute should be interpreted according to their ordinary and grammatical sense as used in the Oxford Dictionary.

(b) **The Golden Rule.** This rule is a modification of the literal rule. It states that if in using the literal rule, this would lead to absurdity or some repugnancy or inconsistency with the rest of the statute, then the grammatical and ordinary meaning of the word should be modified so as to avoid that absurdity or inconsistency. For example, in **Adler v. George (1964)** the defendant was charged with obstructing members of the air force on their RAF base. It was an offence under the Official Secrets Act 1920 to obstruct H.M. Forces 'in the vicinity' of a prohibited place. The defendant argued that he had not committed an offence under the Act because 'in the vicinity' meant 'surrounding' the base and not 'in' the base. However, Lord Parker C.J. said 'in the vicinity' should not be read literally but should be used to include 'in' the prohibited place itself as it would otherwise lead to absurdity.

(c) **The Mischief Rule or Rule in Heydon's Case.** It states that to find out the true meaning of a statute, four matters must be considered: the common law before the Act was passed; the mischief and defect for which the common law did not provide; the remedy Parliament had resolved to cure the defect; and the reason for the remedy. The court may have regard to the preamble of the statute, the long title, headings and to extrinsic sources such as Royal Commissions and Law Reform Committees to ascertain the mischief which the statute was intended to correct. The Mischief Rule was used in **Gorris v. Scott (1874)** where the plaintiff suffered loss when his sheep were washed overboard while the defendant was engaged in carrying them by sea. The plaintiff contended that he was entitled to bring a civil action against the defendant as the latter had breached a statute which required shipowners to provide pens when carrying animals on board their ships. However, the court said that the reason for the rule to provide pens was not to prevent loss overboard but to minimise the spread of contagious disease by animals and as such the plaintiff's loss did not fall within the mischief of the Act.

(d) **The *Eiusdem Generis* Rule.** This rule states that where general words follow specific words, the general words should be taken as referring to those things of the same class as specifically mentioned. In **Powell v. Kempton Pk. Racecourse Co. (1899)** The Betting Act 1853 prohibited the keeping of a 'house, office, room, or other place' for betting with persons resorting thereto. The court held that 'other place' did not apply to an uncovered enclosure adjacent to the racecourse. For the *Eiusdem Generis* rule to apply, there has to be at least two specific words to create a genus. Thus, in **Allen v. Emmerson (1944)** where a statute referred to 'theatres and other places of amusement', it was held that a funfair was within the Act even though not within the same class as 'theatres'.

(e) **The *Noscitur a Sociis* Rule.** It states that a word in isolation has no absolute meaning. Its meaning is relative to the context in which it is used.

3

Apart from rules, there are also presumptions used as aids for interpretation of statutes. The following are among the most important ones:– *the presumption that an Act does not alter the law unless the contrary is shown:* thus when the Criminal Evidence Act 1898 was passed making a wife competent to give evidence against her husband when formerly she could not do so, the House of Lords in **Leach v. R. (1912)** held that because of the absence of express provision, the Act did not intend to make her compellable to give evidence; *the presumption that an Act does not bind the Crown:* this presumption extends to the Crown's agents and servants though not to nationalised industries **(Tamlin v. Hannaford 1950)**; *the presumption that an Act does not have retrospective effect;* and *the presumption against the imposition of liability without fault.*

QUESTION 3 (a) What is delegated legislation?
(b) What are its advantages and disadvantages when compared with Acts of Parliament?

A.C.C.A. 1982

ANSWER (a) In so far as domestic law is concerned, Parliament is the supreme lawgiver and the judges must follow laws made by Parliament. These laws are made by the passing of 'bills' which, on receiving the Royal Assent, become Acts of Parliament. Once made they bind everyone and the court has no power to question their regularity. Moreover, they remain law until repealed by a subsequent Act of Parliament. This supremacy of Parliament is called the 'sovereignty of Parliament'.

Because of the lengthy process of making statute law, Parliament is obviously overworked. Thus, it is usual to delegate this legislative authority to subordinate bodies such as the Privy Council which make laws by issuing orders-in-council; to Government Ministers who issue statutory instruments and to local authorities which make by-laws. These orders-in-council, statutory instruments and by-laws are termed 'Delegated Legislation'. A vast amount of laws is made in this way and the main feature which distinguishes it from Acts of Parliament is that while Parliament is sovereign these subordinate bodies with legislative power are not.

(b) There are various reasons for the increased delegation of legislative powers by Parliament in modern times. It eases the pressure on parliamentary time to deal with other important and pressing matters. Legislative authority is frequently given to subordinate bodies because the subject matter requiring regulation may be too technical for ordinary Members of Parliament. For example, if Parliament wants to regulate traffic in Piccadilly Circus it will be prudent to leave this to Westminster Council which has first hand knowledge of the traffic congestion in the area and the desired remedy, rather than to leave it to a Member of Parliament, say from the Isle of Wight. As parliamentary procedure is slow and cumbersome, Parliament may delegate its powers to another body if immediate action is required, especially in times of national crisis. Such powers are frequently exercised by orders-in-council.

Despite its advantages, various arguments have been raised against delegated legislation. Too much power is given to subordinate bodies who in many instances are non-elected bodies removed by a considerable distance from Parliament itself (e.g., the five-tier authority of the Emergency Powers Act 1939). Because delegated legislation is so easy to make (e.g., many statutory instruments take effect once placed before Parliament) it can lead to uncertainty in the law. Moreover, it can lead to an abuse of power, since its sheer volume makes it difficult for Parliament to control.

Two types of control exist over the use of delegated legislation – parliamentary and judicial. Parliamentary control is exercised by the scrutinising of statutory instruments laid before Parliament by the Select Committee on Statutory Instruments set up under the Statutory Instruments Act 1946. This Committee is made up of M.P.s and its function is to check statutory instruments to see that Ministers do not exceed the authority given them by Parliament. The Act also requires publicity of such instruments. For example, Section 3(2) of the Act provides that where a person is charged with contravening the provisions of a statutory instrument it shall be a defence to prove that the instrument had not been issued by Her Majesty's Stationery Office at the date of the alleged contravention unless it is proved that at that date reasonable steps had been taken for the purpose of bringing it to the notice of the public. Judicial control is exercised by the court which has power, on the application of a member of the public to make a declaration that a law made by a subordinate body is ultra vires and void. A recent example of the exercise of the court's power in this area is in **G.L.C. v. Bromley Borough Council (1981)** where the House of Lords held that the G.L.C. cheap fares policy of running London Transport was null and void.

QUESTION 4 (a) Explain what is meant by *ratio decidendi* and *obiter dicta.*
(b) What are the advantages and disadvantages of the doctrine of binding precedent?
(c) When, if at all, can or should a court refrain from following a binding precedent?

A.C.C.A. 1983

ANSWER (a) The decision of a judge in a superior court on a point of law which has not been reversed on appeal, or overruled, binds all judges of an inferior court when faced with similar facts and may even bind the superior court itself. This is known as the doctrine of judicial or binding precedent. This doctrine developed from the decision of William I to preserve Anglo-Saxon laws. Judges were required to declare the law either as a process of example or analogy, or by virtue that it was declared earlier by a competent court and must therefore be followed. This is the Declaratory Theory of the Common Law and it affected only this branch of the law.

Accordingly every judgement would, and still does, include two basic ingredients, namely, the material facts of the case together with the decision reached by the court (this is binding on the parties seeking a solution from the court to their problem and is *res Judicata*); and the legal principle used by the court in reaching that decision (this will bind all future cases with similar facts and is known as *ratio decidendi*). Thus the *ratio decidendi* may be defined as the statement of law applied by the court to the legal problems raised by the material facts upon which the decision is based.

Occasionally, judges will anticipate variation of the material facts and will state the legal principles which would then apply. This is known as *obiter dicta* and is only of persuasive authority. Thus, the *obiter dicta* may be defined as things said by way of illustration or analogy. An example of *obiter dicta* is Denning J.'s famous judgement in **Central London Property Trust Ltd v. High Trees House Ltd (1947)** on promissory estoppel. In that case, although the plaintiffs did not ask for arrears of rent, the learned judge said that had they done so, they would not have succeeded because of their promise to the defendants to take a reduced rent. *Obiter dicta* may also be used to mean statements of law in support of dissenting judgements.

(b) The advantages of the doctrine of binding precedent are that it makes the law more certain, precise and predictable. If the legal problem raised had been solved before, then persons contemplating litigation will know what the result is likely to be. Precedent allows for detailed solution to innumerable factual situations which would not be possible with an Act of Parliament. The law grows and develops according to the changing needs of society and can be altered comparatively easily without requiring lengthy parliamentary proceedings. Precedent is more practical in that there exists no legal rule for which there cannot be found practical illustrations.

The obvious disadvantages of precedent are bulk and complexity. Too many laws are made by judicial precedent with the result that basic principles tend to become obscure. In many instances, the *ratio decidendi* of a case cannot easily be identified with any degree of certainty. This is particularly true where conflicting reasons are given for reaching a decision (e.g., as in **Grunwick Laboratories Ltd v. ACAS & APEX 1978**). Adherence to previous decisions may cause injustice and although there is always the possibility of the precedent being overruled, this may itself create uncertainty.

(c)   In certain circumstances, the court need not follow a binding precedent. The House of Lords need not follow its own *ratio decidendi* in a previous case and the Court of Appeal **may** follow suit in exceptional cases, such as where there are two conflicting decisions of the C.A.; where, in a criminal case, it would lead to injustice **(R. v. Gould 1968);** and where it is only an interlocutory order made by two Lord Justices sitting as the C.A. **(Boys v. Chaplin 1968).** The Court of Appeal **must** refuse to follow the *ratio decidendi* of its own previous decision if it is inconsistent with a later House of Lords one; or if it is *per incuriam* i.e. made in ignorance of a relevant statute or earlier precedent in the House of Lords **(Young v. Bristol Aeroplane Corp. 1944);** or if it is overruled by a higher court. A precedent created by a single High Court judge is not binding on another High Court judge.

QUESTION 5 Explain what you understand by the term 'equity' and outline the chief contribution of equity to English Law.

I.C.S.A. 1973

ANSWER The concept of equity is based on 'justice and fairplay'. In its narrower sense equity means the law administered in the Court of Chancery before the passing of the Judicature Acts 1873-75.

Equity's main contribution to English law is that it filled in the gaps left by common law. Early common law was based on local customary laws which were consolidated and administered generally in the King's Courts. It had major defects. A plaintiff was often unable to obtain a remedy in the King's Courts because of intimidation, or bribery of court's officials by his powerful opponent and even when a remedy was available it often proved inadequate as the only remedy common law could give was damages. Moreover, because of its rigidity, there were several wrongs for which common law did not provide a remedy.

When the plaintiff could get no remedy at common law, it became customary to seek redress from the King by petition. The petition was passed on to the Lord Chancellor who was a clergyman and based his decision on 'conscience' and 'fairplay'. The practice of petitioning became so popular that the Lord Chancellor set up his own Court of Chancery with its own equitable jurisdiction.

Equity as administered in the Court of Chancery filled in the gaps left by common law in three ways:

With its exclusive jurisdiction, it recognised rights which the common law failed to enforce e.g. trusts and mortgages.

With its concurrent jurisdiction, it introduced remedies which the common law failed to provide e.g. specific performance of a contract; an injunction to stay or restrain the repetition of an injury; and the appointment of a receiver to protect property until the outcome of a hearing. These remedies were very useful as an alternative to common law damages.

With its auxiliary jurisdiction, equity introduced new procedures to supplement common law procedures which proved defective. For example, it acted *in personam* and compelled a defendant to give evidence when at common law he could not be ordered to do so.

In the late nineteenth century, equity became a complete system of law in itself so much so that Jessel M.R. in **Re National Funds Assurance (1879)** remarked "This court is not, as I have often remarked, a Court of Conscience, but a Court of Law."

QUESTION 6 Outline the more important changes brought about by the Judicature Acts of 1873-75 and say why they were thought to be necessary. A.C.C.A. 1976

ANSWER The Judicature Acts 1873-75 were passed to implement the recommendation of the Judicature Commission set up in 1867, that the numerous courts with overlapping jurisdiction should be rationalised as they led to duplication of judicial work and caused great inconvenience and financial hardship to Her Majesty's subjects seeking redress.

The Acts made three important changes. They abolished the old common law courts and Courts of Chancery – replacing them with the Supreme Court of Judicature; and merged the administration of common law and equity. Under the new structure there were to be two branches of courts – the upper branch consisting of the Court of Appeal, and the lower branch consisting of the High Court of Justice with its various divisions. All the divisions of the High Court were empowered to administer both common law and equity and could grant both types of remedy. However, certain matters were specifically reserved for each division corresponding roughly with the matters falling within the jurisdiction of the courts they had replaced. Thus, equity and trust were dealt with in the Chancery Division and contract and tort in the Queen's Bench Division. Until 1970 the structure of the Supreme Court remained as it was then, but in 1970 the Administration of Justice Act and in 1971 the Court Acts made further changes in the structure of the jurisdiction of the courts.

It should be emphasised that the Judicature Acts did not merge common law and equity but only the *administration* of common law and equity.

The second important change bought about by the Acts was to resolve the problem where there was a conflict between common law and equity. Each had said that it would supersede the other. However, the Acts provided that where there was a conflict between a rule of common law and a rule of equity, the latter was to prevail.

Finally, the Judicature Acts abolished the forms of action and introduced new rules of procedures for the courts which they create. In effect, the procedure relating to the issue of writs and to other stages of litigation became considerably simplified.

Chapter 2

Courts, Procedure and Evidence

QUESTION 7 (a) Describe the work of the County Court and explain its importance within the English legal system.

(b) Briefly outline the procedure for bringing a case in the County Court up to the date of trial.

A.C.C.A. 1983

ANSWER (a) With the disappearance of the medieval local courts, there was very little provision for the hearing of minor civil claims until the County Courts were created by the County Courts Act 1846. This Act set up a network of courts to make available to the public cheap and speedy justice. Originally, they dealt with cases involving small sums of money until their jurisdiction was extended by subsequent statutes.

County Courts are now governed by the County Courts Act 1959, the County Court Rules and County Court Jurisdiction Orders. There are more than four hundred County Courts in the country grouped into circuits and presided over by county court judges sitting without a jury. Each court has a County Court Registrar who is a solicitor of at least seven years standing, who acts as an assistant judge dealing with pre-trial matters, small claims and the arbitration procedure.

County Courts deal only with civil cases and the limits of their jurisdiction are normally based upon the amount of the claim and the courts' area of operation. Actions in contract and tort, with a few exceptions, are limited to cases where the amount claimed is under £25,000. Claims of an equitable character such as the administration of estates, carrying out of trusts and mortgages matters are limited to £30,000. Actions concerning the title to land and the recovery of possession of land are limited to cases where the net annual value for rating purpose does not exceed £1000. Contentious probate matters are limited to cases where the net value of the estate at the date of death was less than £30,000. Most County Courts can deal with bankruptcy matters without any limit although in the case of the winding up of a company jurisdiction depends on the company's paid up capital. County Courts also have jurisdiction in certain family matters such as undefended divorce cases, guardianship and legitimacy.

As a general rule, the plaintiff must bring his action in the court of the district where the defendant dwells or carries on business unless the action involves land in which case it may be brought in the court of the district in which the land is situated. The jurisdiction of County Courts is constantly being added to. Recent additions include the enforcement of claims under the Race Relations Act 1976 and the Sex Discrimination Act 1975, the power to re-open credit agreements under the Consumer Credit Act 1974 and appeals under the Local Government (Miscellaneous Provisions) Act 1976. The High Court can also refer cases to the County Court.

(b) Proceedings in the County Court are commenced by a form of plaint known as a request for summons which will set out the names and addresses of the parties and the nature and amount of the claim. The registrar's clerk fixes a date for a pre-trial review of the case, transfers the information given in the plaint on to a summons which he then issues. Service of the summons is arranged by the court and is made personally or by post on the defendant not later than 21 days before the return day which, in most ordinary actions, is the day set for the 'pre-trial review'. The summons is accompanied by special reply forms which require the defendant to state his defence or admit liability.

On receipt of the summons the defendant may within 14 days pay a sum into court with a view to stay the proceedings or serve a defence and/or counter-claim or simply turn up on the return day and dispute the claim. Where a defence is filed the registrar will send a copy to the plaintiff.

Most County Court actions never actually come to trial, either through settlement out of court, or through judgement at the pre-trial review where judgement may be given for the plaintiff if the defendant does not file a defence and does not attend, or if a defence has no substance in an action for a liquidated sum up to a prescribed limit (unless an objection is made). Unless the action is disposed of in this way, the trial day is fixed.

If on the day for the trial, the plaintiff does not appear the action is removed from the list and the plaintiff may apply for it to be reinstated subject to explaining the reason for his absence and payment of additional costs. If the defendant does not appear, the plaintiff will set out his case orally or by affidavit and will generally obtain judgement.

QUESTION 8 State the composition and jurisdiction of the following courts: (a) House of Lords (b) Crown Court (c) Family Division of the High Court

A.A.T. (I.A.S.) 1978

ANSWER (a) **House of Lords.** When sitting as a court the House of Lords consists of five judges to deal with a case at any one time. These judges are called Lords of Appeal in Ordinary, and the current Lord Chancellor and former Lord Chancellor can also act as judges. There are up to eleven Lords of Appeal in Ordinary in the House of Lords with one specialising in Scots Law, and another in Irish Law coming from Northern Ireland.

The House of Lords have both a criminal and civil appellate jurisdiction. It may hear appeals in criminal cases from the Court of Appeal (Criminal Division) and from the Divisional Court of the Queens Bench but only where the lower court certifies that the case concerns a point of law of general public importance. It may hear appeals in civil cases from the Court of Appeal (Civil Division), the High Court through leap-frogging procedure, and the Scottish and Northern Ireland Courts. In all cases of appeal to the House of Lords, leave to appeal may be given by the House of Lords itself. The House of Lords is still regarded as the final court of appeal in the land, but its decision on matters relating to the interpretation of the EEC treaties, and on rights conferred on individuals by Common Market Law is not final as appeals may be made to the European Court of Justice.

(b) **Crown Court.** The Court Act 1971 set up the Crown Court when it abolished the Quarter Sessions and Assizes. Cases are tried before a jury and a judge appointed from among High Court judges, Circuit judges and Recorders. Only a barrister of at least 10 years standing may be appointed as a Circuit judge. A Recorder is a part-time judge and must be a barrister or solicitor of at least ten years standing.

The jurisdiction of the Crown Court is to try indictable crimes which are classified into 4 grades of seriousness: **Class 1** offences e.g. treason, murder, genocide; **Class 2** offences e.g., manslaughter, rape, abortion; **Class 3** offences e.g., burglary, theft, robbery; and **Class 4** offences e.g. S.18 Offences Against the Person Act 1861, and forgery in excess of £1000.

The Crown Court also hears appeals by defendants against conviction or sentence from magistrates' courts; and also hands out sentences against defendants committed for sentence from magistrates' courts.

(c) **Family Division of the High Court.** This Division was created by the Administration of Justice Act 1970. It has a President and some sixteen 'puisne' (lesser) judges. Cases are heard by a judge sitting without a jury. Its jurisdiction involves matrimonial matters, proceedings in respect of wardship of minors, adoption and guardianship proceedings, claims concerning S.17 Married Women's Property Act 1882 and Matrimonial Homes Act 1967, and non-contentious probate matters.

The appellate jurisdiction of this Division is exercised by a Divisional Court consisting of two or more judges sitting without a jury. Appeals are heard from Magistrates' Courts in matters relating to matrimonial orders, such as maintenance orders, and guardianship from Magistrates' Courts in affiliation cases, and from Juvenile Courts in adoption cases.

QUESTION 9 State the composition and jurisdiction of the following courts:
(a) European Court of Justice
(b) The Restrictive Practices Court.

ANSWER (a) **European Court of Justice.** It is above the House of Lords, but for most cases arising in the United Kingdom, the House of Lords remains the final court of appeal. In the U.K. the courts must take notice of any decision of, or expression of opinion by the European Court on any question as to validity, meaning or effect of any of the treaties or of any community instrument.

The European Court consists of judges assisted by Advocates-Generals who are not members of the Court and who act *amicus curiae*, by putting before the Court reasoned submissions on all matters which are up for decision. The judges are chosen for a period of six years from judges or jurists and appointed by State Governments.

The jurisdiction of the Court of Justice includes, inter alia,
(i) Giving preliminary rulings concerning:
    (a) interpretation of the treaty
    (b) validity and interpretation of acts of the institutions of the Community. In this way the legality of, for example, the Commission may be challenged.
    (c) interpretation of statutes of bodies established by an Act of Council, where these statutes so provide.
(ii) Where such a question is raised by any Court of a member

state, that Court may, if it considers it necessary in order to give judgement, request the Court of Justice to give a ruling thereon. (iii) Where such a question is raised by any Court of a member state against whose judgement there is no judicial remedy under National Law that Court must bring the matter before the Court of Justice.

(b) **The Restrictive Practices Court.** It has the same status as the High Court of Justice. Under the Restrictive Practices Court Act 1976, it consists of three judges of the English High Court, nominated by the Lord Chancellor, one judge of the Scottish Court of Session, nominated by the Lord President of the Scottish Court and one judge of the Supreme Court of Northern Ireland, nominated by the Lord Chief Justice of that province. It also has ten non-judicial members who have expert knowledge in commerce, industry and public affairs. Cases are normally heard by one judge and two non-judicial members.

The Court's function is to decide whether a restrictive trading agreement is against the public interest. Such an agreement has to be registered with the Director of Fair Trading, a post created under the Fair Trading Act 1973, who will then bring it before the Court for a decision on its validity. The Court's decision will be based mainly on the likely social and economic effects of the agreement.

Appeal lies to the Court of Appeal (Civil Division).

QUESTION 10 Explain the advantages as methods of settling legal disputes of:
(a) arbitration under the Arbitration Acts 1950 to 1979, and
(b) Administrative tribunals.

A.C.C.A. 1983

ANSWER (a) Arbitration is the reference of a matter in dispute to the decision of one or more persons called arbitrators and is an alternative to settling disputes, especially those of a commercial nature, by litigation in the courts. It can arise by contract in which case the procedure is governed by the Arbitration Acts 1950 and 1979. This type of arbitration is called voluntary arbitration, and it requires the consent of both parties. Voluntary arbitration is preferred to litigation because of its informality, economy, speed and privacy.

Legal representation for the parties is prohibited and the parties plead their case in person although they may bring a friend to assist them. This ensures that one party is not placed at a disadvantage to the other party having a solicitor to put his case. Normal judicial procedure including the rules of evidence apply to arbitration but in practice the parties dispense with this, thus ensuring that the proceedings do not become formal or legalistic as with litigation.

By its very nature voluntary arbitration is a cheap method of settling disputes since the expense that is normally incurred in litigation through legal fees does not arise. The parties also decide the time and place for the arbitration and, unlike litigation, do not have to wait on the convenience of the court. By having control of the arbitration, the parties are able to keep the proceedings private and so their business affairs are not published in the press.

(b) Administrative Tribunals are bodies outside the hierarchy of the courts, with judicial or quasi-judicial powers. They are, in the main, set up by statute to ease the pressure of the courts and they deal with disputes arising in certain areas of the law affecting government policies such as rent, national health, tax and conditions of work. Although lawyers may sit on them, in practice they are staffed by laymen with specialised knowledge of the matter with which each tribunal is dealing.

As a method of settling disputes, administrative tribunals are relatively cheaper than the courts and since they only deal with one kind of dispute (e.g. rent) disputes are resolved quicker than in the courts which deal with all kind of disputes with the result that there is always a long waiting list of cases to be heard. As the members of the tribunals are specialists in their field, matters involving a public service are better judged by them rather than be left to the courts. Proceedings in tribunals are not too formal and matters such as social conditions which would normally carry less weight in the ordinary courts, are taken into consideration by the tribunals in arriving at a decision. Because the strict rules of evidence are relaxed, the parties are encouraged to present their own case, rather than forced to obtain legal representation. The decisions of statutory tribunals are subject to the supervision of the High Court.

Tribunals therefore combine all the advantages of speed, flexibility, informality and expertise, with the additional safeguard of the court's supervision.

QUESTION 11 What steps should be taken in an action in the Queen's Bench Division for the price of goods sold and delivered:

(a) on behalf of the plaintiff who believes that the defendant has no defence, and

(b) on behalf of the defendant who wishes to defend the action?

ANSWER (a) Proceedings in the Queen's Bench Division are commenced by writ of summons. So the plaintiff should start by issuing a writ in the High Court. Two copies are needed; one will be filed in the Court Office, and the other will be returned to the plaintiff for him to serve on the defendant. The purpose of the writ is three-fold. It informs the defendant that High Court proceedings have been commenced against him, that he must either satisfy the claim or return to the Court Office the accompanying acknowledgement claim form stating whether or not he intends to defend the action and that his failure to do so may result in judgement being given against him. Since the claim is for a liquidated sum, there must be a formal indorsement of the writ by the plaintiff setting out his claim. He can state on the writ either the general nature of his claim or a detailed statement of claim. The latter is the desired step since it saves time by dispensing with the need for the plaintiff to file his statement of claim in the action before he could obtain summary judgement against the defendant under Order 14.

If the defendant fails to acknowledge service by not returning the Acknowledgement of Service form within 14 days after receiving his copy of the writ, the plaintiff can apply for judgement in default of appearance. But, the plaintiff must first satisfy the court that the defendant did in fact receive service of the writ. This is done by affidavit.

If the defendant enters an appearance (i.e., indicates his intention to defend the action) the plaintiff can still obtain summary judgement under Order 14. This procedure ensures that the matter is brought to a speedy conclusion where the defendant has no triable defence to liability. An affidavit is required from the plaintiff setting out his cause of action, the amount claimed and his belief that the defendant has no defence. This affidavit is filed in court and is followed by a summons which is served on the defendant who is then given at least 10 days notice of the hearing of the summons for summary judgement. The summons is heard by a Master (a senior barrister appointed by the Lord Chancellor, who performs various functions in the

High Court) who will give judgement for the plaintiff unless the defendant can show that he has a defence which merits a full trial.

(b) Assuming that the defendant had entered an appearance, he can at any time before the date of the trial pay a sum of money into court if he disputes the amount claimed by the plaintiff. Written notice to this effect should be served on the plaintiff and if he continues with his claim and recovers a smaller sum, he will have to meet the defendant's costs from the date of payment into court to the date of the trial. If the defendant disputes liability (e.g., the goods delivered were defective) he must serve a defence on the plaintiff within 14 days after entering an appearance or receiving the statement of claim whichever is the later. This defence must deal with each allegation contained in the statement of claim and it may incorporate a counter-claim by the defendant for damages for breach of contract. Any ambiguity in the plaintiff's pleadings can be clarified by written request, and if necessary by summons for further and better particulars.

The parties will have to disclose to each other, not later than 14 days after the last pleading, a list of all relevant documents in their possession; and they may with leave of the Master ask each other questions on matters raised in the pleadings. After the discovery, but before the full trial, the Master will hear a summons for direction taken out by the plaintiff, the purpose being to provide a thorough 'stocktaking' of the action and to set down a time and place for the trial. If the plaintiff fails to take out a summons for direction within one month of the close of pleadings, the defendant can apply to have the action dismissed for want of prosecution or he may take out the summons himself and serve it on the plaintiff.

QUESTION 12 (a) What are the main provisions to be read into an arbitration agreement unless specifically excluded by the agreement?
(b) How are the costs of arbitration dealt with?

I.C.S.A. 1967

ANSWER (a) The following provisions must be read into an arbitration agreement unless they are specifically excluded by the agreement:
(i) If no other mode of reference is provided, the reference must be made to a single arbitrator.
(ii) If the reference is to two arbitrators, they must appoint an umpire immediately after they are themselves appointed.

(iii) If the arbitrators have delivered to any party to the submission, or to the umpire a notice in writing, stating that they cannot agree, the umpire must enter on the reference in lieu of the arbitrators.

(iv) The parties to the reference and all persons claiming through them respectively must, subject to any legal objection, submit to examination on oath by the arbitrators and must produce all documents which the arbitrators may require.

(v) The witnesses must be examined on oath if the arbitrator or umpire so requires.

(vi) The award to be made will be final and binding on the parties.

(vii) The arbitrator or umpire has the power to award costs and settle their amount.

(viii) The arbitrator has the same powers as the High Court to order specific performance of a contract other than contracts concerning land or interests in land.

(ix) The arbitrator or umpire has the power to make an interim award if this is required.

(b) Under Section 18 of the Arbitration Act 1950 an arbitrator has a discretion to decide how costs will be awarded and he need not give reasons for the exercise of this discretion. This discretion is a judicial discretion and must be exercised in a judicial manner **(Lloyd del Pacifico v. Board of Trade 1930).** The costs awarded are taxable in the High Court.

Section 18(3) makes void any provision in the arbitration agreement that the parties must bear their own costs. However, if the provision that the parties should pay their own costs is part of an agreement to submit to arbitration a dispute which arose before the making of the arbitration agreement, it will be upheld by the court.

Should the arbitrator fail to consider the matter of costs, either party may apply to him within 14 days after the award is made, to determine the issue.

QUESTION 13 (a) What is meant by the 'rule against hearsay'? Are there any exceptions to it?
(b) In a court action what matters are there of which proof is not required?

ANSWER (a) The rule against hearsay provides that assertions of persons other than the witness who is testifying, and assertions in documents produced to the court when no witness is testifying are inadmissible as evidence of the truth of the fact which was asserted. Thus, in **Patel v. Comptroller of Customs (1965)** where the accused was charged with making a false entry in a customs' form by stating that the country of origin of certain imported goods was India when the goods were in bags found to be marked 'produce of Morocco', the appeal court held that the marked bag was inadmissible evidence to show that the goods in fact came from Morocco since the person who marked the bag was not in court to testify. The reasons against statements of hearsay are that the makers of the statements are not in court to testify as to the truth of the facts stated; that the statements were not made under oath; and that hearsay is not the best evidence and to allow it may give the statements much more importance than they deserve.

In civil cases, the hearsay rule has been significantly modified to allow its inclusion. The Evidence Act 1968 allows the admissibility of hearsay evidence contained in written statements provided it is first-hand hearsay (i.e., the maker of the written statement who is not a witness in the case had personal knowledge of the facts stated).

Statements forming part of the same transaction are admissible evidence even though they infringe the hearsay rule providing they relate to a fact in issue and were contemporaneous and explanatory of that fact and not just made by way of narrative of a detailed prior event. Such statements are said to constitute the *res gestae* (things done) and are admissible as part of the same story. Thus, in **R. v. Bedingfield (1879)** where the deceased whose throat was cut uttered words to the effect "see what Bedingfield has done to me" just before he died, the court held that it was hearsay and not part of the *res gestae* since it was something said after the event. The court also said that if at the time the act was done the deceased had been heard to cry out "Don't Harry. Don't Harry" that would have been admissible as part of the *res gestae*.

Other exceptions to the hearsay rule include confessions, dying declarations, declarations against interest, declarations in the course of duty and statements in public documents.

(b) As a rule facts are only accepted in court by way of proof, but this requirement may be dispensed with in the following cases:
Formal Admissions. In civil cases formal admissions are frequently made before trial in order to save cost of proof. In criminal cases, by a plea of guilty the accused admits the material

ingredients of the charge against him. The Criminal Justice Act 1967 also provides that any fact of which oral evidence may be given in a criminal case can be admitted by the prosecutor or the defendant and the admission of such a fact will be conclusive evidence of the fact admitted.

Judicial Notice. Certain matters are accepted by the court without proof on ground that they are in the court's own knowledge. Both judge and jury take notice of common notoriety, such as currency, weight and measures, meantime and summertime and a point of nature. In **Burne v. Edman (1970)** the court took judicial notice that life of a criminal is not a happy one. The power to take judicial notice may be obligatory or discretionary. Notice of English Law is obligatory and some other matters are made obligatory by statute. In the majority of cases, the taking of judicial notice is discretionary.

Presumptions. Upon proof of certain facts, a court may or must presume that another fact exists. When the court must find that the presumed fact exists, the presumption is one of law; when it may so find, the presumption is one of fact. The former includes the presumption of innocence of someone charged with a crime, the presumption of sanity of all persons before the court and the presumption of legitimacy of a child born while its mother's valid marriage subsists. Presumption of fact arise where a similar set of facts has repeatedly led to the same conclusion and these include the presumption of continuance (a fact in existence at a particular time may be presumed to have continued thereafter), and the presumption of wrongdoer (when evidence is concealed or destroyed by a party to a case, it may be presumed that it would be to his disadvantage if produced).

QUESTION 14 (a) On what occasions can the prosecution give evidence of bad character or convictions of the accused before conviction?

(b) Discuss, with illustrations, the senses in which the term 'burden of proof' is commonly used. Is it true to say the burden of proof never shifts?

ANSWER (a) The general rule is that evidence of the accused's bad character or previous convictions cannot be used by the prosecution before conviction if the only reason why it is relevant is that it shows a disposition towards wrongdoing in general by the accused. There are four main exceptions to this rule:

(i) Where the evidence is admissible as a relevant similar fact (e.g., the previous conduct has a bearing on the question whether the acts alleged to constitute the crime charged in the indictment were designed or accidental).

(ii) Where the accused gives evidence of his good character (i.e. puts his character in issue). The prosecution may call evidence in rebuttal.

(iii) Where the evidence is admissible as a relevant fact under a particular statute (e.g., S.27 Theft Act 1968 provides that on a charge of handling stolen goods, evidence of a conviction for theft or handling stolen goods within the preceding 5 years is admissible).

(iv) Where the accused, after attacking the character of the prosecution or prosecution witnesses, gives evidence as a witness (S.1 Criminal Evidence Act 1898).

(b) The primary meaning of 'burden of proof' is the obligation of proving a fact. But this expression can be used in at least two different senses. It is used to signify the obligation of a party to prove a fact in issue (the legal burden). It is also used to mean the obligation of producing sufficient evidence to support that fact in issue (the evidential burden) and to require the judge to leave that fact in dispute to the jury if there is one, or to consider the evidence when he comes to decide whether the legal burden has been discharged.

In civil cases the legal burden is on the party who asserts a fact and not on the party who denies it. Thus, in an action for negligence where the defence of contributory negligence is raised, the plaintiff has the legal burden of proving negligence and the defendant the legal burden of contributory negligence. In criminal cases, a plea of not guilty puts in issue every material allegation contained in the indictment. The prosecution asserts the facts in issue and, subject to statutory exceptions and the defence of insanity, the burden lies on it to prove them **(Woolmington v. DPP 1935).**

In practice, the evidential burden follows the legal burden; but exceptionally those burdens may be on different parties. For example, in a prosecution for murder where the defence of provocation is raised, the legal burden of proving murder and negativing provocation is on the prosecution, but the accused must adduce some evidence of provocation (unless it is implicit from the prosecution case) before the jury can consider this defence. Hence the defence has the evidential burden.

The legal burden never shifts. In criminal cases, the burden is always on the prosecution to prove the accused's guilt and in civil cases an obligation to prove a fact in issue by one party remains throughout the case. However the obligation of proving different facts may move from one party to another and when this happens it is said that the burden has shifted from one party to the other.

QUESTION 15 Explain how the following High Court judgements may be enforced:

(a) Rod has been awarded £1000 damages against Ivor.

(b) Harold has been granted an injunction against David to pull down a shed in which he keeps his antiques, within 14 days.

(c) Harshad has been awarded possession of a house with a rateable value exceeding £2000 against his tenant Zaffer.

ANSWER (a) There is no automatic enforcement of civil judgements by the courts. The initiative rests with the successful party to decide how best to enforce his judgement debt. High Court judgements for the payment of money can be enforced in the High Court itself or in the County Court. Should Rod go to the High Court, there are various avenues open to him. If Ivor owns property, Rob may ask for a writ of *fieri facias* (fi-fa) requiring the bailiff of the county in which such property is situated to seize it in satisfaction of the judgement. Property so seized is then sold, usually by auction, and the proceeds used to discharge the judgement debt after deduction of execution expenses by the bailiff. This method of enforcement is not available for the seizure of land, goods on hire purchase, wearing apparel and bedding of the debtor and his family to the value of £100, and tools of trade to the value of £150. If Ivor is owed money by a third party (e.g., he has a credit balance at a bank) Rod can institute garnishee proceedings for an order that the third party (the garnishee) pay him the money instead. This method of enforcement is only available for legal debts presently due including accrued earnings, and cannot be used to claim any money standing to the credit of the judgement debtor in court. If Ivor owns land, securities or there are monies standing to his credit in court, Rod may apply ex parte on affidavit for a charging order. The charge takes effect as a general equitable charge and if necessary the property charged could be sold to satisfy the debt. If Ivor has any income-earning property which cannot be reached by a writ of fi-fa (e.g., rented premises) Rod may apply to the High Court for the appointment of a receiver to collect the income or profit from the property.

Should Rod find that Ivor has insufficient assets to satisfy the judgement, he could register the High Court judgement in the County Court for the district where Ivor resides. He will then be able to obtain an attachment of earnings order from the County Court. This order enables him to deduct the debt from Ivor's wages and is addressed to Ivor's employer.

(b) High Court judgements requiring the defendant to perform an act other than the payment of money or the delivery of goods or land can be enforced either by an order of committal or a writ of sequestration. Harold can seek a committal order if David's failure to pull down the shed within the specified time was not casual or unintentional. The effect of this order is to commit David to prison until he purges his contempt. As an alternative to imprisonment, Harold may wish David's assets to be taken from him until he complies with the judgement. A writ of sequestration has this effect. It commissions at least four persons to enter and take possession of the judgement debtor's real and personal estate until the judgement is satisfied.

(c) Judgements for the possession of land can be enforced directly by a writ of possession or indirectly by an order for committal and a writ of sequestration. The usual method of possession is a writ of possession. Harshad may ask the court to issue this writ which will give the bailiff power to evict Zaffer from the house so that Harshad may have possession of it.

Chapter 3
Law of Contract

QUESTION 16 (a) In what circumstances may an offer (i) lapse and (ii) be revoked?
(b) Brian enters a supermarket, picks up one of the wire trolleys provided and fills it with groceries from the shelves. He then remembers that he has left the money at home and begins to replace the goods on the shelves. The Manager of the supermarket stops him and says that Brian has bought the goods and must pay for them. Advise Brian.

A.C.C.A. 1977

ANSWER (a) Lapse terminates an offer by operation of law; and revocation terminates an offer by act of the offeror. With the former, the offer automatically comes to an end. With the latter, the offeror has to take steps to bring the offer to an end.

There are three ways in which an offer may lapse. If the offeree does not accept the offer within the time prescribed by the offeror, or where no time is prescribed, if the offer is not accepted within a reasonable time as in **Ramsgate Victoria Hotel Co. v. Montiflore (1866)** where an offer to buy shares was not accepted until some five months later, the offer will automatically lapse. What is a reasonable time will depend on the nature of the subject-matter and the means used to communicate the offer. For example the value of shares is likely to fluctuate more quickly than most other chattels so an offer to sell or buy them would lapse after a very short time. The same may be true with an offer made by telegram so acceptance of that offer by letter may be too late **(Quenerduaine v. Cole 1883).** An offer will also lapse on the death of the offeree, and on the death of the offeror if the offeree is aware of the offeror's death. If the offeree is not aware of his death, then the offer will only lapse if the contract was to be one which required the personal performance of the offeror **(Dickinson v. Dodds 1876).** Finally; an offer may lapse on the failure of a condition upon which the offer was made **(Financing Ltd v. Stimson 1962).**

An offer may terminate by revocation. Revocation means that the offeror has changed his mind and has decided to withdraw the offer from the offeree before the latter has accepted it **(Payne v. Cave 1789).** The offeror is at liberty to withdraw his offer at any time before acceptance notwithstanding that he had declared himself ready to keep the offer open for a given period **(Routledge v. Grant 1828).** For revocation to be effective it must be communicated to the offeree; and if it is sent by post it takes effect when the letter of revocation reaches the offeree or his last known address **(Byrne v. Van Tienhoven 1880).** The communication of revocation need not come directly from the offeror himself; so long as it comes from a reliable source before acceptance, the offer to the offeree will be revoked. A public offer made by advertisement in a newspaper can be revoked by a similar advertisement in the journal **(Shuey Case 1875).**

(b) One of the requisites for a contract is that there must be an offer and acceptance. An offer is a promise to be bound by stated terms if acceptance is made. It must be distinguished from other similar statements, such as an invitation to treat, since these are not capable of being accepted to constitute a contract.

It has been established from decided cases such as **Timothy v. Simpson (1834)** and **Fisher v. Bell (1961)** that a display of goods inside a shop with a price attached or in a shop window is not an offer but an invitation to the public to make an offer. In **Pharmaceutical Society of Great Britain v. Boots Cash Chemist (1953)** the court held that a contract was not made when a customer picked up articles from shelves in a supermarket but only when the cashier accepted the offer of the customer by accepting payment.

Accordingly, Brian should be advised that he has not accepted the supermarket's offer for the goods and is within his rights to refuse to pay for them.

QUESTION 17 Discuss with reasons whether the offers in the following cases have been validly accepted:

(a) *A* advertises his antique clock for sale in the Sunday Glean. *B* visits him on Monday and says that he will give *A* £600 for the clock. *B* tells *A* to let him know by Friday. On Tuesday *B* changes his mind and posts a letter to *A* informing him that he is no longer interested in the clock. *B*'s letter is lost in the post. On Thursday *A* posts a letter accepting *B*'s letter, but soon after changes his mind and telephones *B* the same day informing him that he does not want to sell the clock and that *B* should ignore his letter when it arrives. *A*'s letter reaches *B* two days later.

(b) *A* advertises his red sports car for sale in the Sunday Glean for "£3000 for quick sale – best offer secures". *B* sees the advertisement and immediately writes to *A* as follows: "I am willing to purchase your red sports car for £2500. I will consider the car mine if I don't hear from you to the contrary and will collect it at the weekend". Two days later *C* who has also seen the advertisement telephones *A* accepting *A*'s offer to sell the car for £3000. *A* informs *C* that the car is already sold to *B*. *B* now informs *A* that he no longer wishes to buy the car.

(c) *A* sends his latest volume of poetry to *B* with a covering letter in which *A* informs *B* that unless the volume is returned to *A* within a week *B* will be deemed to have accepted *A*'s offer to sell the book to him for £5. *B* wraps up the book with a view to returning it, but forgets to do so.

(d) *A* advertises in the Sunday Glean that he will pay £20 for the return of his lost watch. *B* who has not read the advertisement finds the watch and hands it in to the nearest police station. *C*, a police constable returns it to *A*.

(e) *A*, by letter, offers to sell goods to *B* upon certain terms. Upon receipt of the letter, *B* posts his letter of acceptance by handing it to the postman who mislays it.

(f) *A* and *B* occupy farms facing each other on either side of the river. *B* says to *A* who is visiting *B*, "Will you buy my cow Buttercup for £200?" *A* says, "I'll consult my wife and let you know tomorrow. If I hang a white sheet from my window between 10 and 11am, it will mean I accept. If not, I refuse." Next day, *A* hangs a white sheet from his window at the agreed time, but as it is misty *B* cannot see it.

ANSWER (a) Where an offeror uses the post to revoke his offer the offer is revoked when the revocation letter reaches the offeree, and not when it is posted (**Byrne v. Van Tienhoven 1880**). So *B*'s letter to *A* informing him that he is no longer interested in purchasing *A*'s antique clock has no legal effect.

A's letter to *B* accepting his offer will constitute a contract only if the postal rule applies. The postal rule states that where it is reasonable for the offeree to use the post to send his acceptance to the offeror a contract is concluded as soon as the letter is properly posted (**Household Fire Insurance v. Grant 1879**). The postal rule does not apply where the terms of the offer require acceptance to be communicated to the offeror or where its application would result in manifest inconvenience and absurdity (per Lawton L.J. in **Holwell Securities Ltd v. Hughes 1974**). It may be that by requiring *A* to let *B* know of his acceptance 'by Friday,' *B* is insisting on actual knowledge of acceptance before a contract can be concluded, in which case the postal rule does not apply. If this is the case then *A*'s telephone conversation with *B* amounts to a rejection of *B*'s offer and *A*'s letter will have no legal effect when *B* receives it.

If the postal rule does apply, then *A*'s telephone conversation amounts to a revocation of his acceptance and the legal effect of the revocation of a postal acceptance will have to be considered. There is no English authority on this type of revocation. On the strict application of the postal rule, once acceptance is complete there is a contract, so that it would be too late to revoke acceptance. As against this, is the view that if the offeror agrees to acceptance by post then he voluntarily accepts the hazards of his choice, the risk of the letter of acceptance being lost or delayed in the post as well as the letter being overtaken by speedier means of communication (see Hudson 82LQR at 170). However, it would seem severely harsh to allow the offeree to have the best of both worlds: to impose liability on the offeror once acceptance is posted and at the same time to avoid liability himself by revoking his acceptance before it reaches the offeror.

(b) As a first step, it is necessary to consider the legal effect of *A*'s advertisement in the Sunday Glean. The general rule as laid down in **Partridge v. Crittenden (1968)** is that an advertisement is only an invitation to treat unless it is couched in very firm words (as in **Carlill v. Carbolic Smokeball Co. 1893**). The words 'best offer secures' is sufficient evidence to conclude that *A*'s advertisement comes within the **Partridge v. Crittenden** type of advertisement.

Both *B* and *C* have made offers to purchase *A*'s red sports car even though *C*'s telephone call is couched in acceptance terms. *B*'s offer is made in such a way as to impose liability on *A* unless *A* rejects the offer and the court has ruled in **Felthouse v. Bindley (1863)** that silence cannot amount to acceptance. However, that rule was only intended to protect the offeree from having to reject an offer or otherwise incur liability, and not where an offeree has clearly manifested his intention to accept the offer, as with *A* when he informed *C* that he had already sold the car to *B*.

It was stated in **Carlill v. Carbolic Smoke Ball Co.** that the offeror may legitimately waive the need for communication of acceptance in which case a contract is concluded as soon as the offeree has shown his intention to accept the offer. The terms of *B*'s offer show clearly that he is waiving his right to receive knowledge of *A*'s acceptance. Accordingly, there is a contract between *A* and *B*, and *B* can be sued for breach of contract.

(c) Acceptance requires some overt act on the part of the offeree to show that he is accepting the offer. This external manifestation of assent may take the form of words or conduct. But the offeror cannot present the offeree with the alternatives of repudiation or liability. In **Felthouse v. Bindley (1862)** where an uncle wrote his nephew offering to buy the latter's horse for £30.75p and added "If I hear no more about him, I consider the horse mine at the price", the court held that even though the nephew intended to accept, the uncle could not arbitrarily impose contractual liability on the nephew by proclaiming that silence would amount to acceptance. Thus, *B* has not accepted *A*'s offer to sell the book to him for £1. Moreover, under the provisions of the Unsolicited Goods and Services Act 1971, *B* will be entitled to keep the book without liability if he did not request the book in the first place and *A* did not take steps to recover it within six months.

(d) The general rule is that an offer must be communicated to the offeree before it can be effective. If services are rendered which in fact fulfil the terms of an offer but are performed in ignorance that the offer exists, there can be no valid acceptance of the offer and consequently no contractual liability **(R. v. Clarke 1927,** and **Bloom v. American Swiss Watch Co. 1915)**. So *B* cannot claim the reward of £1 for the return of *A*'s lost watch. However, if *B* had seen the advertisement offering the reward after he had handed *A*'s watch to the police station but before *C*, the police constable had returned it to *A*, *B* would have been able to claim the reward. In **Gibbons v. Procter (1891)** the defendant published a handbill offering a reward of £25 to anyone giving information to a Superintendent Penn leading to the arrest of a person who assaulted a young girl. Before the handbill was published the plaintiff gave the information to a fellow policeman who passed it on to his superior. The latter in turn passed it on to Penn – but only did so after the handbill had been published. The court found that the information passed through the plaintiff's fellow policeman as his agent to forward the information to the proper officer Penn. The information ultimately reached Penn at a time when the plaintiff knew that the reward had been offered.

(e) One of the exceptions to the rule that acceptance must be communicated to the offeror before it is effective is where the postal rule applies. The postal rule states that if it was in the contemplation of the parties that the post might be used as a means of communicating acceptance, acceptance is complete when the letter is posted, regardless of whether it arrives at the right place or on time or at all **(Household Fire Insurance v. Grant 1879).** A letter is posted when it is in the control of the Post Office or of one of its employees authorised to receive letters. So handing the letter to a postman authorised to deliver letters is not posting **(Re London Northern Bank 1900).**

As *B* did not properly post his letter of acceptance to buy *A*'s goods, the postal rule does not apply and acceptance is not valid because it was not communicated to *A* (the letter was mislaid).

(f)   Acceptance is generally not effective unless there is communication of it to the offeror. 'Communication' means knowledge by the offeror that his offer is being accepted. Since *B* could not see the white sheet which *A* hung from his window as an indication that he was accepting *B*'s offer to sell him the cow, there cannot be said to have been communication of acceptance **(Entores Ltd v. Miles Far East Corp. 1955).** Hence, *A*'s acceptance is not valid.

QUESTION 18   (a)   In the law of contract, explain the importance of intention to create legal relations. How does the court ascertain the intention of the parties?
(b)   Tom agreed to sell his house to Harry. The agreement was 'subject to contract'. Tom sold the house to Joe for a higher price. Advise Harry whether he can sue Tom for breach of contract.

A.I.A. 1978

ANSWER   (a)   All contracts are based on agreements but not all agreements are contracts. Agreements will only be legally enforceable if they are of a contractual nature; and this depends on whether or not the parties intended to create legal relations. Basically, there are two types of agreements; domestic and social agreements, and commercial agreements. With the former, there is a presumption against legal relations, unless, although the background is informal the intention is obviously contractual. With the latter, there is a presumption in favour of legal relations, unless the parties 'contract out' of the agreement.

Examples of domestic agreements are agreements between husband and wife **(Balfour v. Balfour 1919)** unless made with a view to separate permanently **(Merritt v. Merritt 1970);** and agreements between parent and child **(Jones v. Padavatton 1969).** Examples of social agreements are the provision of free residential accommodation for close friends **(Heslop v. Burns 1974)** and 'car-sharing' arrangements between friends or neighbours where one party contributes to the running cost of the other's vehicle **(Coward v. M.I.B. 1963).** With social agreements the presumption may be rebutted by showing that one party has fundamentally altered his position as a result of the agreement. In **Parker v. Clark (1960)** the plaintiffs sold their house to live with the defendants who were relatives, on the understanding that the defendants will leave a share of their house to them. The parties subsequently quarrelled and the defendants repudiated the agreement. The court held that the plaintiffs would not have taken the important step of selling their house on the faith of a mere social agreement, so the defendants were liable in damages. In **Connell v. M.I.B. (1969)** Sacks L.J. accepted the views of Cheshire and Fifoot as such "The test of contractual intention is objective, not subjective. What matters is not what the parties had in their minds. but what inferences reasonable people would draw from their words or conduct".

The parties may 'contract out' of commercial agreements by using such terms as 'binding in honour only' **(Jones v. Vernon's Pools 1939),** 'subject to contract' **(Chillingworth v. Esche 1927),** and 'Gentleman's Agreement'. In this context, it should be noted that although the parties are free to use words to rebut the presumption of legal relations, any form of words which seek to oust the jurisdiction of the court will be declared null and void **(Baker v. Jones 1954).** The intervention of the law may also result in a commercial agreement having a non-contractual effect. For example, the Trade Union and Labour Relations Act 1974 S.18 presumes against intention to create legal relations with collective agreements unless such agreements are in writing and expressly provide the contrary **(The Rosso 1982).**

(b) Agreements for the sale of land are usually made 'subject to contract'. Such agreements are not legally binding as they lack completeness and so the parties are able to withdraw from them without liability. In **Winn v. Bull (1877)** an agreement for a lease 'subject to the preparation and approval of a formal contract' was held to have no contractual effect.

Accordingly, Harry should be advised that any action he may wish to bring against Tom will fail.

QUESTION 19 (a) How may the courts make an apparently vague agreement sufficiently certain and enforce it as a contract? (b) By letter, Paula offered to sell her motor cycle to Jeff at a price to be determined by her brother Tom, and added "you can buy it on ordinary hire purchase terms". Jeff accepted the offer. What is the legal position if:

(i) Tom refused to fix the price,

(ii) Tom fixed the price but Paula refused to deliver the motor cycle because she considered that the price was too low?

ANSWER (a) An agreement will not be enforced as a contract if it lacks certainty. Uncertainty may make the agreement so vague that it has no meaning whatsoever. Clauses such as 'subject to war... lockout or strike... force majeure' are all too vague because there is no trade custom for the use of these terms.

The court may make an apparently vague agreement sufficiently certain and enforce it as a contract by the use of custom. Such custom may be either trade custom or local custom. In **Shamrock SS Co. v. Storey Co. (1899)** a contract to load coal at Grimsby 'on the terms of the usual colliery guarantee' was upheld on proof of the terms usually contained in such guarantees at Grimsby.

The court may also use the concept of reasonableness to enforce an agreement. In **Hillas & Co. Ltd v. Arcos Ltd (1932)** the standard of reasonableness was applied to uphold a contract for the sale of timber 'of fair specification' between persons well acquainted with the timber trade.

Finally, the court may ignore meaningless phrases if the agreement is otherwise sufficiently clear. In **Nicolene Ltd v. Simmons (1953)** a clause in the contract for the sale of steel bars stated that the sale was subject to 'the usual conditions of acceptance'. The court held that as there were no usual conditions of acceptance, this phrase could be severed from the contract. However, only if a phrase is mere verbiage can it be cut out from a document. Sometimes, although a phrase is meaningless, it is relevant to the contract.

(b) An agreement may be incomplete if there are any points still unagreed. If such points are vital to the agreement, it would not be enforced as a contract. However an agreement does not have to be worked out in meticulous detail in order to be complete. Thus a contract for the sale of goods is often complete as soon as the parties have agreed to buy and sell, the remaining details being determined by the concept of reasonableness or by law. Section 8(2) of the Sale of Goods Act 1979 provides that in the absence of the parties to settle the issue as to price, a reasonable price should be paid. A similar provision applies under S.15 of the Supply of Goods and Services Act 1982 to services. Where the parties agree to settle the issue of price by reference to the valuation by a third party, then the contract is avoided if for some reason he does not make the valuation (S.9 Sale of Goods Act 1979). If he does make the valuation, then the agreement is an enforceable contract and should the seller fail to deliver the goods, an action may be brought by the buyer for non-delivery.

Quite apart from the issue as to price, it would appear that the agreement between Jeff and Paula is vague as it is expressly stated to be 'on ordinary hire purchase terms'. In **Scammel v. Ouston (1941)** an agreement to buy goods 'on hire purchase terms' was held by the House of Lords to be too vague to be enforced since there were many kinds of hire purchase agreements in widely different terms.

QUESTION 20 (a) State and explain the kind of contracts which a minor can lawfully enter into.
(b) Bloom, a money lender, makes a loan to Ade on Ade's representation that he is nineteen years old. Ade is in fact seventeen years old. Ade refuses to pay the loan. Bloom wants to sue Ade and he seeks legal advice from you. Advise Bloom of his legal rights, if any.

A.B.E. 1977

ANSWER (a) A minor is any person under the age of eighteen years (Family Law Reform Act 1969) and he is deemed to have attained his majority at the first moment of time on his eighteenth birthday. Generally, there are two types of contracts which a minor may enter into: those that are binding on him and those which are voidable at his option.

Contracts which are binding on a minor are contracts for necessaries and contracts of service for the infant's benefit. 'Necessaries' does not mean 'bare necessities' such as food, clothing and shelter. It means goods or services which are reasonably necessary to maintain a minor in his station of life. In the case of goods, necessaries have been defined in the Sale of Goods Act 1979 S.3 as 'suitable to the condition in life of the infant, and his actual requirements at the time of the sale and delivery'. There are three questions to be answered in ascertaining whether the goods are necessaries:

(i) Are they capable, **in law,** of being necessaries for any infant? Food, clothing, medicines, school books and watches have all been held capable in law of being necessaries, (ii) Are they capable, in law, of being necessaries for the particular infant? This will depend on the infant's station in life and whether or not he had already been adequately provided for. If the answers to (i) and (ii) are 'yes', then (iii) are the goods, **in fact,** necessaries? In **Nash v. Inman (1908)** a tailor sued for the price of eleven fancy waist-coats supplied to a diplomat's son attending Cambridge as an undergraduate. It was held that as the plaintiff did not adduce any evidence that the infant had not enough clothes, the case could not be put to the jury. Question (ii) had not been answered affirmatively. In **Elkington v. Amery (1936)** it was held that a lady's engagement ring and an eternity ring were necessaries but a lady's gold vanity bag was not. An infant is only liable to pay a reasonable price for necessaries. Moreover, the contract must, on the whole, be for his benefit. In **Fawcett v. Smethurst (1914)** an infant hired a car to collect his luggage from a station a few miles away, but there was a clause making him absolutely liable for damages to the car, even in the absence of negligence. It was held that the clause made the contract onerous, therefore it was not a contract for necessaries and not binding. Contracts of service are binding on a minor if they are, on the whole, beneficial to him. Education and apprenticeship contracts may fall under this head. In **Doyle v. White City Stadium (1935)** an infant boxer was disqualified and claimed his purse. It was held that the contract was analogous to a contract of service and was beneficial, on the whole, to the infant, although it operated against him in this instance.

Voidable contracts are binding on a minor unless repudiated by him within a reasonable time after reaching his majority. There are four main types of voidable contracts:- (i) land contracts (sale or lease); (ii) shares; (iii) partnership contracts between partners only; and (iv) marriage settlements. What is a 'reasonable time' is a question of fact. The minor is given sufficient time after attaining majority to consider his status and reconsider the contract. The effect of repudiation is that the minor is relieved from all future liabilities.

(b) Contracts for the repayment of loans are unenforceable against a minor at common law, so the contract between Bloom and Ade is unenforceable and the question is whether Ade is liable for his fraudulent misrepresentation about his age.

A minor is liable for any tort distinct and separate from his contract **(Burnard v. Haggis 1863).** But he cannot be sued in tort where the action would be an indirect way of enforcing a contract upon which no action lies against him **(Jennings v. Rundall 1799).** Thus, it was held in **Leslie v. Sheill (1914)** that an infant could not be sued in deceit for fraudulently inducing an adult to lend him money. An action in quasi-contract for money had and received to their use will also fail if it would indirectly enforce an invalid contract.

So neither an action in the tort of deceit nor an action in quasi-contract may be brought against Ade. Moreover, the money cannot be recovered under the equitable doctrine of restitution as 'restitution stops where repayment begins'.

QUESTION 21 Nina, aged 17, takes a secretarial post away from home.
(a) She takes a two year lease on a flat in Chelsea at £3000 per annum, pays a quarter's rent and enters into possession.
(b) She orders a week's groceries, the bill amounting to £65 but refuses to take delivery or to pay for them.
(c) She orders a sports car valued at £5800. By giving her age as 23, she persuades the seller to deliver it before any payment is made.
(d) After working for one week she gives up her job and borrows £600 from her uncle for an advanced secretarial course. She uses £75 for enrolment on the course at the London Polytechnic and then takes a hectic holiday on the Continent with the balance of the loan.

She eventually arrives at her parent's home, exhausted and penniless and repudiates all her liabilities.

Advise her numerous creditors.

ANSWER (a) The Law of Property Act 1925 prohibits an infant from acquiring a legal estate in land but a lease for a term of years absolute gives him an equitable interest for the agreed period. While he is still in possession he is liable under the contract for non-payment of rent **(Davies v. Beynon-Harris 1931).** However, the contract may be repudiated by him during his infancy or within a reasonable time after reaching majority. The effect of repudiation is that he is relieved from all future liabilities, but any money handed over to the landlord cannot be recovered unless there is a total failure of consideration **(Steinberg v. Scala Ltd 1923).** Consideration means 'benefit'. It is unsettled whether repudiation has retrospective effect. If it does not then the infant will be liable for rent which has become payable before repudiation. In the Irish case of **Blake v. Concannon (1870)** where an infant tenant repudiated a lease after he fell in arrears with the rent the court held that he was liable for rents already due before repudiation.

Since Nina had entered into possession of the flat, she cannot claim that she received no benefit from the contract. Accordingly, the lessor could retain the £750 paid by Nina but she cannot be sued for rent which may be due subsequent to repudiation.

(b) Assuming that the groceries are necessaries, the contract is still executory as Nina has not yet taken delivery of them. There are two schools of thought as to whether an infant can incur liability on an executory contract. In **Nash v. Inman (1908)** Fletcher Moulton L.J. said that an infant's liability for necessaries arises because he had been supplied with the things and not because he had contracted, and so the law imposes an obligation on him to make a fair payment in respect of needs satisfied. In the same case Buckleigh L.J. took the opposite view. He said that the infant's liability is contractual so he is liable to pay for the goods, even though he has not taken delivery. In the case of goods, the Sale of Goods Act 1979 S.3(2) refers to necessaries as goods 'sold and delivered'. It would therefore appear that as the contract is still executory, it is unenforceable and any action for non-acceptance would fail.

(c) The sports car ordered by Nina is *prima facie* non-necessaries. As against the infant, non-necessary contracts entered into by him for goods supplied or to be supplied (other than necessaries) are unenforceable. Thus, the dealer will not succeed in an action for the price of the car. However under the Minors' Contracts Act 1987, the dealer can recover the car from Nina since she obtained it by misrepresenting her age **(Stocks v. Wilson 1913).**

(d) Contracts entered into by infants for the repayment of money lent are unenforceable. However, if the money is used for the purchase of necessaries, the lender is subrogated to the rights of the seller and is allowed in Equity the same right of recovery that the seller would have possessed had he not been paid **(Lewis v. Alleyne 1888).** Uncle may therefore recover the £75 used for enrolment on the secretarial course at the London Polytechnic.

QUESTION 22 (a) Distinguish the following terms:
  (i) Past Consideration;
  (ii) Executed Consideration;
  (iii) Executory Consideration.
  Why is this distinction necessary?

(b) Monsieur has dug Elizabeth's garden for her. At the time of doing the work no mention of payment was made, but after Monsieur had completed the job Elizabeth promised to pay him £30 for the work. State with reasons and reference to decided cases where appropriate, whether Monsieur will be able to enforce this promise against Elizabeth if:

  (i) Monsieur is a jobbing gardener or

  (ii) Monsieur is Elizabeth's neighbour and she is extremely attractive.

ANSWER (a) (i) **Past consideration** is consideration wholly executed and finished with before a promise is made to do something in return. Thus if *A* saves *B*'s life and sometime later, *B* promises *A* £100 for saving his life, *A* cannot rely on his past act as consideration to enforce *B*'s promise because consideration is the price for a promise and *A* was not, by his act, buying *B*'s promise as no such promise was in existence at the time. In **Roscorla v. Thomas (1842)** *A* bought a horse from *B* and afterwards *B*, in consideration of the previous sale, warranted that the horse was sound and free from vice. *A* sued for breach of his promise. The court held that the express promise was made after the sale was over and as such was made for past consideration.

(ii) **Executed consideration** is the performance of an act for a promise. A good example of executed consideration is an act for the promise of a reward. So in **Gibbons v. Procter (1891)** the information supplied by the plaintiff which resulted in the arrest of the person who assaulted a young girl constituted both acceptance of the plaintiff's promise to give a reward of £25 for such information, and executed consideration for it.

(iii) **Executory consideration** is a promise to do something in the future in return for the other party's promise. However, the promise of the future performance will only be regarded as consideration if the performance itself would be so regarded **(Thorp v. Thorp 1702).** Thus the promise of an employee to accept an ex gratia payment is not consideration for a promise by his employer to give it. All agreements between seller and buyer for the sale of goods for future delivery on credit terms are examples of executory consideration.

The distinction between past, executed and executory consideration is important because while the last two are consideration in law, past consideration is not consideration to enforce a promise.

(b) There are three instances where past consideration may be relied on to enforce a promise. Under the Bills of Exchange Act 1882 a person who has given past consideration for a bill is treated as a holder who has given value for it, with the result that he may be able to sue on the bill if it is dishonoured. Similarly, the Limitation Act 1980 allows a statute-barred debt to be revived by written acknowledgement, with the result that this acknowledgement may be enforced even though the consideration (the antecedent debt) was past. Finally, a past act may be treated as consideration to enforce a promise if it can be shown that (i) the past act was done at the request of the promisor and (ii) it was reasonable to contemplate payment. The first condition was laid down in **Lampleigh v. Brathwait (1616)** where at the request of *A*, *B* obtained a royal pardon for him and *A* subsequently promised to pay him £100. The court held that *B* could sue *A* on the promise because *B*'s act was done at the request of *A*. The second condition was added in the nineteenth century by **Re Casey's Patents (1892)** where *A* and *B*, the joint owners of certain patent rights, wrote to *C* stating that they would give him one-third share of the patents because of his services as the practical manager in working their patents. The court held that the past service raised an implication that, at the time it was rendered, it would be paid for.

Monsieur will only be able to rely on his past service to enforce Elizabeth's promise if he comes within the third exception. If Elizabeth did not request him to dig her garden, then on account of the matters discussed above, he cannot enforce payment and his status would be irrelevant. If, however she did request the work, then it would be reasonable for Monsieur to expect payment if he is a jobbing gardener. If he was only her next door neighbour and did the work because she is attractive, the court is likely to hold that payment was not contemplated at the relevant time and that he did the work for mere sentimental reasons.

QUESTION 23 (a) 'Consideration must be sufficient but need not be adequate'. Explain the meaning of this statement.
(b) Tom has lent Fred £500 which is due for repayment on December 1. Tom asks Fred in early November for immediate

repayment because he is short of money. Fred replies that he can give Tom £400. Tom agrees to accept £400 in full settlement of the debt.

Would Tom be able to sue for the outstanding £100? Would your answer be different if Fred had asked to settle the debt by giving Tom a cheque for £400 on December 1?

ANSWER (a) Consideration is the price for a promise. This price may take the form of an act or forbearance or promise to do either but it must have some economic value. Natural affection in itself and mere sentimental motive for promising will not be enough to enforce a promise not made under seal. In **White v. Bluett (1853)** the court held that a son's promise not to bore his father with complaints was not consideration to support the father's promise to refrain from suing him on a promissory note. Similarly in **Thomas v. Thomas (1842)** where a widow was promised by her husband's executor that she could live in a house because of her late husband's wishes and on the payment by her of £1 a year, the court held that the husband's wishes alone would not have amounted to consideration in the eyes of the law.

As long as the consideration provided by the promisee has some economic value it does not matter that it is of little or no value to the promisor. In **Chappell & Co. Ltd v. Nestlé Co. Ltd (1960),** where chocolate manufacturers sold gramophone records for 1s 6d plus three wrappers of their 6 pence bar of chocolate, the court held that the wrappers formed part of the consideration even though they were useless to the manufacturers. **Thomas** and **Chappell** cases also show that in the absence of fraud, the court will not measure the comparative value of the promisor's promise and of the act or promise given by the promisee in exchange for it. In other words, the court will not enquire into the 'adequacy of consideration'.

Sufficiency of consideration is a legal concept. It means that the consideration must be real to the promisor and must not be something he is entitled to as of right, regardless of his promise. Thus the performance of an existing contractual obligation due to the promisor from the promisee is not generally sufficient consideration for a promise by the promisor to give something extra to the promisee if he performs that obligation. In **Stilk v. Myrick (1809),** a seaman under an existing contract to work a ship, failed in his claim to extra wages promised by the defendant shipowner if he would work the ship home when it was two short of its crew.

The principle in the **Myrick** case has been modified by the Court of Appeal in **Williams v. Roffey Bros and Nicholls Ltd (1990)** where the court decided that if the promise to give something 'extra' was not extracted by threat and the promisor obtained a practical commercial benefit or avoided a disadvantage by the contract being performed, the performance of the contractual obligation will be sufficient consideration to enforce the promise of something 'extra'. In **Roffey Bros. & Nicholls,** subcontractors were on the verge of insolvency and were having difficulties in performing their contractual obligations to the main contractor in time. The main contractor would have incurred penalties for any delay in completing the contract, so it promised to pay something 'extra' to the subcontractors if the contract was performed in time. The Court of Appeal held that in the circumstances the subcontractors were entitled to the extra payment when they completed the contract in time.

Performance of an obligation owed at law (as opposed to contract) is not sufficient consideration to enforce a promise to pay for its performance. So in **Collins v. Godefroy (1831)** where the plaintiff was under a legal duty by subpoena to attend court and give evidence for the defendant in another case, the court held that the plaintiff's court attendance was not sufficient consideration to enforce the defendant's promise to pay him six guineas for his lost time. It would be otherwise if the promisee does something more than he is legally obliged to do **(Glasbrook Bros. v. Glamorgan CC 1925).**

(b) The general rule at common law is that a creditor is not bound by an undertaking to accept part payment in full settlement of a debt. This rule was established in **Pinnel's Case (1602)** and was confirmed by the House of Lords in **Foakes v. Beer (1884)** where Mrs. Beer promised Dr. Foakes to forgo interest on a judgement if he paid the principal sum by instalments. This common law rule does not apply if the smaller sum is paid earlier, or at a different place if it is for the convenience of the creditor **(Vanbergen v. St. Edmund's Properties Ltd 1933),** or in a different manner or form, or if paid by a third party **(Hirachand Punamchand v. Temple 1911),** or if the debtor entered into a composition of creditors agreement **(Wood v. Roberts 1818).**

The acceptance by Fred of £400 from Tom at the earlier date is voluntary and not subject to any pressure as in **D. & C. Builders v. Rees (1965).** Accordingly, payment of this smaller sum will provide sufficient consideration for Fred's promise to discharge the debt **(Pinnel's Case).**

Payment of a debt by cheque only acts as a conditional discharge of the debt, the actual discharge occurs when the cheque is honoured. In this respect, a cheque is no different from cash and so the payment of a smaller sum by cheque at the date when the debt is due is not sufficient consideration for a promise by the creditor to discharge the debt **(D. & C. Builders v. Rees).**

A cheque is also a negotiable instrument and in this respect it has certain advantages over cash (e.g., greater ease of portability and transferability). A creditor may therefore wish to accept a cheque for a smaller sum in absolute discharge of his debt for these reasons. In this respect, part-payment of a debt by cheque will provide sufficient consideration for a promise to discharge the debt **(Sibree v. Tripp 1846).**

Thus, if Fred had asked to settle the debt by giving Tom a cheque for £400 on December 1, the debt would not have been discharged if Tom accepted the cheque as conditional payment. It would be otherwise, if Tom accepted the cheque in absolute discharge of the debt and not just as conditional payment.

QUESTION 24 Explain the meaning and effect of the doctrine of promissory estoppel otherwise known as the doctrine of waiver in the law of contract.

A.C.C.A. 1982

ANSWER In **Central London Property Trust Ltd v. High Trees House Ltd (1947)** Denning J. said obiter that if one party promises another without consideration that legal rights due from the latter to the former will be suspended or extinguished then the promisor will not be allowed to break his promise if the promisee relies on the promise and acts thereon. This principle is also called promissory estoppel or doctrine of waiver and should not be confused with 'equitable estoppel' which includes both promissory estoppel and proprietary estoppel.

In the **High Trees Case** *C* let a block of flats to *H* for 99 years at a rent of £2500 per year and in 1940 *C* agreed to reduce the rent to £1250 because few flats were sub-let by *H* owing to the war. In 1945 when the war difficulties of letting were over, *C* again demanded the full rent. It was held that *C* was entitled to the full rent since the agreement to accept the lower rent was only intended to apply while war conditions lasted. It was also stated that if *C* attempted to claim the full rent for the years 1940–45 the claim would have failed. The **High Trees** principle was justified by **Hughes v. Metropolitan Ry Co. (1877)** where a landlord by his conduct led a tenant to believe that during negotiations over the sale of the reversion he would not enforce his right to forfeit the lease for failure to carry out repairs of the premises.

In the main, the **High Trees** principle only operates to suspend legal rights and so the promise will continue to operate until reasonable notice has been given by the promisor that he proposes to resume those rights (see **Hughes v. Metropolitan Ry, Foakes v. Beer, Ajayi v. T.R. Briscoe Ltd 1964**). In **Tool Metal Manufacturing Co. Ltd v. Tungsten Electric Co. Ltd (1955)** it was held that an agreement made during the war not to seek compensation operated in equity to prevent a claim for such compensation until reasonable notice had been given of an intention to resume those legal rights. Exceptionally, the **High Trees** principle may be used to extinguish legal rights if the promise was intended as such (per Lord Denning in **High Trees House Case** and **D. & C. Builders v. Rees).** However, this can only arise in the case of a continuing obligation, such as the payment of rent under a lease, with the result that past rent at the original rate cannot be recovered but the right to future rent can be revived by reasonable notice.

There are various limitations on the **High Trees** principle. It does not afford a cause of action but only operates by way of defence. In **Combe v. Combe (1951)** a husband, during divorce proceedings, promised to pay his wife £100 per year. The wife relying on this promise, forbore from applying to the court for a maintenance order and later sued to enforce the husband's promise. Her claim failed. The promise must also be given freely without the use of threats **(D. & C. Builders v. Rees);** and the court must be satisfied that it is inequitable to allow the promisor to go back on his promise although it is not necessary for the promisee to show that he has acted to his detriment (per Denning MR in **Brikom Investments Ltd v. Carr 1979**).

Promissory estoppel has been introduced in equity to mitigate the harsh common law rule in **Pinnel's Case (1602)** that a creditor is not bound by his promise to accept part payment of a debt in full satisfaction. This common law rule conflicts with business practice and frequently causes inconvenience and hardship. Thus, a plea of promissory estoppel is permitted, in appropriate cases, where the promisee has not furnished any consideration for the promise.

QUESTION 25 Advise Lorraine, Brenda and Dominique in each of the following situations relevant to them:

(a) Lorraine attended a car auction after reading an advertisement in her local newspaper that cars to be auctioned were 'without reserve'. She was the only person to bid for a Golf sports car but the auctioneer withdrew the car from the auction since Lorraine's bid was three times below the market value of the car.

(b) Brenda whose house was on fire telephoned the police of the neighbouring county who passed on the message to their local fire station which then responded to the call in the belief that it was rendering gratuitous service in its own area. Two days after putting out the fire, the fire chief learnt that he was entitled to payment for the services since Brenda was not living in the county. So he sent Brenda a bill for £1000.

(c) Dominique was promised a radio by Max if she repaid Tom the £60 which she borrowed from him. Dominique has repaid the loan from Tom but Max is refusing to part with the radio which he promised Dominique.

ANSWER (a) An advertisement that an auction of specific goods will take place on a certain day is only an invitation to treat, not an offer, so that if the auction is cancelled a member of the public cannot claim travelling expenses for turning up at the place where the auction was to be held **(Harris v. Nickerson 1873).** However, if the advertisement also states that the auction will be 'without reserve' and the auction does in fact take place, the auctioneer will have to sell the goods on auction to the highest bidder even though his bid is below the market value of the goods **(Warlow v. Harrison 1859).**

From what has been said above, Lorraine has a very strong claim against the auctioneer for non-delivery of the sports car.

(b) The test to decide whether a contract exists between Brenda and the fire chief is what inferences a reasonable person would conclude from their words or conduct. In **Upton RDC v. Powell (1942)** where the facts were similar the court concluded that a contract did exist between the parties.

Brenda may not necessarily have to pay the full bill. Section 15 of the Supply of Goods and Services Act 1982 provides that where the parties have not agreed on the price in their contract, only a reasonable price has to be paid for the services. The court may feel that in the circumstances £1000 is unreasonable and may reduce the bill accordingly.

(c) The basic rule is that the performance of an existing contractual obligation is not sufficient consideration to enforce a promise of something 'extra'. This rule is laid down in **Stilk v. Myrick (1809)** as modified by **Williams v. Roffy Bros. & Nicholls Ltd (1990).** However, where the promise to give something 'extra' is made by a third party then the performance of the contractual obligation will be sufficient consideration **(Shadwell v. Shadwell 1860).**

Accordingly, Dominique can sue Max for failure to give her the radio.

QUESTION 26 Consider the nature of an accountant's duty of care towards his client and third parties. To what extent can he exclude or limit liability for breach of this duty?

ANSWER The relationship between an accountant and his client is contractual based on a contract for the supply of services. Section 13 of the Supply of Goods and Services Act 1982 implies a term in the contract that the services will be carried out with reasonable care and skill where the supplier is acting in the course of a business. Liability under Section 13 is not strict, the supplier only has to exercise reasonable care. The standard of services that can be expected will depend on any special skill or expertise that the supplier professes to have. In the case of an accountant he must "bring to bear on the work he has to perform that skill, care and caution which a reasonably competent, careful and cautious auditor would use" (per Lopes L.J. in **Re Kingston Cotton Mill Co. 1896**).

Where the contract is to provide advice of a speculative nature it may be difficult to establish a lack of care simply because the desired result is not achieved. Thus in **Luxmoore-May v. Messenger May Baverstock (1990)** auctioneers who had exercised reasonable care and skill were held not liable for failing to attribute a painting to be the work of a little known artist when they were asked to research its value with a view to it being auctioned, even though their valuation resulted in the painting being sold for less than one hundredth of its actual value.

The supplier also has a duty of care to third parties where he provides advice which he knows will be relied on by such persons. However in such a case his liability will not be in contract, but rather in the tort of negligence. For this tort to arise there must be a special relationship between the parties. A special relationship exists where the statement maker possesses special skill or expertise and knows that his statements will be relied on by the recipient. In **Hedley Byrne & Co. Ltd v. Heller & Partners Ltd (1964)** a bank negligently gave a reference regarding the credit worthiness of one of its customers to an advertising firm and would have been liable for losses incurred in consequence of the reference, but for a disclaimer notice protecting the bank from liability.

The **Hedley Byrne** principle could result in accountants being exposed to a liability in an indeterminate amount for an indeterminate time to an indeterminate class for investors, creditors, banks and government authorities all rely on accounts. However, in **Caparo Industries plc v. Dickman & Others (1990)** the House of Lords held that the duty of care for negligent statements causing economic loss should be restricted to situations where the statement maker is actually aware of the transaction which the recipient of the statement has in contemplation, and knows that the statement will be communicated to him and that it is likely that he will rely on it in deciding whether or not to engage in the transaction contemplated. Accordingly, there is no general duty of care on an accountant to shareholders and the general public.

Hedley Byrne & Co. Ltd v. Heller & Partners Ltd shows that where a duty of care exists, the accountant may exclude or limit liability for its breach by using a 'disclaimer notice'. However, the use of such notices is subject to the provisions of the Unfair Contract Terms Act 1977 which regulates exemptions clauses. In **Harris v. Wyre Forest District Council (1990)** the House of Lords held that a disclaimer notice used in a surveyors report could not protect the surveyors from liability since it was subject to the 1977 Act and on the facts of the case was unreasonable.

QUESTION 27 Advise *A* in the following cases:

(a) *A* intends to take his family for a motoring holiday in Cornwall. He discovers that his friend *B* is also going for a holiday in Cornwall and offers to give him a lift, there and back, in his car. In return, *B* offers to share the cost of the petrol.

(b) The *B* Company advertises for tenders for a specified number of bricks for houses which the company is building, to be delivered 'as and when required'. *A* submits a tender which the company accepts. The company does not order any bricks from *A*.

(c) *B* agrees gratuitously to take *A*'s greyhound to a race meeting. He forgets to do so, and the dog remains in the kennel. The dog was favourite for the race in which it was entered.

(d) *A* promises *B* £100 if he stops smoking for a year. After *B* has refrained from smoking for three months *A* informs him that he was withdrawing his offer.

ANSWER (a) Social arrangements are not legally enforceable as they are not of a contractual nature. In **Coward v. M.I.B. (1963)** a worker informally arranged to carry a neighbour/workmate to and from work in return for some consideration. The Court of Appeal held that the arrangement was not intended to have legal consequences. **Coward Case** was followed in **Connell v. M.I.B. (1969)** on an extra-contractual ground. So *A* is advised that the arrangement is not a contract and will not be enforced in a court of law.

(b) A request for tender is a request to state the lowest price at which tradesmen can supply goods or do a specific piece of work. Such a request is not an offer but simply an invitation to treat. If, however, the request also states that the lowest tender will be accepted, then it is treated as an offer with the result that the lowest tender will have to be accepted **(Spencer v. Harding 1870).** If, on the other hand, the request states that the tender is to supply goods 'as and when required' the tender amounts to a standing offer. However, the 'acceptance' by the other party does not constitute acceptance in the legal sense to produce a binding contract. Each requisition by the offeree is an individual act of acceptance and creates a separate contract **(G.N.R. v. Witham 1893).** If the tradesman revokes his offer, he will not be made liable for future deliveries **(Offord v. Davies 1862)** unless he had bound himself to meet any orders which might be placed and there was consideration for the undertaking **(Miller v. F.A. Sadd & Son Ltd 1981).**

    A is therefore advised that the company will incur no liability for failure to place an order for bricks.

(c) The law will not enforce a gratuitous promise unless it is made by deed. As *A* did not provide any consideration for *B*'s promise to take his greyhound to the race meeting, *A* cannot sue *B* for breach of this promise. The agreement also appears to be of a social nature and so the onus of proof will be on *A* to show that the parties intended to create legal relations.

(d) In this transaction, *A* is binding himself by a conditional promise, leaving *B* free to perform the condition or not as he pleases. This type of transaction is called a unilateral contract because only one party is bound by it. It is doubtful though, whether that party can withdraw his promise before performance is completed. In **Carlill v. Carbolic Smokeball Co. (1893)** Bowen L.J. said that acceptance and performance constitute one act. So on general principles, the offeror should be able to withdraw his offer at any time before performance is completed. Support for this view is found in **Offord v. Davies (1862).** However, in **Errington v. Errington (1952)** Denning L.J. disagreed and said that acceptance is complete as soon as the other party commences performance although he is not entitled to any payment until he has completed performance. In **Daulia Ltd v. Four Millbank Nominees Ltd (1978)** the Court of Appeal said obiter that once performance has started, it would be too late to revoke the offer. So although the law is far from clear on this point, it would appear that *A* will not be allowed to withdraw his offer.

QUESTION 28 (a) What is the significance of the distinction between conditions and warranties?
(b) What implied conditions and warranties are imported into contracts governed by the Sale of Goods Act?   A.B.E. 1979

ANSWER (a) Traditionally, the terms of a contract have been split into conditions and warranties. A condition is a term of a contract which is so important that any breach entitles the injured party to claim damages and repudiate the contract. The term must go to the root of the contract. A warranty is a term of the contract which is not as important as a condition and only gives rise to a claim for damages.

   Whether a term is a condition or warranty is a question of the intention of the parties and that intention is deduced from the circumstances of the case. If the intention of the parties cannot be ascertained, the court will address itself to the commercial importance of the term. In **Poussard v. Spiers (1876)** an actress failed to turn up for the first few performances of a play owing to illness. It was held that her promise to perform from the first night was a condition and as it was broken, the management could terminate her contract. On the other hand, in **Bettini v. Gye (1876)** a singer was four days late for rehearsals. It was held that the rehearsal clause was only subsidiary to the main purpose of the contract and so the management could only claim damages and not terminate the contract. In the case of sale of goods, conditions and warranties are defined by the Sale of Goods Act 1979. In insurance law, 'warranty' means condition.

Certain contractual undertakings cannot be categorised as 'conditions' or 'warranties', and so the right to rescind will only arise if the breach is sufficiently serious. These terms are described as 'innominate' or 'intermediate' terms and there is judicial support for the view that they form a separate category from 'conditions' and 'warranties' (see for judicial comment Diplock L.J. in **Hong Kong Fir Shipping Co. Ltd v. Kawasaki Kisen Kaisha Ltd 1962**). An innominate term can only arise where the parties have not declared their intention as to whether the term is to be a condition or a warranty and as to its effect on the contract, if broken. Thus, in **Bunge Corp. v. Tradax Export S.A. (1981)** Lord Wilberforce recognised "the modern approach of not being over-ready to construe terms as conditions unless the contract closely required the court to do so."

The significance of the distinction between conditions and warranties then, is the legal consequences that follow the breach. A breach of the former entitles the innocent party to repudiate and claim damages. A breach of the latter only entitles him to claim damages. In certain cases, the innocent party has to treat a breach of condition as though it was a breach of warranty. If the condition is there solely for the benefit of the innocent party and it is broken, the innocent party may ignore it. If, with the knowledge of the breach, he chooses not to repudiate, he loses his right to repudiate in which case he is said to be able to sue on a warranty ex post facto – he can sue only for damages. In other cases, he has to sue on a warranty ex post facto if he received a substantial benefit. Section 11(4) of the Sale of Goods Act 1979 states that if a contract for sale is not severable and the buyer has accepted the goods or any part thereof, the breach of any condition is to be treated as a breach of warranty. 'Accept' means that he intimates acceptance to the seller or the goods have been delivered to him and he does any act inconsistent with the ownership of the seller or he keeps the goods after a lapse of time.

(b) The terms implied under the Sale of Goods Act 1979 are contained in sections 12–15. They are implied, so that the buyer need not ensure that they are written down. Moreover, in a consumer sale, the seller cannot exclude them by use of an exclusion clause. In essence, they provide two categories of protection, namely, against failing to get ownership and against getting defective or unsuitable goods.

Under section 12, there is an implied condition that the seller has a right to sell the goods. It would appear from case law that the right to sell is much wider than having title to the goods. Thus, in **Niblett v. Confectioners' Materials Co. Ltd (1921)** where the seller could have been prevented by law from selling, because he had infringed a trade mark of another company, the court held that the seller was in breach of section 12 (the same section under a previous Act) even though the seller had title to the goods. Since the passing of title is the central feature of the contract, the buyer will be in a very strong position if section 12 is broken. In **Rowland v. Divall (1923)** the defendant sold a car to the plaintiff which neither party knew to be stolen. After four months use, the police took it away. In an action to recover the price the seller argued that (a) an allowance should be made for the four months' use and (b) by using the car for four months, the buyer had 'accepted' the goods within the meaning of S.11(4) so that he was compelled to treat the breach of the condition as a breach of warranty and could not recover the full contract price. However, the court of appeal held that (a) the buyer had paid for the property in the goods and had not received it; (b) the four months' use was irrelevant; (c) as the buyer did not receive the property in the goods there was nothing to accept; (d) accordingly, the buyer was entitled to recover the full price. Section 12 also implies the following warranties: the goods will be free from any incumbrance in favour of a third party (e.g. a hire purchase agreement) and the buyer will enjoy quiet possession of the goods. A seller who is doubtful about his title to the goods may expressly sell them on the basis that he is transferring 'only such title as he may have'. To this extent the implied condition that he has a right to sell and the implied warranties can be modified (S.12(3)). However, an exemption clause cannot be used to exclude Section 12.

Section 13 states that in a sale by description, there is an implied condition that the goods will correspond with the description. All sales of unascertained goods are sales by description and even a sale of specific goods which the buyer has seen can be a sale by description. In **Beale v. Taylor (1967)** a car which was described as a 'Herald convertible, white 1961' was sold to a buyer who subsequently discovered that while the rear half of the car was part of a 1961 Herald convertible, the front half was part of an earlier model. The court held that the seller was in breach of S.13. 'Description' is very wide and covers such matters as ingredients, measurements, method of packing, quantity, quality and date of shipment.

Section 14(2) states that where goods are sold in the course of a business, there is an implied condition that they will be of merchantable quality. 'Merchantable quality' means suitable for the purpose(s) for which such goods are commonly bought. The standard of quality expected from the goods will depend very much on the price paid and the description given to the goods **(Cehave NV v. Bremer Handelgesellschaft m.b.h. 1976).** This condition as to merchantable quality will not be implied for defects drawn specifically to the buyer's attention before the contract is made and, if he had examined the goods, for defects which would have been revealed to him. Section 14(3) implies a condition as to fitness for purpose but for this condition to apply, the seller's business must have been to sell such goods, the buyer must have made known to him the special purpose for which he intended to use the goods and it must have been reasonable in the circumstances to assume that the buyer was relying on the seller's skill and judgement.

Section 15 states that where goods are sold by sample, there is an implied condition that the bulk will correspond with the sample, the buyer will have a reasonable opportunity of comparing the bulk with the sample and the goods will be of merchantable quality.

QUESTION 29 (a) Explain the meaning and importance of the 'officious bystander' test in relation to ascertaining the existence of contractual terms.
(b) Mrs. Cobbing takes her expensive evening gown to the shop of Williment Dry Cleaning Ltd to be cleaned. Inside the shop is a notice which states 'customers are advised that compensation for loss or damage to garments is limited to a maximum of £10 per item'.

Mrs. Cobbing queries this notice with the manager who assures her that she will get adequate compensation for any loss or damage incurred. Mrs. Cobbing leaves her gown with Williment Dry Cleaning Ltd who lose the gown. Mrs. Cobbing receives a cheque for £5 but the dry-cleaners refuse to consider any further claim. Advise Mrs. Cobbing.

A.C.C.A. 1977

ANSWER (a) The terms of a contract define the rights and duties arising under it. These terms may be express or implied terms. Implied terms are of three types – terms implied in fact, that is to say terms which the parties must have had in mind when they were contracting although they did not expressly say so; terms implied by custom (trade or local); and terms implied by law (e.g. under the Sale of Goods Act 1979). The 'officious bystander' is only relevant to terms implied in fact. He is a fictitious and more interested person than his dull colleague 'the reasonable man', invented by the court to give a contract such business efficacy as the parties had intended. If while the parties were making the contract, this fictitious person was to ask whether a particular term was part of the contract and the parties were to sharply retort 'Yes, of course it is', then the court would imply the term in the contract.

The principle on which a court will imply terms in fact was stated in **Shirlaw v. Southern Foundries Ltd (1929)** by Mackinnon L.J. as follows "Prima facie that which in any contract is left to be implied and need not be expressed is something so obvious that it goes without saying, so that, if while the parties were making their bargain, an officious bystander were to suggest some express provision for it in the agreement they would testily suppress him with a common 'Oh, of course!'" In **The Moorcock (1889)** where a ship while unloading settled on a ridge of hard ground beneath the mud and was damaged, the court implied a term into the contract of an undertaking by the wharfingers that the river bottom was in such a condition as not to endanger the ship. In **Pettitt v. Pettitt (1970)** Lord Diplock said that "the officious bystander... may pose the question but the court, not the parties gives the answer".

For a term to be implied in fact both parties must have known of the matter to be implied. In **Spring v. National Amalgamated Stevedores & Dockers Society (1956)** the plaintiff who had been a member of another trade union, joined the defendant union. In accepting his membership the defendant union was acting in breach of the TUC's Bridlington Agreement which stated, inter alia, that no union should accept workers previously belonging to another union without inquiry. The defendant union ultimately expelled the plaintiff in obedience to the Bridlington Agreement and tried to justify the expulsion on the ground that it was an implied term of the contract of union membership that the union should be able to comply with its lawful agreements. The court rejected this argument with Sir L. Stone V.C. referring to the officious bystander test as follows "If that test were to be applied to the facts of the present case and the bystander had asked the plaintiff at the time he signed the acceptance form, 'Won't you put into it some reference to the Bridlington Agreement?' I have no doubt that the plaintiff would have answered, 'What is that?'"

If it is clear that one party would not have agreed to the matter to be implied because, for example, it was detrimental to his interest, the court will not imply the term. In **Shell U.K. Ltd v. Lostock Garage Ltd (1976)** an oil company agreed in writing to supply oil to a garage which undertook to buy its supplies solely from the company. After the oil company had reduced the price of oil supplied to neighbouring garages during a price war, the garage claimed that there was a term implied in its contract with the company that the latter would not normally discriminate against it. The court refused to imply such term because the oil company would not have agreed to it.

(b)   A clause attempting to exclude or limit liability is only valid if it is incorporated in the contract and covers the type of loss or damage that has occurred. The clause is incorporated if it is set out or referred to in a contractual document which the parties signed **(L'Estrange v. Graucob 1934);** or if the document is un-signed, then if either the person against whom it is being relied on knows of its existence (e.g., through a consistent course of previous dealings as in **Kendall v. Lillico 1969**) or if reasonable steps are taken to bring it to his notice before or at the time the contract is made. If notice of the clause is given after the contract is made, the clause will not be effective (see **Olley v. Marlborough Court Ltd 1949;** and **Thornton v. Shoe Lane Parking Ltd 1971**).

From what has been said above, the clause limiting the dry cleaners' liability for loss or damage to customers' garments has been effectively incorporated in the contract with Mrs. Cobbing. However, this customer may seek to avoid the clause on two grounds.

She may rely on the Unfair Contract Terms Act 1977 in which case, the dry cleaners will have to prove that the clause was reasonable if it is to be upheld. Secondly, she may rely on the oral representation by the manager that she would be adequately compensated for any loss or damage to her gown. At common law, a misrepresentation about the extent of an exemption clause (see **Curtis v. Chemical Cleaning & Dyeing Co. Ltd 1951,**and an oral undertaking inconsistent with an exemption clause and given by the person to benefit from such clause, will override the clause (see **Evans & Son Ltd v. Andrea Merzario Ltd 1976).**

In light of the above authorities, Mrs. Cobbing is advised that the limitation of liability clause displayed inside Williment Dry Cleaning Ltd will not affect her claim for full compensation for the loss of her evening gown.

QUESTION 30 (a) Define misrepresentation. Distinguish between (i) fraudulent and (ii) innocent misrepresentation.
(b) Brenda bought a pony from Harry for £3,000 and soon after the sale the pony collapsed and died from exhaustion. The vet's certificate indicated that the pony was suffering from a rare heart disease which could not have been known by the seller. Brenda informs you that while she was examining the pony before the sale Harry had said to her "You need not look for anything; the horse is perfectly sound. If there was anything the matter with the horse I would tell you." Advise Brenda.

ANSWER (a) A misrepresentation is a false statement of fact which induces a contract. Fact must be distinguished from expressions of opinion **(Bisset v. Wilkinson 1927)** as the latter are not representations. However, a statement of opinion may be a representation if, by implication, it involves a statement of fact. If an opinion is based on facts and those facts are particularly within the speaker's knowledge, then there is a representation that he had reasonable grounds for this opinion **(Brown v. Raphael 1958)**. Mere vague expressions (sales talk) are not representations.

A misrepresentation is only actionable if it actually induced the innocent party to make the contract. Thus no cause of action will lie if the representee did not allow the representation to influence his decision to enter into the contract, or if he did not know of the representation **(Horsfall v. Thomas 1862)**. Similarly, a misrepresentation will not be actionable if the innocent party relied on his own judgement.

A distinction must be made between fraudulent and innocent misrepresentation. The test of fraud is the absence of honest belief, knowingly making a false statement or being reckless as to its veracity **(Derry v. Peek 1889)**. Negligence is not sufficient for fraud. A statement may be fraudulent although it was made without bad motive and without intention to cause loss **(Polhill v. Walter 1832)**. Innocent misrepresentation is one that is not fraudulent. It may be negligent.

For a fraudulent misrepresentation the action is brought in the tort of deceit and the innocent party will always get damages. The object of damages in tort is to put the plaintiff in the position he would have been in had the misrepresentation not been made. Consequential loss is also recoverable as long as it is not too remote; but the rule of remoteness in an action for deceit is not the normal one of foreseeability. "The defendant is bound to make reparation for all the actual damages directly flowing from the fraudulent inducement. ...It does not lie in the mouth of the fraudulent person to say that (the damages) could not reasonably have been foreseen" (per Lord Denning M.R. in **Doyle v. Olby (Ironmongers) Ltd 1969**). The contract is also voidable at the option of the misled person. If he rescinds, the contract is terminated back to the beginning (ab initio). Rescission can be effected by simply taking back goods obtained by fraud or by simply notifying the representor within a reasonable time. If the representor intentionally disappears and cannot be found, the victim must only do his best to show that he is giving up the contract **(Car & Universal Finance Co. Ltd v. Caldwell 1965).**

For a negligent misrepresentation the action is brought either for common law negligence **(Hedley Byrne v. Heller & Partners Ltd 1964)** or under the Misrepresentation Act 1967. Section 2(1) of the 1967 Act imposes an absolute obligation on the representor not to make representations unless he has reasonable grounds for believing them to be true. This subsection awards damages to the victim of the misrepresentation who must have contractual relations with the representor. The measure of damages under S.2(1) is the tortious measure and not that applicable to breach of contract **(Sharneyford Supplies v. Edge 1985).** Whether negligent or non-negligent (other than fraudulent) section 2(2) provides that where the facts are such that the victim of the misrepresentation can rescind the contract the court may prevent him from rescinding the contract and award him damages instead if rescission would be inequitable. Damages are awarded instead of, and not in addition to, rescission under subsection 2. So in the case of a non-negligent misrepresentation if rescission is not possible (because the parties cannot be restored to their pre-contractual position where the subject-matter has perished or third parties' rights are involved) the victim will be without a remedy.

(b) Harry's statement to Brenda while she was examining the horse could be a representation or a contractual statement. Although the remedies for misrepresentation namely rescission and damages, are the same as for breach of contract they differ in several respects and Brenda may be worse off if she bases her claim on misrepresentation rather than breach of contract.

Rescission for misrepresentation is based on the assumption that the formation of the contract is defective and its purpose is to put the parties substantially back to their pre-contractual position. This will only be done if restitution is possible and the court does not exercise its discretion under S.2(2) of the 1967 Act to award damages in lieu of rescission. On the other hand, rescission for breach is based on the assumption that the performance of the contract is defective and allows the innocent party as of right to terminate the contract from the date of breach where the breach is sufficiently serious. Damages for misrepresentation are available as of right only on proof of fault (fraud or negligence) by the statement maker and are assessed according to tort principles which require the victim to be put in the position he would have been in had the tort not been committed. Damages for breach are available as of right, regardless of fault, and are assessed according to contract principles which require the victim to be put in the position he would have been in had the contract been performed (i.e., had the representation turned out to be true).

Brenda cannot obtain rescission for misrepresentation since restitution is not possible. She cannot return a live pony to Harry. Nor can she obtain damages for misrepresentation since Harry's statement was made innocently and the court has no discretion under subsection 2 to award damages in such cases. However, Brenda can recover damages for breach of contract. The court is prepared to treat a statement as contractual rather than a mere representation where, as in Brenda's case, the maker of a statement, knowing that the other party places great importance on a certain fact, states that the fact is true **(Schawel v. Reade 1913).**

QUESTION 31 (a) 'Silence does not amount to misrepresentation.'

Comment.

(b) Biggles wished to take out a comprehensive motor insurance. On the proposal form he stated, in response to a question, that he had never previously been refused motor insurance by any other company. This was untrue. The insurance company later discovered this and refused to pay him any compensation after he had been involved in an accident. Advise Biggles.

What would your advice be if the question as to previous insurance had not been asked on the form and Biggles did not reveal the refusal?

ANSWER (a) A misrepresentation takes an active form and may be expressed as a positive assertion of fact or inferred from conduct. Thus, as a rule, silence cannot amount to misrepresentation. In **Bell v. Lever Bros Ltd (1932)** Lord Atkin said "The failure to disclose a material fact which might influence the mind of a prudent contractor does not give a right to avoid the contract."

There are, however, some instances where silence or non-disclosure would afford a ground for relief. These are where silence distorts a positive representation; where the contract is a contract of utmost good faith; and where a fiduciary relationship exists between the contracting parties.

In the first instance, if a person makes a representation and it is not a full and frank disclosure then it may be a misrepresentation if what he withholds makes it a half truth. Even if the statement is true at the time it is made, then if the situation changes at the time the contract is made so that the statement is no longer true, failure to inform the other party of such change, may amount to a misrepresentation **(With v. O'Flanagan 1936).**

Contracts *uberrimae fidei* also impose an obligation to disclose to the other party material facts known to a contractor. Silence in such cases amounts to a misrepresentation. Examples of contracts *uberrimae fidei* are insurance contracts.

Finally, where the relationship between the parties to a contract is a confidential one the law also imposes a duty of disclosure.

(b) It is necessary as a first step in considering Biggles claim for compensation under the motor insurance policy to ascertain whether the proposal form which he filled in contained a 'basis' clause. If it did, then the answers given by Biggles would form the basis of the contract and any inaccuracy in his answers would entitle the insurance company to repudiate liability. If it did not, then the untrue statement made by him would not entitle the insurance company to repudiate liability unless it amounted to the non-disclosure or misrepresentation of a material fact **(Dawsons Ltd v. Bonnon 1922).** A fact is material if it would guide a prudent insurer in determining whether he would take the risk and, if so, at what premium and on what conditions.

On the assumption that the proposal form did not contain a 'basis' clause, the insurance company could only avoid liability if Biggles fraudulent misrepresentation related to a material fact. In **Locker & Woolf v. Western Australian Insurance (1936)** it was decided that, where the insurers asked a question as to previous refusals in a proposal form for fire insurance, a previous refusal in respect of an application for motor vehicle insurance was material and ought to have been disclosed. The insurance company is therefore entitled to repudiate liability and Biggles has no course of action against them.

Even if the insurance company did not ask the question as to previous insurance, Biggles would have been under a legal obligation to disclose this refusal since non-disclosure of a material fact would entitle the insurers to repudiate liability. Insurance contracts are contracts *uberrimae fidei*.

QUESTION 32 (a) In what circumstances, if any, will proof of mistake render a contract void?
(b) *A* had notepaper printed showing the address of some large but non-existent factory premises and a whole string of offices abroad. Using this notepaper, he ordered and obtained from *B* a quantity of goods which he promptly resold to *C*, who acted in good-faith. *A* has now disappeared with the proceeds of the sale. Advise *B*. A.C.C.A. 1976

ANSWER (a) Generally speaking, where mistake operates, it renders the contract void. There are several classification of mistakes which would affect a contract. The most modern, and the one readily accepted by the courts is the classification between common, mutual and unilateral mistakes.

A common mistake exists where both parties make the same mistake about one subject matter. An example of this type of mistake is where the parties contract over a subject-matter which they believe to be in existence but which does not in fact exist. In **Galloway v. Galloway (1914)** a husband and wife entered into a separation agreement under the mistaken belief that they were legally married. The court held that the contract was void. A common mistake as to the quality of the subject-matter will not however affect a contract at common law **(Leaf v. International Galleries 1950).** To mitigate the harshness of this principle, the Court of Appeal in **Solle v. Butcher (1950)** stated that equity will in appropriate cases, regard the contract as voidable and set it aside, thus relieving the party who has suffered most but only on terms which are fair between the parties. In **Grist v. Bailey (1966)** *G* contracted to buy a house for £850 which both the buyer and seller believed to be subject to a statutory tenancy. Before completion, it was discovered that the tenant was not so protected and that the house with vacant possession was valued at £2,250. It was held that as the mistake was one of quality it did not render the contract void at common law. However, the court was prepared to exercise its equitable jurisdiction and set aside the contract on the terms that *G* should be permitted to purchase the property at £2250 if he so wished.

A mutual mistake exists where both parties make a mistake about different subject-matters. An example of this type of mistake is mistake as to the identity of the subject-matter. In **Raffles v. Wichelhaus (1864)** *W* agreed to buy cotton 'ex Peerless, Bombay' from *R*. There were two ships leaving Bombay both bearing the same name. *W* meant the ship leaving in October, *R* meant the ship leaving in December. It was held that the contract was void.

A unilateral mistake exists where only one party makes the mistake. Examples of this type of mistake are mistake as to the identity of the parties **(Lewis v. Averay 1972);** and mistake as to the nature or character of a document signed **(Saunders v. Anglia Building Society 1970).**

(b) A mistake by one contracting party as to the identity of the other party will only render the contract void if the identity of the other party was material to the contract i.e. if the contract would not have been entered into had the true identity of the other party been known **(Cundy v. Lindsay 1878).** If however, the mistake is only as to an attribute of the other party, the contract is not void for mistake but at the most may be voidable for fraud **(Phillips v. Brooks 1919).**

In **Lewis v. Averay (1972)** the court said that where the parties contract through correspondence and one party fraudulently misrepresents his identity as that of an existing person, there is a presumption that the innocent party intends to contract with the person whom the fraudulent party purported to be. Where however, the parties contract face to face the presumption is that the parties intend to contract with each other and any mistake made will be one as to attributes.

The facts of the problem are similar to those in **King's Norton Metal Co. Ltd v. Edridge (1897).** In that case the plaintiffs received an order from 'Hallam & Co.' which was described as a substantial firm. In fact 'Hallam & Co.' consisted of an impecunious rogue called Wallis. The plaintiff sent the goods to 'Hallam & Co.' on credit. Wallis took possession of them, failed to pay and sold them to the defendants. It was held that the plaintiff had intended to contract with the writer as there was no real 'Hallam & Co.' in existence but only an alias.

B is therefore advised that the contract is only voidable for fraud. However since *B* did not take steps to avoid it before the goods were sold by *A* to an innocent third party *C*, the latter has a good title to the goods.

QUESTION 33 (a) In what circumstances can a person deny his own signature on the ground of mistake?

(b) *M*, a company director, employed *N* as his confidential clerk. *N* placed a document on *M*'s desk and, requesting *M* to sign it, remarked 'You don't need to read it, Sir, it is one of our usual orders to *X* Ltd'. *X* Ltd were well known customers of the company. *M* signed the document. It was really a guarantee of *N*'s overdraft at the *L*. Bank.

N, having failed to clear his overdraft, the *L*. Bank seek to make *M* liable upon the guarantee. Advise *M*.

I.C.S.A. 1979

ANSWER (a) At common law, a person who signs a document is bound by his signature to that document and will incur any liability on it whether or not he reads or understands it **(L'Estrange v. Graucob Ltd 1934).** In appropriate cases, however, equity will permit him to avoid liability by allowing him to plead the defence Non Est Factum (It is not his deed). This defence originated in **Thoroughgood's Case (1584)** and may be raised if the document had been incorrectly read over to him and his mistake is one relating to its nature or character. The defence was successfully raised in **Foster v. Mackinnon (1869)** by a person who signed a bill of exchange, having been told it was a guarantee and in **Carlisle & Cumberland Banking Co. v. Bragg (1911)** by a person who signed a guarantee after he was told that it was a proposal for insurance.

If the party is mistaken only as to the contents of the document and not as to its nature, his plea of 'non est factum' cannot succeed. In **Howatson v. Webb (1907)** the defendant signed a mortgage believing it to be a transfer of land. It was held that the two transactions were, in fact, of the same nature so the defence failed.

Following the decision of the House of Lords in **Saunders v. The Anglia Building Society (1970)** the defence has been severely limited and will not be available to a person who has failed to exercise due care before signing the document concerned. In that case, Mrs. G executed a deed which she was told was a deed of gift to her nephew but which turned out to be an assignment on her sale of her leasehold house to the nephew. Mrs. G was 78 years old at the time, she had mislaid her spectacles and did not read the document which she signed. She would not have signed it had she known the true facts. It was held that the plea of non est factum could not succeed.

(b) Where a person mistakenly signs a document believing it to be something quite different from what it is, he may be able to plead *non est factum* and avoid liability on the document. In **Saunders v. The Anglia Building Society (1970)** the House of Lords said that for this defence to apply three conditions must be satisfied – (i) there must be a fraudulent misrepresentation by one party inducing the other party to sign the document; (ii) the latter must not have signed the document negligently; and (iii) his mistake must be a mistake of the nature or character of the document.

M, the company director would appear to satisfy conditions (i) and (iii) but it is doubtful that he has satisfied condition (ii). *M* ought to have read the document before signing it. By not doing so, this would be prima facie, negligence on *M*'s part. *M* may attempt to dispel negligence by showing that *N* was his confidential clerk who was expected to act honestly.

QUESTION 34 Explain the equitable remedies for a mistake which is not recognised as an operative mistake at common law.

ANSWER There has always been an equitable set of rules for mistake. However, since **Solle v. Butcher (1950)** virtually a new set of rules has developed in equity. Equity can set aside a contract which would not be set aside at common law; and rectify a mistake which common law does not recognise. The mistake need not be fundamental in the common law sense but a trivial mistake would not do. Therefore in equity 'fundamental' means important. To obtain relief in equity, the party seeking it must not himself be at fault and he must act promptly. Time runs from the date of the contract and not from the date of discovery of the mistake. Equity intervenes in three ways to provide relief for a mistake which is not an operative mistake at common law. It may refuse specific performance, it may set aside the contract (rescission) and it may rectify the mistake. Equity may refuse to grant an order of specific performance against the mistaken party even though the contract is valid at common law because the mistake is not one of fact or fundamental in the common law sense. In **Day v. Wells (1861)** *W* instructed an auctioneer to sell cottages, thinking that he had told the auctioneer to put a reserve price on them. The auctioneer sold the cottages without reserve, at a lower price. The successful bidder sought an order of specific performance against *W*. It was refused.

Equity can rescind a contract if to carry out the contract at common law would cause undue hardship to the party who has made the mistake **(Solle v. Butcher).** In **Peters v. Batchelor (1950)** the Court of Appeal set aside on terms a lease of premises on the ground that the parties thought that they had been used only for business purposes when in fact they had been used for residential purposes and thus subject to the Rents Act.

Equity may also give relief by rectifying the mistake although it would not upset the contract. If the parties conclude an **agreement** and later embody that agreement in a contractual document which does not accurately embody their agreement, equity may rectify the document so as to accord with their intention, and if appropriate, order specific performance of the document so rectified. Rectification will only be granted if three matters are established. There must be complete agreement first and it is not necessary that the prior agreement should be an enforceable contract, as long as it is clear. Secondly, it must be proved that the intention was to reduce the prior terms into writing and that that intention continues. Finally, there must be very clear evidence that there was a mistake common to both parties. It follows that if the document accurately records the prior agreement, it cannot be rectified merely because the prior agreement was made under a mistake. **(F.E. Rose Ltd v. W.H. Pim & Co. Ltd 1953).**

QUESTION 35 (a) Explain the difference between duress and undue influence. How do they affect the validity of a contract?
(b) Mrs. Grant threatened to prosecute Mrs. Grey's son (who had stolen funds belonging to Mrs. Grant) if Mrs. Grey did not agree to buy a certain picture from Mrs. Grant at twice its market value. Mrs. Grey at that time agreed to buy the picture but later refused to complete the transaction.

Advise Mrs. Grey.

A.A.T. (I.A.S.) 1977

ANSWER (a) At common law a contract may be avoided on grounds of duress. Originally duress had a very restrictive meaning. It meant actual or threatened physical violence to, or unlawful constraint of the person of the contracting party **(Friedeberg-Seeley v. Klass 1957.** Thus a threat to the goods of a person was not duress **(Skeate v. Beale 1890).** Nor was a threat to prosecute the other contracting party or his close relative for a crime that actually had been committed **(Fisher & Co. v. Apollingris Co. 1875).**

In recent years, the court has been prepared to extend the scope of duress to cover economic duress (i.e., threatening unpleasant economic consequences to a person if he does not agree to contract) as long as the threat is unlawful and prevents consent being given freely. In **Pao On v. Lau Yiu Long (1980)** the Privy Council was prepared to recognise economic duress when the plaintiffs threatened to break a contract with a company unless its shareholders guaranteed any loss resulting from the performance of the contract. On the facts there was no duress because the shareholders considered the matter before giving the guarantee and felt that it was unlikely that they would have to make any payment under it. In **Universe Tankships Inc. v. ITWF (1982)** a plea of economic duress did succeed before the House of Lords. There, trade union officials refused permission for a ship to leave port unless the plaintiffs made a payment to the union's welfare fund. The plaintiffs were able to recover the payment because of economic pressure.

Undue influence is a ground in equity to avoid a contract. It is "some unfair and improper conduct, some coercion from outside, some overreaching, some form of cheating, and generally, though not always, some personal advantage obtained by the guilty party" (per Lindley L.J. in **Allcard v. Skinner 1887).** Undue influence falls under two categories of relationships, namely, (i) where no special relationship between the contracting parties exists; and (ii) where a confidential or special relationship exists.

With the former, the person complaining of undue influence must prove that actual pressure was applied. In **Kaufman v. Gerson (1904),** *G*'s husband misappropriated money entrusted to him by *K. K* threatened *G* that if she did not make good the money he would bring a prosecution against her husband. *G* then agreed in writing to make good the money in return for *K*'s promise not to prosecute. It was held that the contract would be set aside.

With the latter, the law presumes undue influence and it is for the defendant to disprove it. Examples of special relationships are doctor and patient, solicitor and client, trustee and beneficiary, guardian and ward, religious adviser and disciple and parent and child until the child attains his majority and is emancipated **(Lancashire Loans Ltd v. Black 1934).**

The presumption of undue influence is rebutted by showing that the party under undue influence had made a free exercise of independent will. The most usual way of doing this is to show that the other party had independent advice before entering into the transaction.

Undue influence makes the contract voidable in equity but relief may be lost by affirmation of the contract after the influence ceases; by failure to seek relief within a reasonable time after the removal of the influence **(Allcard v. Skinner)**; and by third parties bona fide acquiring rights in the contract.

The principle of undue influence has been extended by statute to cover malpractices like 'high-pressure' salesmanship. Under the Fair Trading Act 1973, the Director-General of Fair Trading may initiate inquiries into trade practices which subject consumers to undue pressure to enter into consumer transactions containing inequitable terms. Such inquiries may lead to an order under the Act forbidding the continuance of the practice. Breach of the order may lead to both civil and criminal sanctions.

(b) Equity will rescind a contract entered into by a person under a threat from the other contracting party to prosecute him or a close relative for a criminal offence. In the leading case of **Williams v. Bayley (1866)** where the facts were similar to those in the problem it was held that the father's agreement to make an equitable mortgage to the bank in consideration of the return of some promissory notes was voidable on the ground that undue influence had been exerted by the bank by playing on the father's fear for his son's safety.

Mrs. Grey is therefore advised that she is entitled to repudiate the contract for the purchase of a picture from Mrs. Grant at twice its market value.

QUESTION 36 (a) In what circumstances, if any, may the legal part of a contract be severed from the illegal part?
(b) Consider whether the following agreement is legally enforceable. Attoh caught Idi stealing cocoa from his store. Attoh agreed not to prosecute Idi in return for Idi's promise to pay for the cocoa.

A.I.A. 1977

ANSWER (a) If a contract is only partly illegal, the court may sever the contract and enforce the valid part and refuse assistance with regard to the illegal part. Severance is only possible if three conditions are satisfied:
(i) The contract must be of such a kind as can be severed. Contracts illegal at common law cannot be severed. Such contracts would include contracts to commit a crime or tort, contracts for immoral purposes, and contracts to trade with the enemy. The

courts are generally more willing to sever contracts in restraint of trade since they are only void on grounds of public policy. Thus in **Bull v. Pitney-Bowes Ltd (1967)** an unreasonable restraint clause was severed from the rest of the contract.

(ii) It must be possible to sever the offending clause by deletion and without the court re-wording the contract. This has often been referred to as the 'blue pencil' test. In **Mason v. Provident Clothing & Supply Co. Ltd (1913)** the contract was an undertaking not to compete within twenty-five miles of London. The House of Lords held that this contract was unenforceable and it refused to strike out 'within twenty-five miles of London' and to substitute 'in Islington' (where the defendant was competing) as this would not have severed the contract but would have redrafted it.

(iii) The effect of severance must not be such as to change the nature of the contract. In **Goldsoll v. Goldman (1915)** the defendant who traded in imitation jewellery in the UK, sold his business to the plaintiff and agreed that he would not trade in imitation or real jewellery for two years in any part of the UK or in certain overseas countries. It was held that references to real jewellery and foreign countries which were too wide could be severed without altering the basic character of the contract.

(b) The rule is that contracts tending to interfere with the administration of justice are illegal at common law on grounds of public policy. Such contracts would include an agreement to stifle a prosecution on a matter of public interest and concern. In **Windhill Local Board of Health v. Vint (1890).** Cotton L.J. stated that the courts would not enforce or recognise any agreement which had the effect of withdrawing from the ordinary course of justice a prosecution for a public offence. In **Clubb v. Hutson (1865)** the court held that obtaining money or credit by false pretence was a public offence for which no compromise was permitted.

The agreement between Attoh and Idi for theft if the latter paid for the cocoa is therefore illegal and so not enforceable.

QUESTION 37 Prunella, a prostitute, hired a chauffeur-driven car from Roger who was unaware that she intended to use it to ply her trade. She now refuses to pay the hire charge. Advise Roger.

ANSWER At common law a contract to promote sexual immorality is illegal on grounds of public policy and will not be enforced by the courts. Where however, the contract is ex facie

63

lawful and is used to effect an unlawful purpose the court will have to consider the state of mind of the parties before deciding on the legal consequences of the contract.

If one party intended that the lawful contract was a means of achieving an unlawful act and this intention was known to the other party then the court would treat the contract as if it was unlawful at the inception and both parties will be remediless. In **Pearce v. Brooks (1866)** plaintiffs let a carriage on hire to a prostitute in the knowledge that she would use it for the purpose of plying for trade. In an action to recover the hire charge the court held that as the purpose for which the carriage would be used was known to the plaintiffs, no relief could be given to them. In **Holman v. Johnson (1775)** the court said that the rule existed not for the sake of the defendant but because the courts would not lend their aid to such a plaintiff.

It follows therefore that if the plaintiff was unaware of the purpose for which the party entered into the contract, then he may be allowed to enforce it. In **Archbolds (Freightage) Ltd v. S. Spanglett (1961)** the defendants contracted to carry the plaintiffs' whisky in a van which was not licensed to carry goods belonging to third parties. It was held that the plaintiffs could recover damages for breach of contract of carriage as they did not know that the van was not properly licensed.

As Roger was unaware that Prunella intended to use the car for the purpose of plying her trade as a prostitute, he may bring an action to recover the hire charges for the use of the car.

QUESTION 38 (a) Discuss the circumstances in which a contract in restraint of trade will be enforced by the Courts.
(b) *A* carried on business as an estate agent in Portsmouth and in London Bridge. He employed *C* as clerk and negotiator at the London Bridge office. *C* signed a covenant whereby he undertook for three years not to set up in business within a radius of seven miles of the Portsmouth or of the London Bridge offices of *A*. After termination of the contract of employment *C* forthwith opened an office of his own within a five miles radius of the Portsmouth office. Advise *A*.

A.B.E. 1979

ANSWER (a) A contract in restraint of trade is a contract which purports to restrict a person's economic activity. Such a contract is prima facie void at common law and will only be enforceable if there is an interest meriting protection, the restraint is reasonable and not contrary to public interest.

Contracts in restraint of trade may be divided into four main groups: restraints in employment contracts; restraints on the sale of a business; restraints in contracts between trade associations; and exclusive dealings agreements (solus agreement).

Employment contracts usually contain a term restraining an employee when he leaves his employer, from competing with him either by employment with a competitor or by competing personally. The courts will not uphold such a restraint unless the employer had a proprietary interest capable of being damaged by the employee and the restraint was reasonable and not contrary to public policy **(Kores Ltd v. Kolok Ltd 1959)**.

Restraints are sometimes imposed by the purchaser of a business on the vendor preventing the latter from competing with the business sold so as to damage the goodwill. Such restraints will be enforceable if reasonable. In **Nordenfelt v. Nordenfelt Guns and Ammunition Co. Ltd (1894),** *N*, a weapon inventor sold his world-wide business to *N* & Co. and promised that for 25 years he would not manufacture guns and ammunition anywhere in the world. It was held that the promise would be enforced.

Agreements between trade associations restricting the supply of goods or on price-fixing will only be enforceable if they are reasonable and do not prejudice the rights of third parties. Third parties are further protected by the Restrictive Trade Practices Acts and the Fair Trading Act 1973. These Acts require agreements to be registered with the Director General of Fair Trading if they are made by parties carrying on business in the production or supply of goods or services or they involve the restriction on pricing of goods or services, conditions of supply etc. The agreements will then be tested by the Restrictive Practices Court which would uphold them if they are reasonably necessary to protect the public; their removal would not be beneficial to the public, they are reasonable to protect the legitimate interests of the parties, their removal would adversely affect employment in the industry and they do not unduly restrict or discourage competition.

Contracts restricting the supply of goods to those from a particular manufacturer are often referred to as 'Solus trading Agreements'. The rule is that they are void if they restrict trade but not if they intend to promote trade **(Esso Petroleum Co. Ltd v. Harper's Garage Ltd 1968)**.

(b) An employee is free to go into competition with his former employer except if he contracts not to do so and that contract is upheld by the court. The court will uphold such a contract only if it is reasonable in all the circumstances. Its reasonableness will depend on a number of factors e.g., the duration of the restraint, the form of activity that is protected and the area the restraint is intended to cover.

In **Mason v. Provident Clothing & Supply Co. Ltd (1913)** a restraint imposed on a canvasser was held to be void as it covered an area about 1000 times as large as the area in which the canvasser was employed.

If *A* can show that although working at the London Bridge Estate Office, *C* had information of *A*'s Portsmouth clients, *A* may be able to get an injunction restraining *C* from carrying on business within the five miles radius of *A*'s Portsmouth office.

QUESTION 39 Under what circumstances can a party sue on a contract for the work which he has done, although he has not completed the work precisely as agreed?

A.A.T. (I.A.S.) 1977

ANSWER As a rule, before a party can sue for work done by him under a contract, his performance must be precise and exact to the letter of the contract. If he has not performed the exact thing he has agreed to do, then he gets nothing for his work. The harshness of this rule was illustrated in **Cutter v. Powell (1795)** where Cutter's widow failed to recover anything, because her husband, owing to his death, was unable to precisely perform his contract when he failed to complete the voyage.

This strict common law rule is subject to exceptions:

(a) **Divisible contracts.** Where performance is by instalments, payment can be recovered for work already done, although an action may lie for breach of contract for failure to complete performance. In **Ritchie v. Atkinson (1808)** a shipowner agreed to carry a cargo at a stipulated rate per ton. He carried only part of the cargo and was entitled to recover freight pro rata. Later he was held liable for failing to carry the rest of the cargo. Whether or not a contract is divisible will depend on the intention of the parties. However unless this intention is manifested, the court will presume that the contract is severable. In **Roberts v. Havelock (1832)** a contract to repair a ship did not expressly state when payment was to be made. The court held that the repairs did not have to be completed before payment could be claimed.

(b) **Prevention of performance by the other party.** Where the other party prevents the work being completed, then payment for the work already done can be obtained on a quantum meruit basis. In **Planché v. Colburn (1831)** the plaintiff agreed to write a book on Costume and Ancient Armour. He was to receive £100 on completion of the book. When the plaintiff had written part of the book the defendant stopped publication of the periodical in which the book was to be serialised. It was held that the plaintiff was entitled to a quantum meruit for the work he had done.

(c) **Acceptance of Partial Performance.** Where the other party accepts partial or imprecise performance, then payment for the work already done can also be obtained on a quantum meruit basis. Acceptance by the other party must be voluntary. If he had no choice but to accept, then no payment for the partial performance can be given. Thus, in **Sumpter v. Hedges (1898)** where *S*, who had contracted to build two houses and stables for £565 on *H*'s land, abandoned the contract after doing part of the work valued at £333 thus causing *H* to complete it, it was held that *S* was not entitled to recover the value of the work done.

(d) **Substantial Performance.** Where the contract is substantially performed subject only to certain minor defects and/or omissions, the performing party is entitled to the contract price less a deduction in respect of such defects and/or omissions. In **Hoenig v. Isaac (1952)** the plaintiff, an interior decorator agreed to decorate the defendant's flat, and to fit a wardrobe and a bookcase for £750. When the work was completed it was found to be defective owing to bad workmanship but which could be put right for £55. The court held that the decorator had substantially performed the contract and was thus entitled to the contract price less the cost of making good the defects.

What amounts to substantial performance is for the court to decide. However in **Bolton v. Mahadeva (1972)** it was held that as the defects amounted to between one-third and one-quarter of the contract price, the contract was not substantially performed.

QUESTION 40 (a) In what circumstances is a party to a contract bound to comply with a term concerning the time for performance of his obligations?

(b) Joseph is employed by Narina to decorate and furnish a flat she has acquired. She asks him to complete the work by 31st March when she intends to move into the flat. When the date arrives the decoration of the flat is only half completed and

Narina therefore tells him that, if the work is not completed within the next two weeks she will refuse to pay him. At the end of two weeks the decoration is almost completed, but no furniture has been installed. Subsequently Narina refuses to pay for any of the decoration or accept delivery of the furniture. Advise Joseph.

A.A.T. (I.A.S.) 1979

ANSWER (a) At common law, time for completion of performance is essential to a contract and a party will be entitled to treat the contract as at an end if the other party fails to perform his obligations within the stipulated time. The common law attitude was illustrated in **Sharp v. Christmas (1892).** In that case, a buyer of potatoes agreed to take delivery 'before Christmas next' but failed to do so. It was held that as time was of the essence of the contract, the seller was justified in reselling the potatoes to a third party.

Equity takes a less rigid view about time for performance and will not as a rule treat it as 'of the essence'. Hence for contracts specifically enforceable e.g. the sale of land, Equity may grant an order of specific performance to a party in spite of his delay in performing his obligations provided it would not result in injustice to the other party. Equity, however, treats time as the essence in the following cases:

(i) where the parties expressly stipulate a time for performance in the contract and indicate that its observance is essential;

(ii) where one party is guilty of undue delay and the other party notifies him that unless performance is completed within a reasonable time, the contract will be treated as broken;

(iii) where the nature of the subject-matter (as in the case of perishable goods and property which fluctuates in value with the passing of time) makes it essential that the stipulated time be met. In order to rationalise the law relating to time for performance S.41 Law of Property Act 1925 now states that equitable rules are to be applied in cases where a contract is capable of specific performance, even though the action is for damage. In other cases the common law rule that time is 'of the essence' prevails. On this principle the common law rule is generally presumed to apply in all mercantile contracts, e.g. with respect to a time fixed for the delivery of goods.

(b) Narina has made time of the essence of the contract by giving notice to Joseph after the time fixed for completion of performance, to complete within a reasonable time **(Charles Rickards Ltd v. Oppenheim 1950).** Since Joseph has failed to complete the work within the two weeks, he has prima facie broken the contract. Narina may lawfully repudiate the contract and need not accept delivery of the furniture. Joseph may, however, be entitled to part of the contract price if he shows that the contract is divisible, i.e., that the obligations relating to furnishing the flat can be separated from the work of decoration, or that his work amounts to substantial performance **(Hoenig v. Isaacs 1952).**

QUESTION 41 Explain what is meant by an anticipatory breach of contract, and discuss the remedies available to the party not at fault.

ANSWER Where a contracting party informs the other in advance that he will not perform his obligation when the time for performance arrives this is known as an anticipatory breach of contract.

When such a breach takes place the other party may either try to keep the contract alive by continuing to press for performance or he may accept the breach, treat the contract as discharged and sue for the appropriate remedy.

The consequences vary according to the choice that he makes. If the innocent party decides to wait for the date for performance to arrive he runs the risk of the contract being discharged in some other way than breach thus relieving the party in default from all liability as was in the case of **Avery v. Bowden (1855).** In that case the defendant chartered the plaintiff's ship and it was agreed that the defendant should load her with a cargo within 45 days. Before this period had lapsed the defendant's agent said that he had no cargo and requested the plaintiff to leave the port. However, the plaintiff remained at the port in the hope that the defendant would fulfil his promise. Before the 45 days had expired the Crimean War broke out. It was held that the contract was discharged by frustration and the parties were relieved from all liabilities.

On the other hand, the innocent party may be able to obtain larger damages by taking this course of action. Thus where the contract is for the sale of goods and the seller commits an anticipatory breach, the measure of damages will depend on the market price of the goods, not at the date of repudiation but at the time fixed for performance. If therefore the goods had appreciated in value, the amount of damages recoverable by the buyer will be higher.

Another advantage of keeping the contract open is that the party in breach may change his mind and perform the contract eventually and this may be more beneficial to the innocent party than damages.

If the innocent party elects to treat the contract as discharged, he may claim a remedy immediately and does not have to wait until the date when performance is due. In **Hochester v. De la Tour (1853)** the defendants agreed to employ the plaintiff as courier for three months from June 1. Before this date arrived, the defendants repudiated the contract. It was held that the plaintiff was entitled to claim damages immediately.

QUESTION 42 (a) State and explain the circumstances in which a contract may be frustrated.
(b) *S*, an exporter, and *B*, an importer, make a contract whereby *S* will supply a large quantity of palm oil to *B*. Before the contract was executed, *S* is prohibited by a government decree from exporting palm oil because of a serious shortage of oil in *S*'s country. *B* sues *S* for non-delivery. Advise *S* as to his legal position.
A.B.E. 1978

ANSWER (a) Frustration is unforeseen circumstances beyond the control of the parties, which make performance impossible. This doctrine originated in the nineteenth century to mitigate the harshness of the absolute rule of contract laid down in **Paradine v. Jane (1647)** that where a supervening event, through the fault of neither party, intervened then in the absence of the contract expressly providing for the contingency, the contract had to stand. Under the doctrine of frustration the parties will be discharged from their obligations provided neither of them was responsible for the events which rendered performance sterile or impossible.

There are a series of categories in which the courts will consider the element of frustration sufficient to discharge a contract. A contract for personal service will be discharged by supervening incapacity. Thus in the case of a contract of employment, death or physical disability of one of the parties will discharge the contract **(Boast v. Firth 1868).**

A contract will be frustrated if subsequent legislation renders its performance unlawful. The illegality must however affect the main purpose of the contract. Thus in **Denny, Mott & Co. Ltd v. James Fraser & Co. Ltd (1944)** where an agreement for the lease of a timber yard was made so that the lessee could buy the timber from the lessor the court held that the contract was frustrated when war-time regulations prohibited dealings in such goods since the main purpose of the contract, viz. trading in timber, had become illegal.

Physical impossibility to carry out the contract will also discharge the contract. Thus, in **Taylor v. Caldwell (1863)** where a music hall which was hired for the performance of concerts was destroyed by fire before any of the concerts had taken place, the contract of hire was held to be frustrated.

A contract will be frustrated where the common venture which the parties had in mind is no longer possible. In **Krell v. Henry (1903)** a room in Pall Mall was let to watch the coronation processions of King Edward VII from the windows of the room. When the King's illness caused the processions to be postponed, the court held the contract to be frustrated.

(b) The facts of the problem are similar to those in **Denny Mott & Co. Ltd v. James Fraser & Co. Ltd (1944)** where government regulations prohibiting the sale of timber rendered the contract frustrated. Accordingly, S is advised that he is discharged from all subsequent liability under the contract for the sale of palm oil and that the action by B for non-delivery will fail.

QUESTION 43 (a) Explain from case law the circumstances in which a contract may be frustrated on the ground that the labour required to carry it out was not available.
(b) Swift Builders Ltd agreed to install a central heating system in Jacqui's flat for £600, the price to be paid on completion of the job. Swift Builders Ltd spent £400 on labour and material for the work, but before the work was completed the flat was accidentally destroyed by fire.

Advise Jacqui whether she is liable to pay the whole or any part of the contract price to Swift Builders Ltd

ANSWER (a) A contract will be discharged by frustration if there are events recognised by law which make performance impossible. Thus, if a contract should become more expensive or onerous to perform, it cannot be treated as frustrated. In **Davis Contractors Ltd v. Fareham UDC Ltd (1956),** the plaintiffs contracted to build 78 houses for the defendants within eight months at a price of £92,425. Owing to labour shortages, the houses took twenty-two months to complete and cost the plaintiffs £115,000. The plaintiffs claimed that the contract had been discharged by frustration and that they were entitled to claim on a quantum meruit basis in respect of the work done. It was held by the House of Lords that while the labour shortages made the contract more onerous to perform, they did not prevent it from being performed and so the contract was not frustrated.

In a contract of personal services where the labour is required to be supplied personally by the promisor the contract will be discharged by frustration if the promisor is unable to perform it through ill-health or death **(Boast v. Firth 1868).**

Again where the labour required to perform the contract is requisitioned by the government in time of war this will be an acceptable ground to the court for the frustration of the contract **(Metropolitan Water Board v. Dick Kerr & Co. 1918).**

(b) As Jacqui's flat in which the central heating system was to be installed was destroyed by fire accidentally, the contract between the builders and Jacqui is automatically discharged and the parties relieved from subsequent liability **(Taylor v. Caldwell 1863).**

Under S.1(2) of the Law Reform (Frustrated Contracts) Act 1943 expenses incurred by one party are recoverable only up to the limit of any monies paid or payable to that party before the frustrating event. Since no money was paid or payable to Swift Builders Ltd before the fire they cannot recover the £400 expenses incurred in labour and materials.

Section 1(3) of the Act allows Swift Builders Ltd to recover a just sum from Jacqui if Jacqui has obtained a valuable benefit under the contract prior to it being frustrated. The court must have regard to all the circumstances of the case, especially any expenses incurred by Swift Builders Ltd before the fire and also whether the circumstances causing the frustration have affected the value of the benefit. The principles for calculating an award under S.1(3) were explained by Goff J. in **BP Exploration Co. (Libya) Ltd v. Hunt (No.2) (1979).** It has to be shown that Jacqui received a valuable benefit which must be identified and valued and this is the upper limit of any award the court can make. Having valued the benefit, the court must then assess a just sum for the person who has provided the benefit.

Swift Builders Ltd have started work on the central heating system, so this is prima facie evidence that a valuable benefit has been received by Jacqui. However, the requirement to have regard to the effect on the benefit caused by the frustrating event, may, in some cases, reduce the benefit to nil. It is submitted that the destruction of the flat, with the partly completed central heating system, means that the benefit to Jacqui has been completely lost. Accordingly, the court will not require her to make any payment to Swift Builders Ltd

QUESTION 44 (a) Explain upon what principles damages are assessed where there has been a breach of contract.
(b) *H* boards an express bus to London to finalise an important contract which will bring him a profit of £50,000. The bus breaks down and is very late and he loses the contract. Discuss the liability of the bus company.

I.C.S.A. 1972

ANSWER (a) When awarding damages for breach of contract, the Court has to consider two questions:– (a) What losses are legally recoverable; and (b) how to assess the damages for those losses.

In a contract for the sale of goods, the Sale of Goods Act 1979 stipulates how such losses are quantified into monetary terms. Where there is a market for the goods the loss is prima facie quantified with reference to it. If the seller fails to deliver the goods sold then the buyer's loss is the difference between the market price for identical goods and the contract price. Thus if the goods can be bought cheaper in open market the buyer prima facie loses nothing. On the other hand, if the buyer fails to accept delivery and to pay for the goods, then the seller's loss is the amount (if any) by which the contract price exceeds the market price at the time the goods ought to have been accepted. Where the goods are subsequently sold to a new buyer, then if the seller is a dealer with plenty of stock for disposal, he is still entitled to the profit which he would have had, had the buyer accepted the goods, for the seller has made a profit on one sale only instead of two sales.

If the goods sold are defective, the buyer's loss will be the difference in value between the market value of the goods actually delivered and the market value which they would have had, had they been in accordance with the contract. If the goods are so defective that they become something quite different from what the parties contracted for, then this would amount to non-delivery and the principle of assessment of damages for non-delivery would apply.

73

Different considerations apply where there is no market for the goods. For failure to deliver goods which cannot be replaced by buying in the market the loss would include cost of the goods and of their carriage and a reasonable profit if they were for resale. For failure to accept delivery of goods which cannot be disposed of in open-market the seller's loss will be the contract price.

The amount of damages awarded may be reduced to reflect a party's duty to mitigate his losses, if this is possible, as by selling or buying goods elsewhere.

(b) The object of damages in contract is to put the plaintiff in the same position as he would have been in had the contract been performed properly. This principle is subject to the rule that only losses which were in the contemplation of the parties at the time the contract was made are recoverable. Special losses are only recoverable if the defendant had knowledge of the special circumstances at the relevant time. Thus in **Victoria Laundry Ltd v. Newman Industries Ltd (1949)** the plaintiff wished to expand their laundry business and bought a boiler which was delivered five months later. As a result, the plaintiffs lost (i) ordinary day to day profits and (ii) certain exceptionally profitable contracts which they could have obtained with the Ministry of Supply. It was held that as the defendants knew that the boiler was needed for immediate use, they were liable for loss of profits that ordinarily result from such use, but they were not liable for the special loss as they knew nothing of those contracts.

Applying the rules to the problem, the loss of the £50,000 profit cannot be regarded as being in the ordinary course of things. If *H* had used alternative transport to get to London (e.g., a taxi) the bus company would have been liable for the cost incurred in taking the alternative transport.

However, if the bus company was aware that *H* was going to London to finalise such a contract, it would have been liable for such loss. The bus company could not have contended that the proposed London contract had not yet been finalised and that it was not certain that *H* would have obtained the contract since it has been held that damages would be awarded for loss of chance (see **Chaplin v. Hicks 1911** where the plaintiff was awarded damages for loss of chance to compete in the finals of a beauty contest).

If *H* has suffered distress or inconvenience by the delays, he may make a claim for this, for although it was held in **Addis v.**

Gramophone Co. (1909) that damages for distress or disappointment are not recoverable, the **Addis** principle is thought to be confined to employment cases for wrongful dismissal. In a number of holiday cases such as **Jarvis v. Swan's Tours (1973)** and **Jackson v. Horizon Holidays (1975)** damages were awarded for distress and loss of expectation where such loss was not too remote.

QUESTION 45 (a) Explain and illustrate the differences between liquidated damages and penalties.

(b) *Z* agreed with *B*, a builder, that *B* should build a house for *Z* for £8,000, the house to be ready for occupation by 1st May. The parties further agreed that for every day's delay in giving *Z* possession of the house, *B* would pay *Z* £10. For various reasons the house is not ready until 31st May. *Z* who has had to store his furniture and accommodate his large family in a nearby hotel claims from *B* by way of damages his actual expenses over this period amounting to £400. *B* offers to pay £300 i.e. 30 days at £10 per day. Advise the parties.

ANSWER (a) It is possible for the parties themselves to agree in the contract on the damages to be paid for its breach. If such damages represent a genuine attempt to pre-estimate the loss they are known as liquidated damages and are recoverable irrespective of the actual loss. If they are not, then they will be considered as a penalty and will be disregarded. A penalty is sometimes said to be *in terrorem* i.e. to compel performance. In **Lamdon Trust Ltd v. Hurrell (1955)** a clause in a hire purchase agreement provided that the hirer should upon determination of the agreement pay to the owner three-quarters of the purchase price of the car for depreciation during the period of hire. The court held this clause to have been inserted *in terrorem* as a penalty.

The question whether a sum inserted in the contract is liquidated damages or a penalty will depend on how the court views it. The fact that the sum is described as 'liquidated damages' or 'penalty' is relevant but not conclusive. In **Kemble v. Farren (1829)** the sum was described in the contract as 'liquidated damages' but it was held to be a penalty. In **Cellulose Acetate Silk Co. Ltd v. Widnes Foundry Ltd (1933)** manufacturers of machinery agreed to install machinery within a period of 18 months and to pay 'by way of penalty £20 per week' if they took longer. A delay of 30 weeks occurred and the plaintiff's actual loss was far greater than the £600 to which they were entitled under the contract. The House of Lords held that although described as a penalty, the sum was a genuine pre-estimation of the loss likely to be suffered and was thus liquidated damages.

In **Dunlop Pneumatic Tyre Co. Ltd v. New Garage & Motor Co. Ltd (1915)** Lord Dunedin suggested the following tests for determining whether the sum inserted in the contract was a penalty or liquidated damages:–

(i) if the sum stipulated for is extravagant and unconscionable in amount in comparison with the greatest loss that could conceivably be proved to have followed from the breach, it is a penalty.

(ii) if the breach consists only in not paying a sum of money and the sum stipulated is a sum greater than the sum which ought to have been paid it is a penalty.

(iii) if a single lump sum is made payable on the occurrence of one or more or all of several events, some of which may be serious and others not, there is a presumption that it is a penalty.

Thus, if the contract simply gives rights contingent on the happening of a certain event, and that event takes places without either party being in breach, the question of penalty does not arise. In **Alder v. Moore (1961)** a professional footballer was insured by his Union against permanent disablement. He was injured and totally disabled and agreed with the insurance company, in return for the benefit money, never to play professional football. If he did play such football he was to be subject to a penalty equal to the amount paid. The insurance company sued for the sum. It was held that the sum was not a penalty, despite its name, because it was not payable on a breach of contract.

(b) Damages for breach of contract may be assessed by the court or may be fixed in the contract by the parties themselves. With the latter, the court will generally uphold them unless they amount to a penalty. In **Cellulose Acetate Silk Co. v. Widnes Foundry Ltd** the liquidated damages amounted to £600 while the actual loss was £6,000. The court upheld the liquidated damages and disallowed the plaintiff from claiming for the balance of the loss.

The sum fixed in the contract between *Z* and *B* is prima facie liquidated damages so the court will uphold it and *Z* will not be allowed to claim his actual loss.

QUESTION 46 Summarise and explain the remedies, other than damages, available to a litigant in an action for breach of contract.

ANSWER Apart from damages, the remedies available to an innocent party for breach of contract are: specific performance, injunction and quantum meruit. All three are equitable remedies and will be awarded at the discretion of the court.

Specific performance is an order requiring a person to carry out his contractual obligation. It may be granted in lieu of or in addition to damages but will generally not be granted where the court is satisfied that damages alone would compensate the innocent party. Nor will it be granted where the contract requires constant supervision such as with building contracts which are of a continuing nature where the performance is usually by stages. Specific performance will not be granted for contracts involving personal skill as the court will be incapable of compelling the complete execution of such contracts properly. In **Lumley v. Wagner (1852)** the court refused an order for specific performance against a lady who had agreed with a theatre manager to sing at his theatre for a definite period. Where a contract lacks mutuality a decree will not be awarded to a party unless the decree could be awarded against him should the need arise. Thus specific performance will not be granted where one of the parties is an infant. Contracts which may be specifically enforced are contracts for the sale of land, contracts for the purchase of shares and debentures in a company and contracts for the sale of unique articles such as heirlooms and great works of art.

An injunction is an order restraining the doing, continuance or repetition of a wrongful act. In the law of contract an injunction may be granted to enforce a stipulation which must be negative in substance though not in form. An injunction is a useful remedy for a contract of personal service where specific performance would not be given. As Lord St. Leonards in **Lumley v. Wagner** said "It is true that I have not the means of compelling her (the defendant) to sing, but she has no cause of complaint if I compel her to abstain from the commission of an act which she has bound herself not to do, and thus possibly cause her to fulfil her engagement." However, an injunction will not be granted to prevent a defendant from working in any other capacity except for the employer, as its effect would drive the defendant to starvation or to specific performance of a positive covenant to serve. In **Warner Bros. Pictures Inc. v. Nelson (1937)** the defendant agreed to (a) act for the plaintiff for a fixed period and (b) not for any third party; and (c) not to engage in any other occupation without the plaintiff's consent. It was held that an injunction would be granted only for (b).

A claim for *quantum meruit* is a claim for the value of work done under a contract. This remedy is given in order to prevent the undue enrichment by one party at the expense of the other party. It rests not on the original contract but on an implied promise through acceptance by the other party of the benefit of the work done. It may be:–

(a) Where one party has performed work under a contract and the other party has chosen to accept the benefit of it although not obliged to do so. Acceptance must be voluntary by the other party.

(b) Where although work has not been completed, it has been substantially performed.

(c) Where the complete performance of the contract has been prevented by the act of the other party **(Planché v. Colburn 1831).**

(d) Where the work has been performed under a void contract as in **Craven-Ellis v. Canons Ltd (1936)** where a managing director did some work under a service contract which was void because the directors who made it did not take up their share qualification.

QUESTION 47 (a) To what extent is it true to say that only a person who is a party to a contract may sue or be sued in respect of its breach.

(b) A contract for the sale of goods includes a provision that the seller will deliver but only at the purchaser's risk. The goods are entrusted to a carrier for delivery and are damaged by the carrier's negligence. Advise the purchaser.

I.C.M.A. 1980

ANSWER (a) At common law no rights or obligations under a contract may arise on anyone except on the parties to the contract. This is known as the doctrine of privity of contract. Thus, a stranger to a contract may not sue or be sued under it even though the contract was made for his benefit. The doctrine of privity in its present form has its origin in **Tweddle v. Atkinson (1861)** and was reaffirmed in subsequent House of Lords cases including **Beswick v. Beswick (1968).** In **Tweddle v. Atkinson** the plaintiff was about to marry the defendant's daughter and the defendant had promised the plaintiff's father that he would pay the plaintiff £200 if the father would pay the plaintiff £100. The defendant died before he had paid the two hundred pounds. In an action by the plaintiff against his estate, the court held that the action could not succeed as the plaintiff was a stranger to the contract. If, as in **Beswick v. Beswick,** the plaintiff is also the personal representative of the promisee he may be able to enforce the promise against the promisor but only in that representation capacity.

There are several exceptions to the doctrine of privity of contract. Rights and duties attached to land can bind future assignees as well as the original lessor and lessee. Similarly, rights attached to a negotiable instrument can be enforced by a holder for value even though he was not a party to the bill (Bills of Exchange Act 1882). A beneficiary under a trust can enforce it against the trustee even though he was not a party to the contract creating it; and an undisclosed principal may enforce a contract against a third party even though the contract was only made by his agent with that party. Under the Road Traffic Act 1972 a third party may sue, not only a driver of a vehicle for injuries caused but also his insurance company.

Sometimes, even the burden of a contract may be imposed on a stranger. A covenant restricting the use of land can bind not only the buyer himself but any later owner of the land who had notice of the covenant **(Tulk v. Moxhay 1848).** Under the Restrictive Trade Practices Act 1956 a supplier of goods may enforce a resale price maintenance agreement against a person who is not a party to it. However, as most resale price maintenance agreements are now void under the Resale Prices Acts, this exception is not now as important as it was a few years ago.

(b) Despite the exemption clause, the purchaser may still be able to bring an action for the damage to his goods against the seller by relying on the provisions of the Unfair Contract Terms Act 1977. Even if the exemption clause was to be upheld, the carrier could not benefit from its protection if he is sued by the purchaser since he was not a party to the contract of sale **(Alder v. Dickson 1955).**

Chapter 4
Consumer Law

QUESTION 48 (a) To what extent, if at all, will a contract which purports to exclude or restrict liability for a defect in the quality of goods sold be enforceable?

(b) *B* Ltd, manufacturers of magnetic toys which were known in the trade to be unreliable in their performance, sold to *A* (a wholesale dealer) a consignment of such toys upon the terms that "the manufacturers accept no responsibility for any defects or malfunctioning of the goods". Half of the consignment proved to be so unreliable that *A* was unable to sell them to retailers.

Advise *A*.

I.C.S.A. 1979

ANSWER (a) The general rule is *caveat emptor* (let the buyer beware). Hence, if goods are sold and they are not of merchantable quality, there is nothing the buyer can do unless there was some express undertaking given by the seller that the goods were merchantable. This is still the rule between private individuals; but in transactions entered into by the seller in the course of business the Sale of Goods Act 1979 states that a condition will be implied that the goods are of merchantable quality. 'Merchantable quality' means that the goods will be fit for their common use. The standard of quality that can be expected of the goods will depend on any description applied to them (e.g., new goods or second-hand goods), the price of the goods (e.g., expensive goods or inferior goods) and all other circumstances. The goods only have to be of merchantable quality at the time the risk passes to the buyer.

The implied condition as to merchantable quality does not apply for defects which are drawn to the buyer's attention before the sale and for defects which an examination would reveal where the buyer did examine the goods prior to purchasing them. In addition, the seller may use an exemption clause to exclude liability for breach of this implied condition or to restrict the remedies for its breach where the buyer does not deal as a consumer and the exemption clause is reasonable (S.6(3) Unfair Contract Terms Act 1977). The buyer does not deal as a consumer if he makes or holds himself out as making the contract in the course of a business, or if the goods sold are of a type not ordinarily supplied for private use or consumption. In **R and B Customs Brokers Ltd v. UDT Finance Ltd (1988)** the plaintiff company which carried on the business of shipping brokers bought a second hand car which was to be used partly for business purposes and partly for the private purposes of the two directors who were husband and wife. The car was unmerchantable and when they were sued the defendants attempted to rely on an exemption clause in the contract. The Court of Appeal held that the exemption clause was not valid under the 1977 Act because the plaintiff company was dealing as a consumer and not in the course of a business. The fact that the car was to be used partly for business purposes did not prevent the plaintiff company from dealing as a consumer rather than in the course of a business; the purchase of the car was not an integral part of the plaintiff's business or there was not sufficient degree of regularity of similar purchases to make it part of the company's normal business activities.

Schedule 2 of the Unfair Contract Terms Act 1977 lays down guidelines to determine the reasonableness of an exemption clause. They include:

(i) The strength of the bargaining positions of the parties, taking into account any alternative means by which the customer's requirements could have been met;

(ii) Whether the customer received any inducement to accept the terms (e.g., reduction in price of the goods);

(iii) Whether the customer knew or ought reasonably to have known of the existence and extent of the terms (e.g., if the contract was a standard form contract between parties belonging to the same trade association the terms might be reasonable because they were not imposed by the strong on the weak);

(iv) Where the term excludes or restricts liability if some condition is not complied with, whether it was reasonable at the time of the contract to expect that compliance with that condition would be practicable. For example, in **R.W. Green Ltd v. Cade Bros Farm (1978)** a clause in a contract for the sale of seed potatoes required the buyer to notify the seller of his rejection of defective seeds within three days after delivery otherwise he would lose his right to reject. The court held that the clause was unreasonable since the buyer could not know whether the seeds were defective until the crop was harvested.

Section 11(4) of the Act lays down two guidelines for the application of the reasonableness test where an attempt is made to restrict or limit liability to a specified sum of money. These guidelines are:–

(i) The resources which the seller could expect to be available to him for the purpose of meeting the liability;

(ii) How far it was open to the seller to cover himself by insurance. For example, a clause limiting the liability of a manufacturer for defects would not be reasonable if he could have taken out an insurance against such liability without having to materially raise the price for his product **(George Mitchell Ltd v. Finney Lock Seeds Ltd 1983).**

(b) The contract between *A* and *B* Ltd is a contract for the sale of goods within the Sale of Goods Act 1979, i.e., a 'contract whereby the seller transfers or agrees to transfer the property in goods to the buyer for a money consideration called the price'. Accordingly, the conditions and warranties implied by the statute apply. These include the condition under section 14(2) that the goods will be of merchantable quality. This condition has clearly been broken since half the consignment was unsaleable. Normally, where a buyer gives an order for a large quantity of goods and on delivery some prove to be merchantable while others are not, the buyer is able to reject the entire consignment unless the contract is severable **(Rapalli v. Take 1959).** However the contract between *A* and *B* Ltd is a non-consumer transaction i.e. a contract between businessmen. In such circumstances, it is possible for the manufacturers (*B* Ltd) to contract out of liability under section 14 of the Sale of Goods Act. To do this they will have to prove that the exemption clause was reasonable. Probably, the court will uphold the exemption clause in view of the fact that the parties were on equal footing and the magnetic toys were known in the trade to be unreliable. *A*'s position could even be weaker if he had been given some inducement such as a reduction in the wholesale price, to enter into the contract.

QUESTION 49 (a) To what extent does existing legislation protect a purchaser of goods against 'phoney guarantee'?

(b) King Wai bought a radio alarm clock from Hui Hardware Store for £56 and was given a guarantee card to sign and return to Leung-Tse (Hong Kong) Radio Manufacturers Ltd in Cherry Tree Rise, Piccadilly. The guarantee card read "We the manufacturers undertake to replace any defective parts of this article for one year provided that this card is signed and returned to us within 14 days of sale. Subject to the aforesaid mentioned, we shall not be liable for any loss or damage however caused, by the use of this article". King Wai forgot to return the guarantee card.

After two weeks' use, the radio alarm clock ceased to work. King Wai complained to Hui Hardware Store but was told "Sorry sir, it is nothing to do with us, you ought to have returned the guarantee card we gave you to the manufacturers".

Advise King Wai.

ANSWER (a) A guarantee is an undertaking given to the buyer to replace certain defective parts of goods purchased within a specified time. Sometimes, the dealer gives this guarantee coupled with a statement restricting the buyer's right to terminate the contract for faulty goods. At other times, the manufacturer gives this guarantee under certain conditions such as that (1) the guarantee card accepting the manufacturer's offer against faulty workmanship or defective materials must be completed and sent back within 14 days; (2) faults due to the buyer's faulty handling or misuse are outside the guarantee; (3) the buyer is liable for all labour, postal or carriage charges; (4) the guarantee excludes all liability to compensate for loss or damage, however caused. This last condition weakens the value of the guarantee considerably as it aims to exclude the manufacturer's liability in negligence. The manufacturer's guarantee gives the buyer valuable extra protection especially if the goods are second hand goods, but it deprives him of his right to an action under **Donoghue v. Stevenson (1932).** This could only happen though, if a contract exists between the manufacturer and the buyer and it can only come about if the buyer is required to sign and return the guarantee card. So, if the card is merely handed over to the buyer and not returned by him he preserves his common law rights against the benefit of the guarantee.

The Sale of Goods Act 1979 implies conditions and warranties in favour of the buyer as against the retailer. These terms cannot be excluded by the retailer if the sale is a consumer sale (S.6 Unfair Contract Terms Act 1977). Similarly section 2 of the 1977 Act states in effect that any clause in a manufacturer's guarantee which restricts liability for negligence resulting in death or personal injuries will be unenforceable against the injured contracting party; and section 5 provides that in a consumer sale any clause in a guarantee which attempts to exclude liability for negligence will be ineffective.

(b) King Wai should point out to Hui Hardware Store that under section 14(2) of the Sale of Goods Act 1979 where goods are sold in the course of a business and they turn out to be unmerchantable it is the seller's responsibility. King Wai is therefore entitled to recover the price for the clock; but he has no legal right to have the clock repaired or replaced. Had he signed and returned the guarantee card to the manufacturers such a right would have existed against them, but not against the retailer.

QUESTION 50 Section 18 of the Sale of Goods Act provides certain rules for ascertaining the intention of the parties in a contract for the sale of goods as to the time at which the property in the goods is to pass to the buyer. State and explain what these rules are.

A.B.E. 1977

ANSWER Under S.17 the property in specific goods passes when the parties intend it to pass. If however the intention of the parties cannot be ascertained then the property is deemed to pass according to the rules laid down in S. 18. These rules are as follows:

Rule 1 – Where the sale is unconditional and relates to specific goods in a deliverable state, property passes when the contract is made even though the time of payment or of delivery (or both) is postponed to a future time. This rule is subject to a contrary intention which will depend on the facts of each case. In **Ward v. Bignall (1967)** a seller unconditionally sold a specific car to the buyer but retained possession until the buyer could pay for it. Diplock L.J. said (obiter) "in modern times very little is needed to give rise to the inference that the property in specific goods is to pass only on delivery or payment". A contrary intention will not however override Rule 1 unless it is present at the time of the contract **(Dennant v. Skinner 1948).**

Rule 2 – Where specific goods are not in a deliverable state, property passes only when the seller has put them in a deliverable state and has notified the buyer of this. Goods are only in a deliverable state when they are in such condition that the buyer would be bound under the contract to take delivery of them.

Rule 3 – Where specific goods are in fact in a deliverable state but something has to be done by the seller to ascertain the price, e.g. weigh, measure or test the goods, the property in them will pass only when this has been done and the buyer notified.

Rule 4 – Where goods are sold on approval or 'sale or return' terms, property passes when the buyer signifies his approval or acceptance of them to the seller or where he retains them without giving notice of rejection beyond the time stated in the contract for their return or beyond a reasonable time.

Rule 5 – The property in unascertained or future goods passes when the goods become ascertained i.e. unconditionally appropriated to the contract by the seller with the express or implied assent of the buyer or by the buyer with the express or implied assent of the seller.

Goods are unascertained if they have no separate identity at the time of the contract. The meaning of 'unconditional appropriation' was considered by Pearson J in **Carlos Federspiel & Co. v. Twigg & Co. Ltd (1957)** when he explained "A mere setting apart or selection by the seller of the goods which he expects to use in performance of the contract is not enough. To constitute an appropriation of the goods to the contract, the parties must have had an intention to attach the contract irrevocably to those goods, so that those goods and no others are the subject of the sale and become the property of the buyer."

QUESTION 51 (a) Henry orders a grandfather clock from Swindale, a local dealer. Henry pays for the clock on 1 May and requests Swindale to deliver the clock on 10 May when Henry will have moved into his new house. On 7 May the clock is stolen from Swindale's shop and Henry seeks your advice as to whether he can recover his money.

(b) Jack leaves his car with Hassan Garage, car dealers, on a 'sale or return' basis on 1 November. The car dealers were authorised to sell for £600. Hassan Garage failed to sell the car and after repeated requests from Jack the car is returned on 30 March in a damaged condition. Advise Jack as to his legal rights, if any.

A.A.T. (I.A.S.) 1979

ANSWER (a) S.20 of the Sale of Goods Act 1979 states that unless a contrary intention is shown the risk of accidental loss or damage to goods remains with the seller until the property in the goods is transferred to the buyer after which they are at the buyer's risk whether delivery has been made or not. In **Tarling v. Baxter (1872)** a haystack was burned down before the buyer took it away. It was held that the loss fell on the buyer and he still had to pay the price because the property had passed to him at the time of the contract, and the fact that the buyer had not yet taken delivery was immaterial. S.20 does not alter the liability of anyone who is a bailee of goods.

In the problem, assuming that there was no agreement as to the time when the property of the grandfather clock should pass to Henry, the Sale of Goods Act 1979 provides that if the goods are identifiable, and are in a deliverable state, property will pass at the time the contract is concluded. As the risk passes with the property, Henry is advised that he will not be allowed to recover his money unless the theft was caused by Swindale's negligence. If the clock was not identified and appropriated to the contract by the time of the theft, the property in the clock would not have passed and Henry would be able to recover his payment.

(b) S.18 Rule 4 states that when goods are delivered to the buyer on approval or 'on sale or return' or other similar terms the property in the goods passes to the buyer when he signifies his acceptance or approval to the seller or does any other act adopting the transaction or, if he does not signify his acceptance or approval retains the goods without giving notice of rejection. If notice of rejection is not given then the property in the goods will pass on the expiry of the time fixed for their return or if no time is fixed on the expiry of a reasonable time. What is a reasonable time is a question of fact to be decided in each case.

However in **Poole v. Smith's Car Sales (Balham) Ltd (1962)** where the facts were similar to those in the problem, the Court of Appeal held that since more than a reasonable time had lapsed, the property in the car had passed to the defendants and they were liable for the price.

Applying the above Rule, Jack is advised that he could reasonably assume that, because of the delay, the property in the car had been transferred to the car dealers and he is entitled to recover £600, the price of the car.

QUESTION 52 (a) Explain the legal maxim 'Res perit domino'. Are there any exceptions to it?

(b) Bob agreed to buy a used car from Ken's Garage on terms that the garage would fit a new engine and have the car available for collection within 14 days. Ken's Garage fitted a new engine in 7 days and wrote to Bob stating that the car was ready for collection. Before Bob received the letter, the car was accidentally destroyed by fire.

Advise Bob (i) whether he is liable to pay for the car and (ii) whether he can receive compensation from Ken's Garage for failure to deliver the car.

ANSWER (a) The maxim 'Res perit domino' means that the risk passes with title. This is the general rule and is contained in S.20 Sale of Goods Act 1979 which states that unless otherwise agreed goods remain at the seller's risk until the property in them is transferred to the buyer. In **Healy v. Howlett (1917)** *B* ordered from *S*, 20 boxes of fish out of a consignment of 190 boxes which were in transit. *S* sent *B* an invoice stating that the fish was being carried at buyer's risk. Before the 20 boxes were appropriated to *B*, the fish went bad. It was held that the invoice was not part of the contract as it was sent after the contract was made; and since the deterioration took place while the goods were still unascertained, the risk did not pass to the buyer.

The passing of risk as defined under S.20 will not apply in the following cases:

(i) Where delivery has been delayed through the fault of either buyer or seller, the goods are at the risk of the party at fault as regards any loss which might not have occurred but for such fault (S.20).

(ii) If after the property in the goods has passed to the buyer, the seller agrees to look after the goods until the buyer wants them, the seller becomes a bailee and will be liable if the goods perish as a result of his negligence (S.20).

(iii) If the parties agree that the risk is to pass at a time before or after the property has passed to the buyer. This agreement may be implied by custom. In **Bevington v. Dale (1902)** furs were delivered on approval and were stolen during the approval period. The sellers proved that there was a recognised custom in the fur trade that goods out on approval should be at the buyer's risk. Thus the buyer was liable to pay the price.

(iv) In C.I.F. contracts risk passes to the buyer once the goods are over the ship's rails although property does not pass until the shipping documents are handed over to the buyer.

(v) Where the seller of goods agrees to deliver them at his own risk to a place other than where they were when sold, the buyer must, nevertheless take any risk of deterioration in the goods necessarily incidental to the course of transit (S.33).

(b) S.18 Rule 2 states that in a contract of sale of specific goods where the seller has to do something to put them in a deliverable state, the property does not pass until such thing is done and the buyer is notified.

The property in the car does not pass to Bob until a new engine is installed in the car and Bob is aware that the car is ready for collection. As Bob received the letter of notification after the car was accidentally destroyed by fire, the risk of accidental loss remains with the Garage. So Bob need not pay for the car. Section 7 of the Sale of Goods Act 1979 states that if goods have perished after the contract is concluded but before the risk passes to the buyer, the agreement is void and neither party will have any right under the contract. Bob therefore, will be unable to obtain compensation from Ken's Garage for the latter's failure to deliver the car.

QUESTION 53 (a) Rita sells a kitchen table to Irene to be collected in three days. The day after the sale Rita sells the table to Catherina. Irene wishes to recover the table from Catherina and seeks your advice as to her legal rights. Advise her.

(b) Peter sells his motor-car to Helen who pays by cheque. The cheque is dishonoured. As soon as Peter discovered the true position he informs the police. Meanwhile Helen sells the car to Nelly who buys in good faith. Peter seeks to recover the car or its value from Nelly. Advise Nelly.

A.C.C.A. 1978

ANSWER (a) The position where a seller sells goods, retains possession and then fraudulently disposes of them again is governed by S.24 Sale of Goods Act 1979. This section states in effect that where a person having sold goods remains in possession of them then any subsequent sale of those goods to a buyer who buys in good faith and without notice of the seller's defective title will pass a good title to the buyer. The second buyer will only obtain a good title if he is in actual possession of the goods.

In light of S.24, Irene is advised that an action to recover the kitchen table from Catherina will fail as Catherina bought the table from Rita in good faith without knowledge of the previous sale and she was in possession of the property. Irene may however bring an action for breach of contract against Rita for non-delivery of the table. The measure of damages would be the difference between the market price and the contract price.

(b) S.23 of the Sale of Goods Act 1979 states that where an innocent third party buys goods under a voidable title from a seller and at the time of the sale to the third party, the seller's title has not been avoided, the third party will obtain a good title. In **Phillips v. Brooks (1919)** a rogue bought a ring from a shopkeeper after fraudulently describing himself as 'Sir George Bullough'.

The rogue pledged the ring with a pawnbroker before the shopkeeper had taken steps to avoid the contract. It was held that the contract was voidable and that the pledge was valid under S.23. This section does not apply if the original contract was void and not voidable **(Cundy v. Lindsay 1878).** In **Lewis v. Averay (1972)** the Court of Appeal said that where parties contract face to face and one fraudulently misrepresents his identity, the contract is only voidable.

The facts in the problem are similar to those in **Car and Universal Finance Co. Ltd v. Caldwell (1965).** In that case the original owner went to the police and to the A.A. as soon as the rogue's cheque was dishonoured and before the rogue sold the car to the innocent third party. It was held that the owner had preserved his ownership and the car could be recovered from the third party.

Peter is therefore advised that he may recover the car or its value from Nelly.

QUESTION 54 (a) In a contract for the sale of goods state the rules concerned with delivery of the goods.
(b) John wishes to re-stock his 'deep freeze' cabinet and orders ten pounds of beef sausages and a leg of lamb, to weigh three pounds from the Frosty Meat Co. at their advertised price. When the meat was delivered he finds that, while the total weight of the sausages is ten pounds, two pounds consist of pork sausages and the leg of lamb delivered weighs five pounds. Advise John.

A.A.T. (I.A.S.) 1978

ANSWER (a) Delivery is the voluntary transfer of possession from one person to another (S.61). It may be actual or constructive. S.27 of the Sale of Goods Act 1979 states that it is the duty of the seller to deliver the goods and of the buyer to accept and pay for them in accordance with the terms of the contract. Unless otherwise agreed, delivery and payment are concurrent conditions. The rules concerning delivery of goods, in the absence of express stipulation, are contained in the 1979 Act and are as follows:
(i) The place of delivery is prima facie the seller's place of business. If the seller has no place of business then it is his place of residence.
(ii) If the goods are specific goods which the parties know to be in another place, delivery should be made at the place where the goods are situated at the time of the contract.
(iii) Where the seller has agreed to deliver the goods he must do

so within a reasonable time, and at his own expense.

(iv) If the goods are in the possession of a third party, there is no delivery until such party acknowledges to the buyer that he holds the goods on his behalf.

(v) Delivery to a carrier whether named by the buyer or not for the purpose of transmission to the buyer is prima facie delivery to the buyer.

(vi) If the goods have to be delivered at a place other than that where they are sold, the buyer must take the risk of deterioration necessarily incidental to the course of transit.

(vii) If the buyer does not take delivery within a reasonable time, the buyer is liable for any loss caused by the delay and for a reasonable charge for the care and custody of the goods.

(viii) If the seller delivers goods by instalments the buyer need not accept them unless he has agreed to do so. In such a case the goods are to be paid for separately and if there is a failure to make or take delivery of one or more instalments the breach may either constitute a repudiation of the whole contract, or a severable breach giving rise to a claim for damages only. The test is the quantity of goods involved in relation to the contract as a whole and the likelihood of the repetition of the breach.

(b) Section 13 of the Sale of Goods Act 1979 states that where there is a contract for the sale of goods by description there is an implied condition that the goods shall correspond with the description. The word 'description' is very wide and it covers such matters as quantity, weight, ingredients and even packing. Every item in a description which constitutes a substantial ingredient of the thing sold is a condition. Therefore liability for breach of this implied term is strict. In **Re Moore and Landauer (1921)** buyers were entitled to reject an entire consignment of canned fruit when some boxes contained 24 tins, after they had ordered 3,100 cases packed in boxes containing 30 tins. And in **Arcos v. Ronaasen (1933)** where buyers were allowed to reject $1/2''$ and $9/16''$ thick when they had ordered only staves $1/2''$ thick, Lord Atkin said "a ton does not mean about a ton, or a yard about a yard. Still less when you descend to minute measurements does half an inch mean about half an inch. If a seller wants a margin he must stipulate for it."

The remedies for breach of S.13 are set out in S.11(3). The buyer may treat the contract as at an end, send back the goods and refuse to pay for them. The right to reject is lost if, in a contract which is not severable, the buyer accepts the goods or part of them (S. 11(4)). The buyer may claim damages for an ex post facto warranty.

As an alternative to an action under S.13, S.30 gives the buyer certain courses of action where the seller has delivered the wrong quantity of goods contracted for. This section states that where the seller delivers less than the quantity of goods he contracted to sell, the buyer may reject them but if he decides to accept them he must pay for them at the contract rate. Where the seller delivers more than he has contracted to sell, the buyer may accept the goods included in the contract and reject the rest or he may reject the whole lot. If he accepts the whole of the goods he must pay for them at the contract rate. Where the seller delivers the goods which he contracted to sell mixed with goods of a different description not included in the contract, the buyer may accept the goods and reject the rest or he may reject the whole lot. If he accepts the goods not contracted for, he must pay for them at their market value.

Applying the above rules to the problem John has two course of action. He may obtain his remedy for breach of S.13 as the sale was a sale by description. If he pursues this course he will have to accept the lot or reject the lot and claim damages (if any) as the contract is not severable. He may however consider an action under S.30 as it gives him more latitude.

Although the differences in each case are, in volume terms, small the principle of 'De minimis non curat lex' (The law does not concern itself with trifles) is unlikely to apply here to prevent John from exercising his right to reject the goods delivered, since in relation to the amount contracted for the differences are significant.

QUESTION 55 (a) Describe in outline the principal exceptions to the rule 'nemo dat quod non habet' whereby a person cannot pass a better title to goods than he himself possesses.
(b) Robin is an absent-minded teacher. One day he goes to work without locking up his house. Sly, a thief, lets himself in and steals a valuable clock which he sells to Tom, a private collector. Tom buys in good faith, paying Sly £1000. Robin now wishes to know whether he can recover the clock from Tom. Advise Robin.

I.C.S.A. 1982

ANSWER (a) It is a general common law rule that no one can give what he does not have. Thus, a person who buys goods from someone other than the owner of the goods cannot obtain title to the goods. This common law rule is embodied in S.21(1) of the Sale of Goods Act 1979 which states that where goods are sold by a person who is not the owner of them and without the authority or consent of the true owner, the buyer acquires no better title than the seller. To this rule there are a number of exceptions of which the most important are:

(i) **Agency.** Whether or not an agent can pass a good title of his principal's goods to a third party depends on the status of the agent. An ordinary agent can pass title of his principal's goods only if he acts within the scope of his authority. Thus, if an ordinary agent is instructed to sell his principal's car for not less than a thousand pounds and he sells the car for a smaller sum to an innocent buyer and absconds with the proceeds of sale, the principal can recover the car from the buyer. A mercantile agent i.e. a professional selling agent such as a car dealer, may pass a good title of his principal's goods to an innocent buyer even if he acts outside the scope of his authority (S.2 Factors Act 1889).

(ii) **Estoppel.** The owner of goods who, by words or conduct, represents to the buyer that the seller has a right to sell the goods is precluded from denying the seller's right to sell (S.21 Sale of Goods Act 1979),

(iii) **Sale in Market Overt.** Where goods are sold in market overt, according to the usage of the market, the buyer will acquire a good title to the goods provided he buys them in good faith and without notice of any defect or want of title on the part of the seller (S.22 Sale of Goods Act 1979). 'Market overt' means every open, public and legally constituted market; and for the buyer to benefit from this section certain conditions must be satisfied. The sale must be by the shopkeeper in the public part of the premises, of goods of the kind normally sold by the shop and it must take place between sunrise and sunset **(Reid v. Metropolitan Police Commissioner 1973).**

(iv) **Sale under a voidable title.** Where the seller of goods has a voidable title to them and his title has not been avoided at the time of the sale, the buyer will obtain a good title to the goods provided he buys the goods in good faith and without notice of the seller's defective title (S.23). A voidable title can be acquired under a voidable contract such as where the seller obtains the goods from the true owner by a misrepresentation.

(v) **Second Sale by a seller left in possession.** Where a seller having sold goods remains in possession of them, or of documents of title to them, any subsequent sale of those goods to an innocent third party will pass a good title to that person (S.24). It

does not matter that the seller had remained in possession of
those goods without the buyer's consent; but the third party must
actually be in possession of the goods if he is to obtain a better
title than the buyer **(Nicholson v. Harper 1895).**

(vi) **Sale by a buyer in possession.** Where a buyer in possession
of goods or document of title to them under a contract of sale and
with the seller's consent, resells them to an innocent third party,
the latter will obtain a good title even though the buyer had no
title because, for example, the seller had reserved the title to the
goods (S.25). The third party must have taken delivery of the
goods in order to benefit from this section.

(vii) **Motor vehicles on hire-purchase.** The hirer or buyer of a
motor vehicle under a hire-purchase or conditional sale agreement who sells the vehicle to a private purchaser taking in good
faith and without notice of the agreement, can pass a good title to
the vehicle (Sch 4 Consumer Credit Act 1974).

(b) Unless Tom can show that he has acquired a good title to the
stolen clock under one of the recognised exceptions to the nemo
dat quod non habet rule, he will have to return the clock to Robin
who will not be under any obligation to compensate Tom. It
makes no difference that Tom bought the clock in good faith.

The only exception under the Sale of Goods Act 1979 which
could confer good title of stolen goods to an innocent purchaser
of them is where the goods are bought in market overt. The onus
(burden) of proof is on Tom to show that he comes under this
exception.

QUESTION 56 (a) Discuss the rights of action which a seller has
for breach of contract against the buyer personally.
(b) James agreed to buy 100 tons of wheat from ABC Ltd, at £50
per ton. James later refused to accept delivery of the wheat as the
market price of wheat had fallen to £30 per ton. ABC Ltd are
now claiming damages. Advise James.

A.C.C.A. 1979

ANSWER (a) The remedies of an unpaid seller against the
buyer personally are contained in the Sale of Goods Act 1979.
S.49 gives him an action for the price and S.50 enables him to
claim damages for non-acceptance.

An action for the price is available to the seller if the buyer
wrongfully fails to pay for the goods. This action is available in
two cases. First, where the property in the goods has passed to

the buyer and he wrongfully neglects or refuses to pay for the goods according to the terms of the contract. Secondly, where the parties expressly state that the price is payable on a fixed date even though the property has not passed or the goods appropriated to the contract and the buyer wrongfully neglects or refuses to do so.

In both cases the buyer's refusal to tender the price must be wrongful. Thus, if the seller is not willing to deliver the goods or if the buyer has been given credit and the credit period has not expired, no action will lie under S.49. An action for the price may be brought even though the buyer cannot get possession of the goods because they have been accidentally destroyed, so long as the risk has passed prior to destruction.

An action in damages for non-acceptance may be brought against the buyer if he wrongfully refuses to accept delivery and pay for the goods. The measure of damages is the 'estimated loss directly and naturally resulting in the ordinary course of events from the buyer's breach of contract'.

Section 50 (3) provides that the measure of damages is prima facie the difference between the contract price and the market price if there is a market for the goods unless the seller is a dealer and the supply of such goods exceeds the demand in the trade **(Thompson Ltd v. Robinson (Gunmakers) Ltd 1955).**

An action for the price may be linked with a claim for damages for non-acceptance where for example, the seller has incurred expenses such as storage charges, by reason of the buyer's default.

(b) Losses resulting from a breach of contract for the sale of goods are recoverable only if they are reasonably foreseeable (S.50(2) Sale of Goods Act 1979). Although **Smeed v. Foord (1859)** decided that loss due to market fluctuations is too remote the modern view is that such loss is foreseeable.

The assessment of damages for such loss arising from the buyer's failure to accept the goods will prima facie be the difference between the contract price and the market price. Where the market price fluctuates, the price to be taken is the price available at the time the goods ought to have been accepted or if no time was fixed for acceptance then at the time of the refusal to accept.

Hence the damages available to ABC Ltd will be the difference between the contract price (£50) and the market price at the time of his refusal to accept (£30). It would not matter if

ABC Ltd at a much later date sell the wheat at a price above the contract price **(Campbell Mostyn Ltd v. Barnett 1954).**

QUESTION 57 (a) Explain the rights of an unpaid seller against the goods sold by him. When will such rights be lost?
(b) By a written agreement entered into in April this year, Shanahan Ltd agreed to sell a boat to Jeff for £15,000. A clause in the agreement reads:

"Until the date of payment, the purchaser is required to hold the vessel in such a way that it shall remain the property of the seller and any fitments or other material added to it shall become the property of the seller."

After delivery of the boat Jeff installed a new engine in it. However, he then went bankrupt before any payment was made to Shanahan Ltd on the boat.

Advise Shanahan Ltd whether they are entitled to recover the boat, together with its new engine, from Jeff's trustee in bankruptcy.

A.A.T. (I.A.S.) 1979

ANSWER (a) An unpaid seller has four remedies against goods sold by him, three of them are statutory set out in the Sale of Goods Act 1979 and the fourth arising out of case law **(Aluminium Industrie BV v. Romalpa Ltd, 1976).** The statutory rights are defined by S.39 and are available whether or not the property in the goods has passed. These rights are: lien, stoppage in transit, and re-sale.

A lien is a right to retain possession of goods until the seller is paid or tendered the whole price. For this right to exist the seller must be entitled to immediate payment. Thus, the goods should not have been sold on credit, or if sold on credit, the term of credit must have expired. The right to a lien is lost where the unpaid seller delivers the goods to a carrier for transmission; where the buyer or his agent lawfully obtains possession of the goods; and where he waives the lien, for example, by agreeing to a sub-sale by the buyer.

A right of stoppage enables the seller to recover possession of the goods and it is exercised by serving a notice of stoppage on the carrier. This right exists if the goods are still in transit. Under S.45 transit is deemed to end when the buyer or his agent takes delivery from the carrier; or if on reaching the appointed destination, the carrier acknowledges to the buyer that he is holding the goods to the order of the buyer; or if the carrier wrongfully refuses to deliver the goods to the buyer. The right of stoppage is only available if the buyer becomes insolvent and it is lost when the goods cease to be in transit; or if the buyer's trustee in bankruptcy tenders the price; or in the case of a foreign sale, when the bill of lading is transferred to a bona fide purchaser for value.

A right of resale exists if the goods are perishable or if the seller serves notice on the buyer of his intention to resell and the buyer does not within a reasonable time pay or tender the price. A resale may also be made if the seller expressly reserves this right in the contract.

A Romalpa-type clause in a contract enables an unpaid seller to obtain a remedy far wider than those under the Sale of Goods Act. It allows him to recover the goods from the buyer upon the latter's insolvency even though the goods were delivered to him and, in certain cases, to trace the proceeds if the goods were resold. A Romalpa-type clause is a reservation of property clause in a contract. It may take one of three forms. It may reserve the legal ownership of the goods in the seller until the payment of the price is met. This is referred to as a simple reservation of property clause and the relationship that exists between the seller and buyer is one of bailor and bailee. The clause may be further extended to make the buyer agent and trustee of the seller with respect to the goods sold and to the proceeds of those goods if resold. This is referred to as an extended reservation of property clause and its effect is to bring into operation the doctrine of tracing as laid down in **Re Hallett's Estate (1880).** The court will infer a fiduciary relationship between the seller and buyer if, for example, the buyer is required to keep the seller's goods stored separately and to keep the proceeds of resale in a separate account. In **Aluminium Industrie BV v. Romalpa Ltd,** AIV sold aluminium foil to Romalpa and reserved the ownership in the foil until the buyer met the purchase price. The conditions of sale included, inter alia, a term requiring the foil to be stored separately. The Court of Appeal held that that particular term imputed a fiduciary relationship between the contracting parties with the result that the proceeds of resale of the foils still identifiable, could be recovered by the seller under the doctrine of tracing.

The reservation of property clause may be so elaborate that it contains indefinite rights, for example, that the property in the goods is not to pass even though the seller has actually received the purchase price of the goods so long as some other payment due to him is outstanding. This is known as an indefinite reservation of property clause and is ineffectual as a reservation of property clause. At the most, it constitutes a charge on vague and indefinite assets and will be enforced as such if registered under S.95 of the Companies Act 1948. In **Re Bond Worth Ltd (1979)** a supplier of acrylic fibre sold a quantity of raw fibre to Bond Worth Ltd, who processed it into carpets with jute and latex backing. The condition of sale included a term to the effect that the equitable and beneficial ownership of the raw fibre sold should not pass until full payment had been received. Slade J. held that the retention clause was an unsuccessful attempt to create a trust so the doctrine of tracing was not applicable and since the clause was not registered under S.95 it was void.

(b) Under S.19(1) of the Sale of Goods Act, where there is a contract for the sale of specific goods or where goods are subsequently appropriated to the contract, the seller may reserve the right of disposal of the goods until certain conditions are fulfilled. In such a case, the property in the goods will not pass to the buyer until the conditions imposed by the seller are fulfilled.

The clause in the contract between Shanahan Ltd and Jeff reserves Shanahan Ltd's rights of ownership in the boat until payment is made for it; but it goes further in claiming to embrace in those rights of ownership anything added to the boat by Jeff. This kind of clause was considered by the Court of Appeal in **Borden (UK) Ltd v. Scottish Timber Products Ltd (1979).** In that case, *B* supplied resin to *S* which the latter used in making chip-board. The contract contained an elaborate reservation of property clause. When *S* went into receivership, *B* attempted to trace the resin. The court held that the reservation of property clause was too wide. On the authority of this decision, Shanahan Ltd should be advised that they cannot recover the boat with the new engine from Jeff's trustee in bankruptcy. However, if the engine can be disconnected from the boat, then Shanahan Ltd can recover the boat without the engine. In **Hendy Lennox Ltd v. Grahame Puttick Ltd (1984)** a supplier sold an engine to the defendants for use in a diesel generator. The engine sold was subject to a reservation of title clause. When the defendants went into receivership the court held that the supplier still had the legal ownership of the engine even though it was incorporated in the generator set, since the engine was still identifiable by its serial number and could be disconnected easily from the set.

QUESTION 58 (a) What is a hire purchase contract? How does it differ from a (i) credit sale contract, and (ii) conditional sale contract?

(b) Charles buys a second-hand sports car from Peter after reading Peter's advertisement in a local newspaper. Charles pays Peter in cash the £500 agreed price and takes delivery of the car. Two days later Charles is visited by a representative of the Bunter Finance Company who informs him that the car is the subject of a hire purchase agreement with Peter who has not paid all the instalments. Charles refuses to surrender the car. Discuss the legal position.

A.C.C.A. 1975

ANSWER (a) A hire-purchase contract is a contract of bailment with an option to purchase the goods. The owner of the goods will transfer possession of them for a stipulated period for payment of a rent. Once the hirer (debtor) pays all the rent for the relevant period he exercises an option to buy and becomes the owner. The hirer (debtor) need not exercise his option to buy and this is done by termination of the contract of bailment before the period expires. Hire-purchase legislation is now contained in the Consumer Credit Act 1974 when the total credit does not exceed £15,000. To determine whether the agreement falls under the Act, section 9(3) declares that from the total price should be deducted any deposit and the total charge for credit.

A credit sale contract is one for the sale of goods, the purchase price not payable immediately but by instalments. Under such contracts the ownership of the goods passes to the credit-sale debtor as soon as the agreement comes into effect. If the credit does not exceed £15,000, the sale becomes a regulated agreement under the Consumer Credit Act 1974.

A conditional sale is very similar to a hire purchase agreement. It is an agreement for the sale of goods, whereby the purchase price is payable by instalments and ownership remains with the creditor until all instalments of the price are paid. The debtor may be given possession of the goods until ownership is acquired. If the credit does not exceed £15,000, the sale becomes a regulated agreement under the Consumer Credit Act 1974.

The distinction between the three types of instalment sales mentioned above becomes important when the debtor disposes of the goods before having paid all the instalments.

With a credit sale the debtor who owns the goods can confer a good title on a buyer or pledgee and the creditor has no right against either **(Lee v. Butler 1893).** With a conditional sale, not regulated by the Consumer Credit Act 1974, although the creditor has reserved the property in the goods, a third party who buys the goods in good faith from the debtor will acquire a good title to the goods defeating that of the seller (section 25(1) Sale of Goods Act 1979). Where the conditional sale falls within the ambit of the Consumer Credit Act 1974 the seller will not lose his title by the buyer's dishonest disposition of the goods. With a hire-purchase agreement, the debtor cannot confer a good title to a third party under S.25(1) of the Sale of Goods Act 1979 as the section only applies to disposition of goods under a contract for sale. The debtor under a hire purchase agreement is in possession of goods under a contract of bailment. Different rules apply for motor vehicle sales.

(b) Under Sch.4 of the Consumer Credit Act 1974 where a motor vehicle held under a hire purchase or conditional sale agreement is disposed by a dishonest hirer or buyer before ownership passes to him, the third party will acquire a good title provided he is a private buyer and buys it in good faith and without notice of the agreement. If the third party is a motor trader he will not obtain a good title even if he buys it for his private use and not for resale in his business **(Stevenson v. Beverley Bentinck Ltd 1976).**

Charles is therefore advised that he has obtained a good title to the car and need not surrender it to Bunter Finance Company.

QUESTION 59 Discuss a hirer's rights
(a) to cancel
(b) to terminate
a hire purchase agreement.

A.I.A. 1977

ANSWER (a) Under Section 37 of the Consumer Credit Act 1974 a regulated agreement may be cancelled by the debtor/ hirer before the end of the fifth day following the day on which he receives a copy of the executed agreement or notice of his rights. The right of cancellation arises if, in antecedent negotiations, oral representations were made in the presence of the debtor by the dealer and the agreement was signed by the debtor/hirer at a place other than the place of business of the creditor.

Where the notice of cancellation is sent by post it becomes effective as soon as it is posted. The effect of cancellation is to bring to an end the agreement and any linked transaction. Moreover all monies paid under the agreement are refundable. Liabilities of the debtor to pay any money due under the agreement will also cease except that he is obliged to pay for work done or goods supplied to meet any emergency or for goods supplied which have been incorporated in any land or thing not forming part of the agreement (section 69(2)).

(b) Under section 99 of the Consumer Credit Act 1974 a debtor (hirer) under a hire purchase agreement regulated by the Act has a right to terminate the agreement before the last instalment falls due. Notice of termination must be sent to the person entitled or authorised to receive payment and where sent by post, it takes effect when received by the creditor or his agent. The effect of termination is to bring the agreement to an end. However the debtor/hirer must pay any sums due on the agreement before termination and any further sum to bring his total payments up to one-half of the total price except where the agreement specifies a smaller sum or where the court considers a lesser sum reasonable. Furthermore, where the debtor has been in breach of the agreement to take reasonable care of the goods, he must compensate the creditor for any loss sustained from his breach of duty.

The distinction between cancellation and termination is that with the latter the agreement has begun to run but with the former the agreement is not yet in force.

QUESTION 60 (a) How does the Consumer Credit Act 1974 seek to protect the hirer against the risk of having the goods taken away when the payments fall into arrears?
(b) Domestic Electrical Ltd, a Hire Purchase Company, has written to Norman threatening to repossess the undermentioned articles held under separate hire-purchase agreements unless all arrears are paid within 7 days. Norman can immediately find £32 but does not wish to lose any of the goods. Advise Norman.

Goods	Total H.P. Price	Amount Paid	Arrears
1. Radiogram	£180	£50	£11
2. Television Set	£150	£30	£20
3. Washing Machine	£200	£110	£30

ANSWER (a) The hirer is protected from having his goods taken away by the creditor when his payments fall in arrears if the goods are protected goods. Goods are deemed to be 'protected goods' under section 90 when they are subject to a regulated hire-purchase agreement and

(i) the hirer is in breach and

(ii) has not terminated the agreement and

(iii) has paid or tendered at least one-third of the total price of the goods and

(iv) has not voluntarily surrendered possession of them. If goods are seized by the creditor after the hirer had abandoned them **(Bentinck Ltd v. Cromwell Engineering Co. Ltd 1971)** or after the hirer had purported to sell them to a third party **(Eastern Distributors v. Goldring 1957)** the goods would no longer be protected. To get the goods back, the creditor must first obtain a court order. Under no circumstances must he enter the hirer's home or other premises to recover possession of the goods. Permission may be granted by the hirer himself or by the court through the issuing of a court order.

Where a creditor contravenes section 90, the hirer is entitled to recover instalments already paid (ss. 91, 92) and the agreement is automatically terminated, although, of course, he has to return the goods.

(b) Goods are deemed to be protected goods if the hirer has paid or tendered at least one-third of the hire-purchase price. Under the three hire-purchase agreements, one of them (the agreement for the washing machine) is protected, but the other two are not protected. The hire-purchase agreement for the radiogram falls short to be protected by £10 and the hire-purchase agreement for the television set needs another £30 before it can become protected goods. Norman may tender, from the £32 he could raise, £10 for the radiogram and £20 towards the television set. It should be noted that even if Domestic Electricals Ltd, were to merge the three agreements into one new agreement, the goods would still have become protected goods without the further payment of £32, since one of the agreements (the one relating to the washing machine) is protected.

QUESTION 61 (a) To what extent is a dealer liable to a hirer for misrepresentations concerning goods which have subsequently become the subject of a hire-purchase agreement between the hirer and the finance company?

(b) Lisa enters Sam's shop and after inspecting the radios on display decides to purchase a transistor radio on hire purchase.

Lisa signs a hire-purchase agreement with F. Ltd, a finance company, to which the set is sold. Shortly after Lisa takes possession of the radio, it ceases to function and she asks you what her rights are.

Advise her.

A.A.T. (I.A.S.) 1979

ANSWER (a) As a general rule where a dealer sells goods to a finance company and the latter lets them on hire-purchase to the customer, the dealer drops out and the contract is deemed to be concluded between the finance company as owner of the goods and the customer. If however, the dealer gives an express warranty as to the condition of the goods (e.g., that a 1934 Standard saloon car is "a good little bus, I'd stake my life on it" – **Andrews v. Hopkinson 1937),** the court is ready to hold it as a collateral contract between the dealer and the customer; the consideration to support the warranty being the customer's willingness to enter into the hire-purchase agreement with the finance company and to accept liability under its terms. If the warranty is broken, the customer may bring an action against the dealer for breach of contract. The measure of damage is the whole damage suffered by the customer, including his liability under the hire-purchase agreement and is not limited to the difference in value between the goods as warranted and as they are in fact. In appropriate cases, the customer may also bring a claim against the dealer in negligence **(Hedley Byrne & Co. Ltd v. Heller & Partners Ltd 1964).**

Under section 56 of the Consumer Credit Act 1974, the dealer is deemed to be the agent of the Finance Company for antecedent negotiations. These negotiations include representations made by the dealer to the customer and any other dealings between them. Negotiations are taken to begin when the dealer and the customer first enter into communication.

The customer under the Act may bring an action for the dealer's misrepresentation against the dealer or the finance company, both of whom are liable to him jointly and severally. By section 56(2) any agreement which provides that the dealer is to be regarded as agent of the customer or that the finance company is to be exempted from liability for the acts or omissions of the dealer is void.

(b) The implied terms governing hire-purchase agreements correspond to those governing consumer sales under the Sale of Goods Act and are contained in Schedule 4 of the Consumer

Credit Act. The Schedule provides that where the finance company bails or hires out goods under a hire-purchase agreement in the course of a business there is an implied condition that the goods will be of merchantable quality. This condition will not be implied in the case of patent defects where the customer did inspect the goods or in the case of latent defects which are specifically drawn to his attention. The Unfair Contract Terms Act 1977 declares void any clause in the hire-purchase agreement which purports to exclude or restrict the finance company's liability under these implied terms in respect of a consumer agreement.

As the radio bought on hire-purchase has proved to be faulty, Lisa may bring an action against F. Ltd for breach of the implied condition as to merchantable quality. She is entitled to repudiate the agreement and to recover all payments made to the finance company. She need not accept a replacement transistor radio. If she decides not to repudiate but to claim damages instead, the measure of damages will be the difference between the value of the goods as they should have been and the value of the goods as they are.

QUESTION 62 (a) Outline the main obligations of finance companies where goods are being acquired on hire purchase terms.
(b) Krug goes to the Downtown Wine Shop to buy six dozen bottles of champagne for his daughter's wedding at a total cost of £600. He presents his Excess Credit Card in payment and signs an Excess voucher. Sometime later, when this champagne has been consumed, Downtown Wine informs Krug that Excess has gone into liquidation and has not paid the £600. Downtown adds that it does not wish to find itself in the position of an unsecured creditor and hence is seeking payment of this sum from Krug.

Advise Krug.

I.C.S.A. 1987

ANSWER (a) The usual method of financing hire purchase agreements is for the supplier of goods to sell the goods to an associated finance company and then for the company to resell the goods on hire purchase terms to the customer. The finance company acts as both supplier of the goods and of the credit, and is under an obligation to observe the formalities for making regulated agreements.

The finance company is required to disclose certain pre-contractual information (as specified by the Secretary of State) so as to assist the customer in deciding whether or not to enter into the credit transaction. The agreement itself must be in writing and in the prescribed form, for example, it must inform the hirer of his rights of termination, the rate of the charge for credit, and the remedies available to the finance company. The agreement must be signed by the customer personally and by the finance company or its agents, after which it becomes executed. Finally, the customer must be given copies of the signed agreement. Sometimes he is entitled to only one copy; at other times he is entitled to two copies. The customer is always entitled to a copy of the agreement as soon as he signs it. If the agreement is not executed when the customer signs it (because it has not yet been signed by the finance company or on its behalf) the customer must be given a second copy of the executed agreement within seven days after the making of the agreement. In the case of cancellable agreements the second copy must be sent by post and must contain details of the customer's right to cancel; or if no second copy is required, notice giving details of the customer's right to cancel must be sent by post to the customer.

Improperly executed agreements are unenforceable against the customer unless the court makes an 'enforcement order' or the customer waives the irregularity.

By S.8 of the Supply of Goods (Implied Terms) Act 1973 as amended by the Consumer Credit Act 1974 the finance company is under an obligation to ensure that it has a right to sell the goods at the time when property in the goods is to pass, and that the goods are not defective and fit their contract description.

By S. 56 of the Consumer Credit Act, the dealer is deemed to be the agent of the finance company for negotiations conducted with the customer and so the finance company will be liable for any representations or contractual promises made by him.

(b) The use of a credit card by a customer to obtain goods from a seller embodies two separate contracts. A contract between the seller and the credit card company whereby the seller undertakes to accept payment by credit card from the card holder in return for payment of the price of the goods less a discount by the credit card company. Also a contract between the credit card company and the card holder whereby the card holder is allowed to pay for the goods by using the credit card in return for paying to the credit card company the full price of the goods supplied to him. The parties become bound when the voucher is signed.

In **Re Charge Credit Services Ltd (1989)** the Court of Appeal ruled that once a retailer allows a customer to pay by credit card for goods the customer's obligation to pay the price is unconditionally discharged and the retailer must recover the money from the credit card company.

Accordingly, Krug does not have to pay the £600 to Downtown Wine Shop. The Shop will have to prove for this sum in Excess's liquidation.

QUESTION 63 (a) In relation to the Consumer Credit Act 1974 explain what is meant by the following:
(i) a regulated consumer credit agreement
(ii) a regulated consumer hire agreement
(iii) an exempt agreement
(b) Jigna buys a second-hand sports car from Car Dealers for £14,000. She uses her Excess Credit Card to pay for the car and signs an Excess voucher. Six months after purchasing the car, the police inform Jigna that the car is stolen property. Jigna is unable to recover her money from Car Dealers who are on the verge of liquidation.

Advise Jigna.

ANSWER (a) (i) A regulated consumer credit agreement is a credit agreement by which the creditor provides the debtor (who must not be a company) with credit not exceeding £15,000. The credit can be a cash loan or instalment credit (as with hire purchase agreements, credit sales and conditional sale agreements). The £15,000 credit limit excludes deposits paid by the debtor as well as interest charges.

The credit may be provided for a specific purpose only (restricted-use credit) such as where the credit funds are transferred directly by the creditor to the supplier (as in the case of hire purchase and credit card transactions), or it may be used for any purpose (as with a credit card which is used to obtain cash). The distinction between these two types of credit is important in relation to linked transactions and the canvassing of loan applications.

The credit agreement may be a debtor-creditor-supplier agreement where the creditor also supplies the goods (two parties only transactions) or has an arrangement with another person to supply the goods (three parties transaction); or it may be a debtor-creditor agreement where there is no arrangement between the creditor and the supplier. The distinction between a

debtor-creditor-supplier agreement and a debtor-creditor agreement is important for liability purposes under section 75 (supplier/creditor liability for misrepresentations and breach of contract).
(ii) A regulated consumer hire agreement is the hire of goods (other than under a hire purchase agreement) to a debtor (other than a company) for a period in excess of three months, for not more than £15,000.
(iii) An exempt agreement is an agreement which is not covered by the Consumer Credit Act so that if a supplier's business only provides credit for exempt agreements, the supplier need not obtain a licence before he can provide credit or observe the formalities for making credit agreements.

The following are examples of exempt agreements: mortgages given on land by building societies and other specified corporate bodies; fixed sum debtor-creditor-supplier agreements (other than hire purchase and conditional sale agreements) where payment is to be made in not more than four instalments; and debtor-creditor agreements where the total charge for credit does not exceed the higher of 13% or 1% above the base rate of the London Clearing Banks in existence 28 days before such agreements were made.

(b) The credit agreement between Jigna and Car Dealers where she uses her credit card to pay for the car is a debtor-creditor-supplier agreement. Section 75 of the Consumer Credit Act 1974 provides that with such agreements where the debtor has a claim against the supplier for misrepresentation or breach of contract, he will have a like claim against the creditor who with the supplier will be jointly and severally liable to the debtor. The section does not apply to non-commercial agreements (i.e., agreements not made in the course of a business carried on by the creditor or owner) or where a claim by the debtor relates to any single item which has a cash price not exceeding £100 or more than £30,000.

Jigna has a claim against Car Dealer for failing to provide her with title to the car (S.12 Sale of Goods Act 1979). For breach of this condition she is entitled to terminate the contract with Car Dealers and recover her money. Accordingly, she may bring an action against Excess Credit Company to recover her loss.

QUESTION 64 Discuss any two of the following:
(a) S.14 of the Trade Descriptions Act 1968, which is concerned with false statements as to services;
(b) the licensing provisions of Part III of the Consumer Credit Act 1974;
(c) the statutory defences to liability provided by S.24 of the Trade Descriptions Act 1968

I.C.S.A. 1990

ANSWER (a) Section 14 contains two offences in relation to false statements as to services to be provided by the statement maker or by a third party. It is an offence for any person in the course of a trade or business to make a statement which he knows to be false or recklessly to make a statement which is false.

'False' means false to a material degree. It must be a false statement about the past or present supply of services. Thus, false statements about the future supply of services are not normally covered by the Act. In **Beckett v. Cohen (1973),** the respondent agreed to build for a customer "within ten days" a garage which was to be similar to an existing one owned by his neighbour. The garage was not built in time and was not like the neighbour's garage. The respondent was charged with recklessly making false statements regarding his services in relation to the building of the garage. It was held on appeal that S.14 did not apply to statements made with regard to the future, which did not have the character of being true or false at the time when made.

False statements in respect of the future supply of services are actionable only if the falsity of the statement can be demonstrated at the time it is made irrespective of whether the services are provided, or if the statement involves an undertaking that services will be provided when the person making the statement has no intention of providing them. In **Cowburn v. Focus Television Rentals Ltd (1983),** the defendants advertised as a promotional offer "Hire 20 feature films absolutely free when you rent a video recorder". This offer expired on the 9th of November 1981 and was replaced by a second offer of free hire of six films. Owing to carelessness, the original offer was still being displayed at their Manchester branch. A customer in Manchester hired a video recorder on the basis of the first offer. Some ten days later, he received a letter setting out his entitlement to the hire of the six films but he was asked to pay for the packing and postage of the films. It was held that the first promotional offer was false when the customer entered the shop; the second promotional

107

offer was also false because customers would reasonably conclude that free hire included free packing and postage.

The false statement need not induce the contract but can be made during the currency of the contract. Thus in **Breed v. Cluett (1970)** where a builder sold an incomplete house which he was building to a buyer and before completing the house recklessly told the buyer that the house was covered by the National House Builders Registration Council 10 years guarantee which was not the case, the court held that he was still guilty of the offence under Section 14.

Section 14 does not cover statements about the standing or capabilities of the person providing the services, statements about the place at which services or facilities are provided, and misleading (as distinct from false) statements or other indications about the provision of services.

(b) Under the Consumer Credit Act two types of business dealing in regulated agreements have to be licensed. They are (1) consumer credit and consumer hire businesses and (2) ancillary businesses. The former include a business in which goods are sold on credit or on hire purchase. Thus, not only must the finance company obtain a licence but also the supplier of the goods. The latter include the business of credit brokerage (as in the case of mortgage brokers), debt counselling (as in the case of solicitors who give advice to debtors about the liquidation of their debts due under regulated agreements), debt collecting and a credit reference agency (i.e., a business which collects information about the financial position of a person and passes it on to potential creditors).

Licences available under the Act are either standard licences or group licences. A standard licence is issued to a named person and it authorises him to carry on business under the name specified in the licence. The Director General of Fair Trading must issue a standard licence if the applicant is a fit person to engage in activities covered by the licence and the name under which he applies to be licensed is not undesirable.

A group licence covers such persons and activities as are covered by the licence and it is issued to those categories of creditors or credit business where personal examination of an individual is not necessary in the public interest, such as the Law Society and the National Association of Citizens Advice Bureau.

Appeals against refusal to grant a licence are made to the Secretary of State and then, on a point of law, to the High Court.

(c) Section 24 of the Trade Descriptions Act 1968 provides two categories of defences, namely, (i) innocent publication and (ii) the general defences available in criminal law.

(i) **Innocent publication.** This means that the defendant did not know and could not have known, after taking due care, that the goods did not conform to the description or that the description had been applied to the goods

(ii) **General defences.** This means that the commission of the offence was due to a mistake or accident or some cause beyond the defendant's control or due to reliance on information supplied to the defendant or due to the act of a third party **and** the defendant took all reasonable precaution to avoid the commission of the offence. In **Simmons v. Potter (1975)** the defendant car dealers were unable to rely on section 24 when they sold a second hand car which unknown to them had a false odometer because they failed to use a disclaimer notice.

Where the defendant intends to rely on the defence that the offence was due to the fault of a third party, he must inform the prosecutor of his defence at least seven days before the hearing in order to enable him to prosecute the other person. A store manager of a company is 'another person' where the action is initially brought against the company **(Tesco Supermarkets Ltd v. Nattrass 1972).**

QUESTION 65 (a) 'Any person who, in the course of a trade or business:

(a) applies a false description to any goods; or

(b) supplies or offers to supply any goods to which a false trade description is applied;

shall, subject to the provisions of this Act, be guilty of an offence.'

(S.1(1) Trade Descriptions Act 1968)

Discuss the meaning and effect of this subsection.

(b) Miss *H* was *J*'s personal secretary. *J* owned a typewriter which he sometimes used himself. Miss *H* asked *J* whether he would sell her the machine. "Yes, certainly," he said, "it's a beauty"; and he sold it to her at a higher price. In fact, the machine was a very bad one.

Consider *J*'s liability, civil or criminal.

I.C.S.A. 1979

ANSWER (a) The subsection contains two separate offences where goods which bear a false trade description are sold in the course of a trade or business. In both cases local authority trading standards officers, and not individuals, have to institute prosecutions against offenders.

'In the course of a trade or business' is not statutorily defined and it is necessary to look to the court for judicial guidance, which makes this part of the Act somewhat uncertain. It would include retail trade, business to business transactions and business to consumer transactions. A transaction is in the course of a trade or business if it is either an integral part of the business or else if there is a sufficient degree of regularity of similar transactions. Thus in **Havering London Borough v. Stevenson (1970)** where, after every two years, it was the practice of the defendant to sell his car which he used for his car hire business and to use the proceeds as working capital, the court held that one such sale where the car had a false odometer reading was a sale in the course of a business and he was liable under section 1. However, in **Davies v. Sumner (1984)** where a self employed courier who used his car for working purposes and claimed tax allowances for its use, later sold the car with a false odometer reading, the High Court overturned the magistrates' conviction since the sale of the car was not part of the courier's normal business activities. "The justices …have asked themselves the question 'was the use of the car an integral part of the business?' and not 'was the sale of the car an integral part of the business?'" said Forbes J. An isolated transaction can constitute a business if it is proved to have been undertaken with the intent that it should be the first of several transactions **(Abernethie v. AM & J. Kleiman Ltd 1970).**

To create an offence under S.1(1)(a) the supplier or offeror must apply the trade description either before the sale is envisaged or at the time the contract is made. Trade descriptions covered by the Act may be given expressly or by implication. They are given expressly where they describe the characteristics of the goods and such matters as quantities, methods of manufacture and previous owners. They are given by implication where, for instance, the goods are displayed in such a way to suggest that they have other attributes. For example, to display raincoats with a photograph of a wearer weathering a downpour of rain without getting wet would simply imply that the raincoats are rain proof and not just shower proof. Similarly, where goods are offered for sale at "cut-price" and a trader adds to the price ticket a higher price which was charged in the past, this could give customers an inaccurate impression of the bargain value of the goods offered, especially if the higher price was charged a long time ago for a very short period. Traders are free to add to the price ticket the higher price only if the goods were identical and were offered during the preceding six months for a continuous period of at least 28 days.

Although it is usually the commercial seller who 'applies a false trade description' to goods the offence can also be committed by commercial buyers such as where the owner of a motor car sells it for a nominal price to a dealer who had falsely described it as worthless and then the dealer does some minor repairs and sells it at a substantial profit **(Fletcher v. Budgen 1974).**

To create an offence under S.1(1)(b) there must be an actual supply or offer to supply the goods involved. Where the application of a false trade description is tied to the supply of the goods in question, then the date of supply is the date of delivery and not the date of the original contract **(Rees v. Munday 1974).** It is a necessary ingredient of the offence that the offender knows that the goods bear a trade description at the time he supplies or offers to supply them, even though he does not have to know that the description is false. The offence under (b) will normally arise where the false trade description is applied to the goods by someone other than the supplier or offeror before the latter supplies or offers to supply them.

(b) *J*'s civil liability should be considered under misrepresentation and under the Sale of Goods Act 1979. A misrepresentation is a false statement of fact which induces a contract. If the misrepresentation is made fraudulently the action is brought in the tort of deceit, otherwise it is brought in contract under the Misrepresentation Act 1967.

By asserting that the typewriter is a beauty, *J* is representing that it is a good typewriter. However *J* will not be liable for his misrepresentation if he can show that Miss *H* did not allow his statement to influence her decision to buy the typewriter or that she did not believe his statement, for example, because she had used the typewriter on previous occasions.

Under the Sale of Goods Act 1979 where goods are sold in the course of a business there is an implied condition that the goods will be of merchantable quality. This condition will not apply if the buyer has examined the goods before the sale was concluded and an inspection would have revealed the defects. In any event, Miss *H* cannot rely on the Sale of Goods Act since the sale of the typewriter was not an integral part of the business **(R and B Customs Brokers Ltd v. UDT Finance Ltd 1988).**

J has applied a false description to goods contrary to S.1(1)(a) of the Trade Description Act by describing the type-writer as a 'beauty' when it was a bad typewriter, and it is well established in law that a prosecution under the Act may succeed even though an action for misrepresentation may fail. However it is submitted that *J* has not committed a criminal offence under the Act since the transaction between *J* and Miss *H* was not an integral part of *J*'s business and so falls outside the scope of 'in the course of a trade or business' (see **Davies v. Sumner 1984**).

QUESTION 66 Explain the role and responsibilities of the Director General of Fair Trading in relation to competition law including monopolies and mergers and anti-competitive practices.

I.C.S.A. 1990

ANSWER The Office of Director General of Fair Trading was established by the Fair Trading Act 1973 to protect the interest of consumers. The Director General's role in the competition field is to oversee the various pieces of legislation aimed at preventing anti-competitive practices by traders.

Under the 1973 Act, the Director General is responsible for monitoring business activities in the United Kingdom and investigating the circumstances leading up to any monopoly or merger situation. With the approval of the Secretary of State, he may refer a monopoly or merger situation to the Monopolies and Mergers Commission and if a business under investigation gives undertakings to the Commission, the Director General monitors the observance of such undertakings.

In the field of restrictive trade practices, the Director General is responsible for keeping a register of agreements which have to be registered under the Restrictive Trade Practices Act 1976 and to refer such agreements to the Restrictive Practices Court to determine their validity. The Director General may also institute exemption proceedings to allow resale price fixing agreements which would otherwise be void under the Resale Prices Act 1976.

The Competition Act 1980 makes the Director General responsible for investigating other trade practices which are likely to be anti-competitive, to require undertakings where such practices exist and in the last resort to refer them to the Monopolies and Mergers Commission. An anti-competitive practice is any practice in the course of a business which is likely to restrict, distort or prevent competition. Such practice may relate to pricing policy, such as where a trader temporarily sells his product below its cost price in order to eliminate his competitors out of the market, and distribution policy (such as where the supplier of one product requires the retailer to purchase another product of the supplier before he can obtain his product).

The Director General is a 'competent authority' for the purpose of assisting the European Commission in ensuring that EEC laws on competition are observed in the United Kingdom.

QUESTION 67 Discuss the extent of a manufacturer's liability in tort where damages or loss is caused by a defect in his product.

To what extent, if any, will liability be incurred where the loss is purely financial or economic?

I.C.S.A. 1987

ANSWER A manufacturer whose product causes injury to person or damage to property may be liable for such loss in a common law action for negligence or in an action for breach of statutory duty under the Consumer Protection Act 1987.

Negligence liability is liability for failing to take proper care to avoid foreseeable loss to others. In **Donoghue v. Stevenson (1932)** a retailer sold a bottle of ginger beer to a customer who gave it to his female companion to drink. After she had consumed most of the ginger beer she noticed the decomposed remains of a snail in the ginger beer bottle and became seriously ill. The House of Lords held that although there was no contractual link between the manufacturer and the customer's friend the manufacturer was still liable to the friend for her illness since he ought to have foreseen that his defective product could cause loss to anyone who used it.

To establish an action in the tort of negligence the plaintiff must prove that the manufacturer owed him a duty of care, broke that duty and as a result he suffered loss. Only in exceptional cases (under the doctrine of *res ipsa loquitur*) is the burden of proof shifted from the plaintiff and on to the manufacturer to disprove negligence. A manufacturer has been held to be negligent not only for producing defective products but also for failing to provide adequate instructions on the use of his products. Defences available to the manufacturer include contributory negligence (where the plaintiff ignores warnings on the use of the product) and consent.

Economic or financial loss is not normally recoverable in an action for negligence **(Muirhead v. Industrial Tanks Specialities**

Ltd 1985) unless there was a special relationship between the plaintiff and the defendant. In **Junior Books Ltd v. Veitchi & Co. Ltd (1982),** specialist subcontractors carelessly laid a concrete floor in a factory and the floor had to be relaid after two years. The House of Lords allowed a claim for loss of profits while the floor was being relaid even though there was no physical damage to the factory because the factory owners had selected the subcontractors who knew that they were being given the job on account of their skill and experience.

The Consumer Protection Act 1987 imposes strict liability (i.e., liability without the presence of negligence) where injury is caused by a defective product. 'Product' includes goods and electricity. A product is defective if its safety is not such as persons generally are entitled to expect (S.3). Factors to be taken into account when considering the safety of a product include any instructions or warnings given by the manufacturer on its use, the marketing aspects of the product, what might reasonably be expected to be done with the product and the state of the art at the time when the product was supplied by the manufacturer.

Liability under the Act rests principally on the producer who includes the manufacturer of the finished product or of a component and any person who won or abstracted the product. However, liability will also attach to any person who holds himself out to be the producer (such as by putting his name or mark on the product), or who imports the product into the European Community or who supplies the product (unless he identifies the producer when requested to do so by the person who suffered the loss).

Apart from the common law defences in tort a number of statutory defences are available where a claim is made under the Act. They include the defence that the defendant did not supply the product, the defect is attributable to compliance with UK or EEC legal requirements, the product was not supplied in the course of a business, the defect did not exist when the product was put into circulation, and the state of scientific and technical knowledge at the time the product was made was such that other producers of products of the same class would not have discovered the defect in their product.

A civil action under the Consumer Protection Act must be brought within three years from the date of the loss. However, no action can be brought where the product was in circulation for more than ten years.

Loss recoverable under the Act includes injury to person

and physical damage to private property. Physical damage to business property and economic or financial loss are not recoverable.

QUESTION 68 What is resale price maintenance. How does the Resale Prices Act tackle the problems by such a practice?

I.C.S.A. 1976

ANSWER Resale price agreements are agreements made between businessmen in the successive stages of production of goods – from the manufacturer down to the ultimate consumer. The manufacturer will agree with the wholesaler and retailer that when the goods actually reach the shop counter they would not be sold for less than an agreed minimum price. This type of agreement is known as a vertical agreement and is distinguished from a cartel which is normally horizontal in form.

At common law, a resale price agreement is known as a contract in restraint of trade and will be unenforceable unless the restraint was to protect only one proprietary article and the minimum price did not adversely affect the public. Thus in **Palmolive v. Freedman (1928)** the Court upheld an agreement which required the defendant to sell the plaintiff's soap for not less than 6d a tablet, on ground that the restraint covered only one article and it did not affect the public interest as neither the defendant nor the public was obliged to buy it.

The Resale Prices Act was passed to discourage such agreements. The 1976 Act requires all such agreements to be subject to judicial scrutiny and it works on the principle that agreements on minimum resale prices between supplier and dealer are void unless made with the view to benefit the consumer.

The Restrictive Practices Court which is seized with the matter will only uphold an agreement if it is convinced that without price fixing the quality or variety of goods would be substantially reduced or that the number of shops would decline or that the servicing of the goods would deteriorate or that there is a danger that the consumer's health would suffer. In **Re Medicaments Reference (1970)** the Court held that an agreement for a minimum price on the sale of medicine and drugs was in the public interest since without the agreement, wholesalers would hesitate to stock a wide range of drugs which were rarely used and only profitable in maintained margins.

Under the Act, it is also unlawful for suppliers to withhold goods from dealers who sell below recommended prices unless during the preceding twelve months the dealers sold the goods at a loss to attract customers (S.13).

QUESTION 69 Explain what is meant by a 'restrictive trade agreement' and describe the legal machinery by which the validity of such agreements is tested.

I.C.S.A. 1979

ANSWER A restrictive trade agreement is an agreement made by trade associations normally tying businesses engaged in the same stage. For example, manufacturers and others may agree on a minimum price on their goods and services and on terms and conditions on which they are prepared to do business with customers.

Under the Restrictive Trade Practices Acts 1956–1976 agreements, whether legally enforceable or not, which restrict goods and services are required to be registered with the Director General of Fair Trading who may then refer them to the Restrictive Practices Court for a decision on their validity.

Agreements on the supply of goods which fall within the provision of the statutes are those made between two or more persons carrying on business in the United Kingdom and which cover the following subjects: (a) prices charged, recommended or paid for goods or for the application of any process of manufacture of them; (b) terms and conditions on which the parties to the agreement will supply or acquire goods; (c) quantities or description of goods to be produced, supplied or acquired; (d) processes of manufacture to be applied to goods; and (e) persons or classes of persons with whom, and areas within which dealings are allowed. Agreements for the exchange of information on prices and on terms and conditions for contracts with customers are also required to be registered. Agreements on services which are required to be registered are those which the Secretary of State may from time to time designate by Order.

Registrable agreements must normally be registered within three months of their making otherwise they are unenforceable between members. On registration, the Director General may either recommend to the Secretary of State that the agreements should be allowed to stand or he may hold dis-cussions with the parties in order to remove objectionable terms. In the absence of a settlement, the Director will refer an agree-ment to the Restrictive Practices Court to determine its validity.

By section 10 of the Restrictive Trade Practices Act 1976, an agreement before the Court is deemed to be contrary to the public interest and is void unless it can escape through one of the 'gateways' provided by the statute. Among the most important 'gateways' are: the restriction is reasonably necessary to protect the public; its removal would deny to the public other specific or substantial benefits; it is reasonably necessary to ensure fair terms when dealing with an outsider who controls a preponderant part of the trade in question; and if the restriction is removed it would cause serious or persistent unemployment or substantially reduce exports.

An agreement which successfully passes through one of the 'gateways' will only be upheld if the Court is satisfied that the restriction is not unreasonable, having regard to the balance between those circumstances and any detriment to the public or third parties resulting or likely to result from the operation of the restriction.

QUESTION 70 Explain the provisions of Articles 85 and 86 of the Treaty of Rome in connection with restrictive trade practices and monopolies.

ANSWER One of the aims of the Treaty of Rome is to provide for the free movement of goods and services across national frontiers. In furtherance of this object, Articles 85 and 86 were enacted.

Article 85 prohibits and makes void any agreement or concerted practice between undertakings, which is calculated to bring about the prevention, restriction or distortion of competition within the Common Market. Article 85(1) states that agreements which are objectionable and void are those relating to price fixing or trading conditions, limiting or controlling production, sharing markets or sources of supply, placing certain trading parties at a competitive disadvantage and imposing on customers obligations which have no bearing on the subject matter of the main contracts such requiring a customer to buy non-essential goods as a condition for being supplied with the goods he requires. Article 85(1) also makes void concerted practices by undertakings, for example, where several undertakings raise prices by identical percentages on identical dates as in **Anilin Dyes and Dyestuffs (1970).**

The Commission decides whether an agreement or conduct of undertakings offends the Treaty provisions but the European

Court of Justice has the final say. Article 85(3) empowers the Commission to allow by way of exemption, agreements and concerted practices between undertakings. Exemptions will be granted where the agreement or practice promotes progress and allows the consumer a fair share in the resulting benefit; and also where the restriction has no noticeable effect.

Unlike Article 85 which prohibits and makes automatically void agreements and other measures which offend the Treaty of Rome, Article 86 simply prohibits an abuse by an undertaking holding a dominant position within the Common Market. By Article 86 an abuse is deemed to exist where unfair price or other trading conditions are imposed on customers; when consumers are prejudiced by production or technical development being limited; when trading partners do not receive equal treatment and when undertakings insist on tying-in clauses.

The effect of Article 86 is not to prohibit the monopoly itself but simply to prevent its abuses.

Chapter 5
Agency

QUESTION 71 (a) What is the purpose of an agency in contract law? In what circumstances may (i) a servant and (ii) an independent contractor be an agent.

(b) *A*, an estate agent, hearing that *B* was planning to sell his house, wrote to *B* offering to act as agent to arrange the sale. *B* replied rejecting *A*'s offer of assistance. Nevertheless, *A* advertised the house for sale and *C* replied to the advertisement and was sent by *A* to see *B*. *B* sold the house to *C* and *A* now claims he is entitled to the standard rate of estate agent's commission on the proceeds of sale. Advise *B*.

Would it make any difference to your answer if *B* had not replied to *A*'s offer of agency services?

ANSWER (a) The purpose of agency in contract law is for someone (agent) to make a contract on behalf of another (the principal) with a third party. In modern commerce, agency is used frequently to effect commercial transactions e.g. through the engagement of brokers, factors, and auctioneers. Usually the principal will employ the agent to make the contract with the third party and when this is done, the agent will drop out without incurring any personal liability and the principal will be in contractual relations with the third party. This type of agency relationship is governed by two separate contracts – the contract of agency proper setting out the relationship between the principal and the agent, and the subsequent contract between the principal and the third party.

An agent differs from a servant and an independent contractor in that while he is mainly employed to make contracts and dispose of property, a servant and an independent contractor are often employed to perform much wider tasks. The cases also suggest that an agent is a person with greater independence and freedom from control than a servant **(Hayman v. Flewker 1863)** and indeed some statutes refer to both servant and agent while others (e.g. the Factors Act 1889) refer only to agent. In contract law, the distinction between an agent and a servant is of little significance.

A servant will be an agent if he is employed by a principal who controls the manner in which the work is to be done. An independent contractor is employed to bring about a given result but the principal does not control the manner in which the result is to be achieved.

A servant can only make a contract on behalf of his employer if he has express or implied authority to do so. The employer will however be liable for the torts of his servant if they were committed within the course of employment or within a period not unreasonably disconnected from the course of employment, even though he does not benefit thereby **(Lloyd v. Grace, Smith & Co. 1912).**

An independent contractor is presumed to be acting on his own behalf in any contract which he makes, but he could act as an agent if expressly appointed or if his action is ratified by the principal or if he acts as an agent of necessity.

(b) In order for the estate agent to be able to claim the commission for introducing the buyer for the purchase of *B*'s house, there must be a contract between the estate agent and *B* appointing the former as agent. No such contract exists between the parties. In fact *B* expressly rejected the estate agent's offer to act as his agent. Even if *B* did not reply to the estate agent's offer of agency service no contract between them could have existed as silence cannot amount to acceptance **(Felthouse v. Bindley 1862).**

The only possibility for the estate agent is to show that he was appointed *B*'s agent by implication. To succeed he would have to prove that *B* saw the advertisement and did nothing to deny the natural inference that the estate agent had been validly appointed as *B*'s agent to sell the house. This may be difficult to prove.

QUESTION 72 (a) Distinguish between actual and ostensible authority of an agent.
(b) Percy appointed Arthur as an agent to buy quantities of goods for him from John and a number of other suppliers. Later, Percy became dissatisfied with Arthur's work and wrote to him on 1st May telling him that he did not wish Arthur to continue buying goods for him. On 1st June Arthur buys goods on credit from John and Percy refuses to pay John for these goods. Advise John.

A.A.T. 1979

ANSWER (a) Actual authority is real authority given by a principal to his agent to enter into transactions on his behalf. It covers three types of authorities – express, implied and usual. If it is express it may be given orally, in writing or under seal. Implied or usual authority is authority to do everything necessary for or incidental to the execution of the authority expressly given to the agent. A principal will not be liable to a third party in the absence of ratification, if the agent exceeds his actual authority.

Ostensible authority is simply a form of holding out by the principal to a third party that his agent has proper authority although in fact such authority does not exist. Explaining this form of authority Slade J in **Rama Corporation Ltd v. Proved Tin and General Investments Ltd (1952)** said "Ostensible or apparent authority… is merely a form of estoppel and a party cannot call in aid an estoppel unless three ingredients are present, (1) a representation made to him, (2) a reliance on the representation, and (3) an alteration of his position resulting from such reliance…" Thus the principal is estopped from denying the authority of his agent where he has allowed a state of affairs to arise or persist which creates the impression with the third party that the agent is cloaked with the authority.

(b) As a general rule an agency contract may be unilaterally terminated by either the principal or agent by giving reasonable notice. This would effectively terminate the agent's power to perform any future acts for the principal, so that any further acts by the agent, purporting to be on the principal's behalf, will render the agent liable to a third party for pretending to possess an authority that has been withdrawn from him. An action will lie for breach of 'warranty of authority' **(Collen v. Wright 1857).**

As regards third parties the problem is not so straightforward because an agent though stripped of actual authority may still have an apparent authority with which to bind his principal unless the third party has been informed that the agent's authority has been terminated. This can only arise though, where through a course of regular and consistent dealings the third party has come to rely on the principal settling his account in the ordinary course of business. In **Drew v. Nunn (1879)** a husband held out his wife as having authority to pledge his credit. She had such authority but it terminated when he became insane. Nevertheless she continued to pledge his credit. On recovery, the husband was held liable for the price of the goods supplied during his insanity.

If, therefore, Percy had regularly acquired and paid for goods from John through the agency of Arthur, John will be able to sue Percy for the price of the goods supplied on 1st June on the ground of Arthur's ostensible authority. If, on the other hand, John was aware of the termination of Arthur's authority he will have no right to sue Percy.

John may nevertheless be able to bring an action against Arthur for breach of warranty of authority if he had relied on Arthur's representation that he had retained Percy's authority. Furthermore, if Arthur fraudulently deceived John, the latter may sue the former in the tort of deceit and recover any loss he has suffered.

QUESTION 73 (a) In what circumstances may an agent lawfully delegate authority conferred upon him by his principal? How are the rights and duties as between the parties determined if delegation is lawful?

(b) Dominique who was about to be married shortly asked Anneliese, a dressmaker of exceptionally high quality and reputation to make her wedding dress. Anneliese agreed, but as she was overworked, she asked a friend Michèle to make the dress on her behalf. Michèle made the dress to the precise specification and quality required and Anneliese paid for it, but when Dominique heard that Anneliese did not make the dress herself she refused either to accept it or to pay for it. Advise Anneliese.

ANSWER (a) The general rule is that an agent is not permitted to delegate performance of his duties. Hence the maxim 'Delegatus non potest delegare'. However this prohibition is not strictly applied and in three cases an agent will be allowed to delegate his duties.

If the principal expressly authorises the agent to do so, then he may lawfully delegate his duties. Authority to delegate may also be implied from the circumstances of the case. For instance, in the construction industry it is customary for a builder to delegate the plumbing and the painting to a sub-contractor. Finally acts of a purely administrative nature where no special skill nor discretion is required may be delegated even though the principal's consent was not obtained.

The fact that delegation of work is lawful does not exonerate the agent from liability to his principal as the responsibility of agency cannot be delegated. Thus there is privity between the principal and his agent.

There is no privity between the principal and the delegate so neither party may sue the other. It would be otherwise if the principal had permitted the appointment of a substitute rather than a sub-agent **(Schwensen v. Ellinger Health Western & Co. 1949).**

(b) Despite the fact that Dominique is getting a wedding dress to the precise specification and quality as she requested from Anneliese, this is a contract requiring special skill. Dominique asked Anneliese to make the dress not just because she wanted a wedding dress made but because she felt that Anneliese, with her reputation of high quality could be relied upon to make the type of dress she required.

As Anneliese did not obtain Dominique's permission to delegate the work to Michèle, Dominique is entitled both to refuse the dress and to pay for it.

QUESTION 74 Discuss briefly the doctrine of the undisclosed principal in relation to Agency.

I.C.S.A. 1971

ANSWER The doctrine of undisclosed principal arises where an agent when contracting with a third party conceals both the identity of his principal and also the fact that he is merely acting as agent. In this case he contracts as if he was the principal.

The importance of this doctrine is in the manner in which the third party may be affected. He would not normally know of the existence of a principal and will regard the agent as the party with whom he is contracting. As such, the primary responsibility is on the agent. If the third party subsequently learns of the existence of the principal he may elect to proceed either against the principal or the agent but not both. His choice is final. However, if the third party has commenced proceedings against the agent without having any knowledge of the principal but only discovers the principal after commencement of such proceedings, he may elect to transfer proceedings against the other **(Clarkson Booker Ltd v. Andjel 1964).** An election can only be made before the third party has obtained judgement, whether or not the judgement is satisfied. Additionally, even where the third party knows of the principal he may be estopped from suing him if he allows the principal to think that the third party will settle the matter with the agent **(Heald v. Kenworthy 1855).**

Of course the principal can always intervene and enforce the contract against the third party personally, though obviously if he does do this he renders himself personally liable to the contract.

In certain circumstances, the right of the principal to intervene and of the third party to elect may not be available. Where the agent's identity is material to the contract the principal will not be allowed to take the benefit of the contract. In **Said v. Butt (1920)** *B*, the manager of a theatre instructed his staff not to sell tickets to *S. S* knew this and sent *A* to buy the ticket for him. *S* went with the ticket but *B* refused him admittance. It was held that the contract was of a personal nature and so *S* could not take its benefit. Again, if the principal allows the agent to contract on terms incompatible with the agency, he will not be able to enforce the contract against the third party. In **Humble v. Hunter (1848)** *P* authorised *A* to make a contract of charter in relation to a ship owned by *P. A* made such a contract with *T* without disclosing his principal's existence. It was held that *P* could not enforce the contract.

The doctrine of undisclosed principal only applies where the agent is acting within the scope of his authority. Thus if he is acting without authority conferred upon him, the principal cannot enforce the contract by purporting to ratify **(Maxsted & Co. v. Durant 1901).**

QUESTION 75   (a) Outline the implied duties of an agent towards his principal.
(b) Your company invites tenders to supply stationery for the forthcoming year and, on the advice of Arthur, your company's purchasing officer, enters into a contract with Thomas who appears to have made the best offer. It is now discovered that Arthur was promised a television set by Thomas as a birthday present shortly before Thomas submitted his tender.
What action, if any, may your company take?

I.C.M.A. 1978

ANSWER   (a) The implied duties of an agent are:–
(i) To use reasonable care and skill in the performance of his task. The degree of care and skill depends on the agency and the standard which the agent professes to have. Thus, if, as in **Keppel v. Wheeler (1927)** he is a professional selling agent employed to sell a block of flats he must obtain the best price reasonably obtainable for his principal's property.
(ii) To account for all monies received during the agency. This includes keeping proper accounts of all transactions made on his principal's behalf and separating 'agency money' from his own. Any money received under a void or illegal contract such as a betting contract must be handed over to his principal **(De Mattos v. Benjamin 1894).**

(iii) To obey lawful instructions of his principal. Unless he is a gratuitous agent, the agent must perform his agency otherwise he will lose his right to remuneration and may even be liable in damages **(Turpin v. Bilton 1843).** Moreover, whether gratuitous or not, if he proceeds to carry out his agency, he must act in accordance with his principal's instructions.

(iv) To act in good faith. The agent is in a fiduciary position towards his principal and so he must not allow his interest to conflict with his duty, nor should he disclose confidential information acquired during his agency **(Lamb v. Evans 1893),** nor should he make a secret profit **(Reading v. Att-Gen. 1951)** or take a bribe **(Armstrong v. Jackson 1917).**

(v) Not to delegate his task. The agent must perform his task personally and should not delegate it unless authorised to do so either specifically or by custom.

(b) An agent occupies a position of trust as between himself and his principal and as such he should not accept bribes or make secret profits. If he does, the principal may dismiss him; or recover the bribe or secret profit from either the agent or the third party in an action for money had and received. Moreover in the case of bribes, as an alternative to an action for money had and received, the principal may sue both parties for deceit as in **Salford Corp. v. Lever (1891)** and will be able to recover the bribe from the agent and damages from the co-defendants.

From the facts of the problem there must be a strong suspicion that the promise of the television set is directly connected with the agency, and to induce Arthur to accept Thomas' offer. Even if it is established that the television set was not intended as a bribe, my company will still be able to claim the television set from Arthur if he has received it, on ground that it is a secret profit. An agent who receives a gift from a third party as a result of his agency, must hand over the gift to his principal unless the latter allows him to keep it. In **Reading v. Att-Gen (1951)** a soldier in uniform rode in lorries carrying stolen goods. He was paid £20,000 for his services. It was held that the Crown as principal was entitled to claim the money even though it suffered no loss from the soldier's act because the soldier had received the money solely because of his service uniform.

QUESTION 76 (a) On 1st February, Jones & Co., in their corporate name, agreed to buy certain goods from Smith & Co. On 2nd February Jones & Co. informed Flint & Co. that they had bought the goods on their (Flint & Co's) behalf. Flint & Co. confirmed the transaction and agreed to treat Jones & Co. as their agents in the matter. Smith & Co. have failed to deliver the goods.

Advise Flint & Co. as to their rights (if any) against Smith & Co.

(b) Bodkin & Co. authorised Hopkins & Co. to buy goods on their behalf from Dobson. Hopkins & Co. made the purchase without disclosing that they were acting on Bodkin's behalf. Thinking, contrary to the truth, that Hopkins & Co. had paid Dobson, Bodkin & Co. paid Hopkins & Co. Dobson has discovered that Bodkin & Co. were Hopkins & Co's principals and now wishes to claim the price from them.

Advise Dobson.

I.C.S.A. 1983

ANSWER (a) There are various ways in which an agency may arise. It may be **express,** such as where one person appoints another to be his agent. The appointment must be by deed if the agent is to contract by deed with third parties. It may be **implied,** such as where the principal places the agent in a situation where it would be normal (either by reason of trade custom or otherwise) for the agent to contract on behalf of the principal although no express authority to do so has been conferred on him; or where the principal permits someone to act as if he was his agent although no principal/agent relationship was intended. This type of agency is sometimes described as agency by estoppel. Agency may also arise by ratification such as where one person without authority expressly contracts on behalf of another and when the latter learns of it, he adopts the transaction; and through **necessity** such as where one person in lawful possession of another's property acts, without authority, during an emergency, to protect that property **(Great Northern Rail Co. v. Swaffield 1874).**

In order to obtain rights under the contract between Jones & Co. and Smith & Co., Flint & Co., will have to show that Jones & Co. were their agents. They are unlikely to succeed by relying on agency by ratification since Jones & Co. contracted in their own name and one of the conditions for ratification is that the person who makes the contract with the third party must profess at the time of making it to be acting on behalf of the person who subsequently ratifies it. In **Keighley, Maxsted & Co. v. Durant (1901),** an agent intending to buy wheat for his principal, bought it in his own name at a price above that at which he had been instructed to buy. The undisclosed principal purported to ratify the transaction but later refused to accept delivery. It was held that ratification was not valid and that the principal could not be sued for failing to accept delivery.

If Jones & Co. were agents of Flint & Co. with their consent and this was known to Smith & Co. then there might be an implied agency for this particular transaction with the result that Flint & Co. would be able to sue Smith & Co. for non-delivery of the goods. The transaction would be based on the ostensible or apparent authority of Jones & Co. and could only arise through a course of dealings with Smith & Co.

(b) The payment of money by a principal to his agent for the benefit of a third party does not discharge the principal's liability to the third party if the agent fails to pass on the money. This is the general rule and it makes no difference whether the agency was disclosed to the third party at the time of the transaction **(Irvine v. Watson 1879)** or whether the third party was unaware of the agency **(Heald v. Kenworthy 1855).** In **Heald v. Kenworthy** an undisclosed principal who had authorised his agent to buy goods on his behalf, was sued for the price by the seller. He pleaded that soon after the sale he had paid the agent in full and that he did so in good faith. The court held that he was still liable to the third party for the price of the goods.

From what has been said above, Dobson is advised that he may successfully bring an action against Bodkin & Co. for the price of the goods sold to their agents, Hopkins & Co. Dobson might have found it difficult to enforce payment against Bodkin & Co. if he had misled them into believing that he had settled payment with their agents, for example, if he had taken a security from Hopkins & Co. and had given them a receipt for the purchase price **(Wyatt v. Marquis of Hertford 1802).**

QUESTION 77 (a) What in the law of agency is meant by warranty of authority? Who provides the warranty and for whose benefit? What is the measure of damages in the event of breach of warranty of authority?

(b) *G*, a resident of Glasgow, is planning to visit London with his family. On Wednesday, *G* sends a telegram to his friend *J*, who lives in London, reading as follows: "Please book five stall seats for Saturday matinee of *Murder Most Vicious*". (*Murder Most Vicious* is a play showing in one of the London theatres). *J* telephones the theatre and books five seats for the Saturday matinee of that week. *G* had been thinking of the following Saturday. The tickets remain uncollected and unsold. State with reasons whether the theatre management may claim payment from *G* or from *J*.

I.C.S.A. 1969

ANSWER (a) Warranty of authority is based on a representation made to a contracting party by the person with whom he is dealing, that the latter has authority from some other person to enter into the transaction. This warranty is provided by the agent for the benefit of the third party. Accordingly, if the agent has no such authority and the third party relies on the representation and as a result suffers a loss, he may bring an action against the representor for breach of warranty of authority. In **Collen v. Wright (1857)** *A,* purporting to act on behalf of *P,* granted a lease of *P*'s land to *T. A* had no authority to do this and *P* was not bound by his act. It was held that *A*'s personal representatives were liable to *T* for *A*'s breach of warranty of authority. The agent will not be liable for breach of warranty of authority if the representation of authority is one of law. Thus if, as in **Rashdall v. Ford (1866),** on the true construction of its memorandum, a company has no capacity to borrow money and one of its directors borrows on its behalf, after misrepresenting the meaning of its memorandum to the third party, he will not be liable for breach of warranty of authority since the construction of a document is a matter of law. It will be otherwise if the memorandum permitted the company to borrow up to a limited amount only; then if a director on its behalf, borrows a sum in excess of that amount, he will be liable for breach of warranty of authority since he will be representing by implication, that the company had not yet borrowed up to that amount; and this will be a representation of fact **Weeks v. Propert (1873).** No action for breach of warranty will lie against the agent if his principal is liable under the main contract either because he ratified the contract or because the agent had ostensible authority **(Rainbow v. Howkins 1904).**

The action for breach of warranty of authority is based on an implied obligation of the agent to the third party. In **Yonge v. Toynbee (1910),** Buckley L.J. said that the agent's liability is based on an implied contract, but another view is that it is based on quasi-contract. The agent will be liable to the third party even though he honestly thought that he had the authority. In **Yonge v. Toynbee** a client instructed solicitors to defend an action. The solicitors entered an appearance and took other steps in the action without knowing of their client's insanity. The proceedings were subsequently struck out and the plaintiff claimed costs against the solicitor for breach of warranty of authority. It was held that they were personally liable.

The measure of damages is the loss suffered by the third party as a result of the contract not being binding on the principal. Thus, if the third party could have obtained full satisfaction from the principal had the contract been binding on him, the agent will be liable in damages to that extent. However if the principal was insolvent, the third party will not be able to recover more from the agent than he would have actually recovered from the principal and this may be very little depending on the degree of the principal's insolvency.

If the agent did in fact know that he did not have the authority which he represented to have, he will also be liable in damages to the third party for the tort of deceit. In **Polhill v. Walter (1832)** the defendant accepted a bill of exchange on behalf of his principal realising he lacked the authority to do so but believing that his principal would ratify his action. The defendant was held liable in the tort of deceit when the bill was dishonoured.

(b) By asking *J* to buy the theatre tickets for him *G* has in effect appointed *J* as his agent to enter into contractual relations with the theatre. The misunderstanding between *G* and *J* as to which Saturday the tickets were required is the result of unclear instructions given by *G* and so the subsequent purchase of the tickets from the theatre will not be affected on ground that it was outside the scope of *J*'s authority.

If when arranging for the purchase by telephone *J* booked the tickets in his own name, the doctrine of undisclosed principal will apply. *J* will be liable primarily for the price of the tickets **(Sims v. Bond 1833).** Normally, where an agent is liable on the contract made on behalf of his undisclosed principal his principal will also be liable subject to an election by the third party. However, since this is a contract of a type which cannot be enforced by the undisclosed principal (see **Said v. Butt**), the agent will be solely liable to the theatre. If *J* had booked the tickets in *G*'s name and had stated that they will be collected by *G* personally from the ticket office, *G* will be solely liable unless the theatre made it clear that *J* as agent will be regarded as responsible for the payment of the tickets.

QUESTION 78 (a) "There is normally a right in the principal unilaterally to revoke the agency at any time before the agency has been completely performed by giving notice." Explain the rule and indicate whether there are any exceptions to it.
(b) Shaw owes Lamb £700. Shaw has appointed Lamb as his agent to collect certain debts owing to Shaw and to retain 20% of each amount collected until his loan to Shaw is fully recouped. The agreement also provides that Lamb should receive a commission of 5% of all gross amounts collected.

Lamb has collected £3000 and thus recovered £600 of his loan. Now Shaw wishes to cancel the arrangement.

Advise Lamb as to his rights in the matter both in respect of the unrecovered balance of the loan and of the commission.

ANSWER (a) Apart from termination by mutual agreement, as a rule an agency can be terminated by the unilateral action of either party. Under this rule the principal may at any time withdraw the agent's authority. Termination of the agent's authority will in effect terminate the relationship of principal and agent, even though it amounts to a breach of contract of the agency proper. But in such a case, the principal may be liable to the agent in damage for loss of the agent's commission or other remuneration and the agent may also be able to restrain by injunction the breach of a negative stipulation in the agency contract, such as an undertaking by the principal not to appoint another agent to conduct the business in question **(Decro-Wall International S.A. v. Practitioners in Marketing Ltd 1971).**

Revocation of the agent's authority does not require any special formality, so that even a deed containing a power of attorney can be revoked orally. The principal will be liable on contracts entered into on his behalf after the termination of the agency, unless he has caused notice of such termination to reach third parties, who may act on the faith of the previous authority.

In certain cases, the principal's right to revoke an agency cannot be exercised and if exercised will be wholly ineffective. If an agent is given authority to act on behalf of his principal as a security for some debt or obligation owed by the principal to the agent, the authority cannot be revoked without the agent's consent. Thus an authority coupled with an interest is irrevocable as long as the authority was intended for the protection of the interest **(Frith v. Frith 1906).** If the authority was given before the interest was created, the authority is not irrevocable. In **Smart v. Sanders (1848)** an agent to whom goods were entrusted for sale later advanced money to the owner. It was held that this authority was not irrevocable.

The principal cannot revoke the agent's authority where the agent is in the process of carrying out his instructions. Similarly, a power of attorney which is expressed to be irrevocable and is given to secure a proprietary interest of, or the performance of an obligation owed to, the donee cannot be revoked without the donee's consent. Furthermore, such power cannot be revoked by any of those events (i.e. death, bankruptcy or insanity of the principal) which normally terminates an agency by operation of law. (The Powers of Attorney Act 1971). This is also true for an agency coupled with an interest.

(b) At common law an agency coupled with an interest cannot be terminated not even if the principal dies or becomes insane unless the agent consents. 'Interest' is usually a debt due from the principal to the agent and the authority is given as security for that debt. In this case, the authority given to Lamb is coupled with an interest. This case must be distinguished from **Doward, Dickson & Co. v. Williams & Co. (1890).** In that case an agent was appointed to collect debts for five years on a commission and the court decided that the authority was not being coupled with an interest and so it was revocable.

Lamb's interest amounts to a form of security and is not a 'mere right to salary or commission'. Lamb is advised that his authority is irrevocable and he is entitled to carry on recovering the debts till his loan has been repaid in full. Furthermore, he is entitled to receive commission at the agreed rate on any amounts he recovers, but once he has been paid in full his agency will terminate.

Chapter 6

Business Organisations

QUESTION 79 (a) What is a partnership? What factors would you take into consideration to decide whether a partnership has been formed?

(b) George and Albert formed a partnership. The partnership agreement contained a clause to the effect that Albert would have the power to introduce into the partnership any of his children on their attaining the age of majority. Albert's daughter, Narina, is eighteen and Albert wishes to make her a partner in the firm. George refuses to consent. Advise Albert.

ANSWER (a) Section 1 of the Partnership Act 1890 defines a partnership as 'the relation which subsists between persons carrying on business in common with a view of profit'. The Act describes a partnership as 'a firm'. However unlike a company the firm is not recognised as a separate legal entity but simply an aggregate of individuals.

The sharing of the profits, as distinct from the gross returns of the business, is the prima facie evidence of the existence of a partnership but it is not conclusive and the whole contract must be looked at together with the real intention of the parties. The Act itself provides guide-lines to decide whether or not a partnership exists. These are as follows:

(i) joint ownership of property does not of itself create a partnership whether or not the joint owners share any profit;

(ii) the sharing of gross returns does not of itself create a partnership, whether or not the persons sharing such returns have a common interest in the ownership of the property producing these returns;

(iii) the receipt by a person of a share in the profits of a business is prima facie evidence that he is a partner in the business but the Act also provides a number of examples where, although there is a sharing of profits, no partnership exists, e.g.

(a) where a person receives payment of a debt out of the profits of the business;

(b) where a servant or agent employed by the business is paid from the share of the profits;

(c) where a widow or child of a deceased partner receives a portion of the profits by way of an annuity;

(d) where the goodwill of a business is paid for by an annuity or other portion of the profits, the seller does not become a partner.

(b) Where a partnership exists, no new partner can be admitted into the firm except with the consent of all the existing partners, since a contract cannot be altered against the wishes of any of the original parties to it (section 24(7)). However, if the partnership agreement contains a clause empowering one of the partners to introduce a new partner, he is deemed to have the tacit consent of all the existing partners and cannot be prevented from introducing a new partner. The facts of the problem are very similar to those in **Byrne v. Reid (1902)** where it was held that the partner who had signed the articles could not prevent the introduction of a new partner by withholding his consent.

Albert is therefore entitled to make his daughter Narina a new partner even if George does not give his consent.

QUESTION 80 (a) "The duties of a partner to his firm are fundamentally the same as those of an agent to his principal." Discuss this statement.
(b) *L, M* and *N* are partners. Having reached the age of 70, *L* wishes to retire from the business and to assign his share to his son, who has worked in the business for 10 years. *M* and *N* object to the assignment and wish to purchase *L*'s share themselves.

ANSWER (a) Section 5 of the Partnership Act 1890 bases the liability of partners for the acts of their partner on agency rules. This section states that "every partner is an agent of the firm and his other partners for the purpose of the business of the partnership; and the acts of every partner who does any act for carrying on in the usual way business of the kind carried on by the firm of which he is a member bind the firm and his partners." The only exception to this rule is where the partner acting has no authority to act for the firm in that matter and the person with whom he is transacting business either knows of his lack of authority or does not believe him to be a partner.

Since he is an agent of the firm he owes it similar duties as an agent owes his principal. Thus he must act bona fide for the firm. This duty extends to making full and frank disclosure to other partners of matters affecting the firm and also to keeping proper accounts (section 28). An agent also owes a duty to disclose any information to his principal which might influence the latter in making a contract; and must render accounts of any transaction in which he has acted as agent **(Dadswell v. Jacobs 1887).** Section 29 imposes a duty on a partner to account to the firm for any benefit derived by him from a transaction concerning the partnership. Similarly, an agent, in the absence of full disclosure, is not allowed to make a profit from his agency **(Hippiesley v. Knee Brothers 1905).**

Section 30 prohibits a partner from competing with the firm unless he obtains the consent of his fellow partners. An agent also must not allow his interest to conflict with his duty **(Nitedals Taendstik fabrik v. Bruster 1906).**

(b) A partner is not permitted to introduce a new partner into the firm without his fellow partners' consent (S.24). However, he may assign his share in the partnership although the assignee does not acquire any right to interfere in the management of the firm or to inspect the accounts of the partnership. The assignee merely receives a share in the profits which the partner would have received had he not transferred his rights. Similarly, if the partnership is dissolved, the assignee is entitled to a share in the assets and to an account as from the date of dissolution (S.31). The assignee is not personally liable for debts incurred by the firm.

M and N are advised accordingly.

QUESTION 81 Give four examples of how illegal partnership may arise. Discuss briefly the contractual rights and obligations of an illegal partnership (a) between themselves (b) with third parties.

A.B.E. 1983

ANSWER The most common way an illegal partnership may arise is where the number of members of the partnership exceeds the statutory maximum. Section 434 of the Companies Act 1948 state that as a rule a partnership formed to carry on a business for gain must not have more than twenty members, or more than ten members in the case of a banking business. Where the membership of the firm exceeds the permitted limits the partnership will be illegal and must be wound up. A partnership is formed to carry on a business at a gain if it is formed with a view to trading at a gain or, as in the case of a mutual insurance association, if it is formed so that its members should have some security **(Re Padstow Total Loss and Collision Association 1882).** Similarly a loan society formed not to make a profit but rather to make loans at interest to its members will be considered as formed for the purpose of a gain and will be declared illegal if the firm's size exceeds the statutory limit for its membership **(Shaw v. Benson 1883).**

An illegal partnership also arises where the firm is formed for an unlawful purpose e.g. for the commission of a crime. In **Foster v. Driscoll (1929)** an agreement was entered into in England, the purpose of which was to smuggle whisky into the United States at the time of prohibition. It was held that the agreement was illegal.

Individual statutes may also result in a partnership being illegal. For example, the Solicitors Act 1957 prohibits a solicitor from entering a partnership agreement, as a solicitor, with an unqualified person.

Again, as in **R. v. Kupfer,** where one or more of the partners resides and trades in a foreign country and war is declared against that country, the partnership becomes an illegal partnership.

(a) The members of an illegal partnership cannot, as a general rule, sue on the contracts to which the illegal association is a party. Nor can they be sued since in law they do not exist. Thus, the court will not direct accounts to be taken nor will it order one partner to contribute to the losses suffered by another.

(b) An illegal partnership may be sued by third parties ignorant of the illegality, provided that the transaction which the third parties are seeking to enforce is not tainted with illegality.

QUESTION 82 (a) In what circumstances may a person ratify a contract made on his behalf but without his authority?
(b) A and B are partners in a small bakery business. Without consulting B, A borrows £10,000 from a moneylender ostensibly for the business and spends the money on his own pleasures. State with reasons whether or not the firm is liable for the debt.

ANSWER (a) Where an agent properly appointed exceeds his authority the principal will incur no liability on the contract but if he ratifies the contract he will be liable to the third party. For ratification to be valid the following conditions must be satisfied:
(i) The agent must have claimed expressly to be contracting as agent and he must have disclosed the existence of a principal. A contract made on behalf of an undisclosed principal cannot be ratified **(Keighley Maxted & Co. v. Durant 1901).**

(ii) The principal must be in existence at the time the contract is made. In **Kelner v. Baxter (1866)** *B*, *C*, and *D* bought wine on behalf of a company which had not yet been formed. On formation, the company purported to ratify the contract made by *B*, *C* and *D*. It was held that ratification was not possible.

(iii) The principal must have contractual capacity both when he ratified the contract and at the time the agent made the unauthorised contract. He cannot, for example, be a minor or alien enemy as in **Boston Deep Sea Fishing & Ice Co. Ltd v. Farnham (1957).**

(iv) The principal must have full knowledge of all material facts at the time of ratification **(Freeman v. Rasher 1849).**

(v) The principal must ratify the whole contract. He cannot ratify only those terms of the contract which are beneficial to him.

(vi) The principal must ratify within the time fixed or if no such period exists, within a reasonable time **(Metropolitan Asylums Board Managers v. Kingham & Son 1890).**

(b) By section 5 of the Partnership Act 1890 every partner is deemed to be an agent of the firm for the purposes of its business and any contract he makes in pursuance of this object will be binding on the firm and his partners. The only exception is where the partner acting has no authority to act and the person with whom he is dealing is aware of this fact or does not know that he is a partner.

Applying the above rules to the problem, if *A* borrowed the £10,000 for the purposes of the firm's business, *B* will be bound with *A* to repay the loan unless the moneylender knew that *A* had no authority to borrow the money or that he was not a partner. The fact that *A* used the money for his private use is irrelevant.

QUESTION 83 (a) On dissolution of a partnership, how in the absence of contrary agreement, are the assets of the firm distributed?

(b) *A*, *B* and *C* are partners sharing profits equally. The capital of the partnership is £24,000 of which *A* has contributed £12,000, *B* £8,000 and *C* £4,000. On the dissolution of the partnership it was found that after outsiders had been paid in full, there was only £12,000 left. Explain how this sum will be shared among the partners.

ANSWER (a) On dissolution of a partnership, every partner is entitled to have the partnership properly applied in payment of the firm's debts and liabilities. In the absence of a contrary agreement, the application of partnership property for payments of the firm's debts and liabilities will be as follows:–

(i) The joint estate is applied in payment of the debts of the partnership and the separate estate is applied in payment of the individual debts of the partner to whom it belongs; if there is a surplus of the latter it goes to the joint estate if it has a deficit; the surplus in a joint estate is dealt with as part of the respective separate estates in proportion to the rights and interest of each partner in the joint estate.

(ii) If one partner only becomes insolvent, the joint creditors may recover all their debts from the solvent partners; the latter may then claim against the estate of the insolvent partner for any sum they had paid, which was over and above the bankrupt's share of the assets.

(iii) If the assets of the firm are sufficient to pay the firm's creditors and partners' advances, but are not sufficient to repay the partners' capital in full, deficiencies are shared in the same way as profits **(Nowell v. Nowell 1869).** However, where partners have contributed unequal capital and agree to share profits and losses equally, then the solvent partners are not liable to contribute the insolvent one's equal share of capital, but the amount available after the solvent partners have made their proper contribution is divided rateably according to the amount of capital standing to the credit of each solvent partner **(Garner v. Murray 1904).** In short, the insolvent partner's share of deficiency is borne by the other partners in proportion to their capital, and not in the proportion that ordinary losses are borne.

(iv) The ultimate residue, if any, will be divided among the partners in the proportion in which profits are divisible.

(b) In this problem there is a deficiency of £12,000 on capital. Each partner must, therefore contribute £4,000. Having contributed £4,000, each of the partners will get back what they had originally contributed. Adjustments would normally be carried out by book entries without actually collecting £4,000 from each partner. So ultimately A will get £8,000, B £4,000 and C will get nothing.

QUESTION 84 (a) On what grounds may a partnership be dissolved by the court?

(b) In order to obtain membership of a partnership, *A* paid the firm a premium of £1,000. The firm was dissolved shortly afterwards.

Can *A* recover any part of the premium.

ANSWER (a) A partnership may be dissolved by the Court on application of any creditor or member of the firm. The former may petition on ground that the firm is unable to pay its debts. The latter may petition on the following grounds:

(i) a partner has become a mental patient under the Court of Protection (Mental Health Act 1959).

(ii) a partner has become in any other way permanently incapable of performing his part of the partnership contract.

(iii) a partner is guilty of such conduct as is calculated prejudicially to affect the carrying on of the business.

(iv) a partner is guilty of wilful or persistent breach of the partnership agreement or otherwise conducts himself in such a way that it is not reasonably practicable for the other partners to carry on business with him.

(v) the business can only be carried on at a loss.

(vi) there are circumstances which render it just and equitable that the partnership be dissolved.

In **Carmichael v. Evans (1904)** the articles of the partnership entitled a managing director to determine the partnership as to any particular partner if that partner was guilty of a flagrant breach of any of the duties of a partner or was addicted to conduct detrimental to the business carried on. The court held that a conviction of one of the partners for travelling without a ticket was conduct which would entitle the managing director to exercise his power of determining the partnership as to that partner.

(b) It is customary when a new partner is introduced into a well-established firm, for that person to pay a sum of money as the price for the privilege of becoming a partner. This money is called a 'premium'. Where such a premium is paid and the partnership is for a fixed term, the court has power to provide for the repayment of a fair part of the premium to the partner who has paid it if the partnership is dissolved before the expiry of that period unless the dissolution is due to the misconduct of the partner who has paid the premium or the dissolution is due to the death of a partner (S.40 Partnership Act 1890).

In the problem if the original partnership agreement provided that part of the premium paid by *A* should be returned to him on the dissolution of the partnership before the expiry of the term he should claim under the agreement. If it did not, and if the circumstances mentioned above apply, *A* should apply to the court.

QUESTION 85 What is meant by a Corporation in English Law? How may a Corporation be created. Explain the rules relating to the contractual capacity of a Corporation.

I.A.S. 1979

ANSWER A corporation is a body or association which is endowed with legal personality and which perpetuates its existence by the admission of new members. There are two types of corporations – sole and aggregate. A corporation sole is represented by one member only at any one time, e.g. the Crown, the Public Trustee. A corporation aggregate has several members simultaneously, e.g. companies.

Although many corporations sole exist by custom, on account of the sovereignty of Parliament, such corporations can only now be created by Act of Parliament. Corporation aggregate may be created by Royal Charter, Act of Parliament, and Registration. Royal Charter is issued by The Crown on the advice of the Privy Council and it is used generally to create corporations for educational and charitable purposes. Examples of corporations created by charter are the Association of Certified Accountants and the Institute of Chartered Secretaries and Administrators. An Act of Parliament is normally used to create corporations to operate nationalised industries. Examples of such corporations are the National Coal Board and the British Steel Corporation. The most popular method of creating corporations aggregate is by registration under the Companies Act 1985. This is done by preparing and filing a Memorandum of Association and Articles of Association, together with certain other documents, with the Registrar of Companies. The corporation is formed when a certificate of incorporation is issued. Examples of such corporations are registered companies.

The contractual capacity of a corporation depends on its mode of creation. A corporation created by Royal Charter has the same capacity as a natural person. A corporation created by an Act of Parliament has its capacity limited by the provisions of the relevant statute. A corporation formed by Registration has its capacity determined by its 'objects clause' in its Memorandum of Association. The 'objects clause' lays down the permitted range of activities which the company may pursue and the powers which it may exercise; any contract which exceeds these activities is ultra vires the company. The other party to such a contract will still be able to enforce it if he acted in good faith. The company can ratify it by special resolution (S.35 Companies Act).

QUESTION 86 Explain the main differences between a limited liability company and a partnership.

A.B.E. 1977

ANSWER A limited company is a business organisation having in law separate legal existence and rights and duties distinct from those of the individual persons who form it. Moreover, in the event of the company being unable to pay its debts, members' liability to make good any deficit will be limited to the amount unpaid on their shares (if the company has a share capital) or to the amount actually guaranteed (if the company is limited by guarantee). A partnership is a business organisation which does not have legal personality. Its structural organisation is simpler, the business vehicle essentially being a specialised form of contract with modification, relying heavily on the law of Agency.

The following are the main differences between these two types of business organisations:

(a) **Numbers.** A public company may have as many members as it desires, but a partnership cannot exceed twenty partners unless it is a specialised partnership e.g. solicitors and accountants (Companies Act 1985)

(b) **Personality.** A company is a separate person in law from its members **(Solomon v. Solomon & Co. Ltd 1897).** A partnership has no legal personality apart from the personality of its members.

(c) **Liability.** Normally the liability of partners is unlimited except in the case of a limited partnership.

(d) **Management.** Management of a company is vested in the Board of Directors while the management of a partnership is vested in the partners.

(e) **Contractual Capacity.** A member of a company is not an agent of the company or his fellow members but a partner is deemed to be an agent of his fellow partners.

(f) **Transfer of Interest.** A shareholder of a public company can freely transfer his shares but a partner needs the consent of existing partners before he can transfer his interest with a view to introduce new partners in the firm.

(g) **Property.** Company's property vests in the company's name but partnership property must be held in the partners' names.

(h) **Formation.** A company is created by compliance with the provisions of the Companies Act 1985, but a partnership can be created quite informally.

(i) **Dissolution.** A company has to be dissolved according to the rules of the Insolvency Act 1986, but a partnership may be dissolved either by agreement or by operation of the law.

QUESTION 87 Advise the following on the forms of business association most suitable for their purposes, pointing out briefly the advantages and drawbacks in each case:

(a) The owner of a chain of laundries who wishes to raise money on the Stock Exchange for further expansion.

(b) An old established orchestral society which wishes, if possible, to avoid having to add the word 'LIMITED' to its name.

(c) Three law students planning to open a boutique in London but who are anxious that their competitors should know as little as possible about its affairs.

ANSWER (a) The owner of the chain of laundries should incorporate his business as a public company limited by shares. The business will then obtain all the advantages of incorporation. It will have its own name ending with the abbreviation 'p.l.c.', it can own its own property and will have perpetual existence. In addition, it will be able to raise capital from the investing public generally, by a prospectus and through a stock exchange 'listing'. Its main drawbacks are that it can start business only when it obtains a trading certificate (S.117, Companies Act 1985), must have a minimum issued share capital of £50,000 and must maintain it. Shares cannot be issued for services – (S.99, Companies Act 1985) and when issued for assets there must be a proper valuation of those assets by an independent expert, and a copy of the valuation report must be sent to the proposed allottee and later to the Registrar of Companies with the return of allotment.

(b) The only way in which the old established orchestral society can be corporated as a limited company and avoid using the word 'LIMITED' after its name is to be incorporated as a private company limited by guarantee. The Registrar has power to allow such a company to dispense with 'LIMITED' subject to compliance with certain basic requirements in its memorandum (S.30 Companies Act 1985). An additional advantage of this type of company is that the members will not become personally liable for company debts until the company goes into liquidation; and even then, only to the extent of the amount actually guaranteed by them. Its main drawbacks are that incidental profits cannot be distributed to members in the form of dividends, and the company will still be required to display 'limited' on its letterheads and order forms (S.9 E.C.A. 1972).

The society may instead, become a limited partnership in which case it need not display 'LIMITED' after its name. Not being incorporated, it will not be subject to provisions of the Companies Act 1985. The ultra-vires doctrine will not affect its activities and its accounts need not be audited. However, it must have at least one partner who will be personally liable for its debts, should there be an insufficiency of partnership assets to meet the firm's liabilities.

(c) The business vehicle most suitable for the purpose of the law students is a registered company. It could be a private company limited by shares, for if qualified by its size it will have partial exemption from publishing – by delivering a copy to the Registrar – its full accounts. Otherwise it may be registered as an unlimited company. An unlimited company need not publish **any** accounts, and can make capital distributions to members free from the usual legal impediments; but personal liability is attached to members for its debts.

If the company is to be limited by shares, its name must end with 'LIMITED', or in the case of an unlimited company with 'UNLIMITED'.

Additionally, the business may be run as a partnership where published accounts are not required but then the firm will be unable to raise loans by the provision of a floating charge (a security peculiar to companies).

QUESTION 88 (a) With reference to companies limited by shares, compare Preference Shares with Debentures. For what reasons are Preference Shares considered more like Debentures than Ordinary Shares?

(b) In connection with the issue of shares by a company, explain:

(i) the meaning of the terms 'Rights Issue' and 'Bonus Issue';

(ii) the purposes for which such issues are made, indicating the effect of each kind of issue on the balance sheet of a company.

A.A.T. 1982

ANSWER (a) The legal distinction between a share and a debenture is that a share may make the holder a member of the company, whereas the holder of a debenture is only a creditor of the company. The money raised by the issue of shares is capital which the company cannot generally reduce; but that raised on debentures is a debt which the company may redeem at any time subject to the terms of issue. Nevertheless, they are both long-term investments in the company.

A Preference Share gives preference over all other shares as to dividend and/or capital. It often carries a fixed rate on dividend and is frequently issued as redeemable. This allows the company to terminate membership by repaying capital to the shareholder without the court's consent (S.159 C.A. 1985). To this extent, a preference share is similar to a debenture. Neither would carry the right to share in a capital surplus on liquidation. They both produce a fixed income but no capital appreciation. In addition, the preference share suffers disadvantages which the debenture does not have. The earning of income is dependent on a dividend being declared. The non-cumulative preference shareholder can therefore lose his year's income for good but the debentureholder can claim his, if necessary, by enforcing his security. Membership rights on preference shares are mostly illusory, since voting rights are in practice restricted to matters directly affecting the shares. Accordingly, preference shareholders are denied the right to participate in the 'democratic' process of the company. Voting power at general meetings is normally vested in the ordinary shareholder who bears greater risk in the company because he will only be paid his dividend after the debentureholder and the preference shareholder are paid what is due to them.

(b) (i) A 'Rights Issue' is given by a company to its existing shareholders to take up new shares in the company in proportion to their current holding. In practice, the shareholders will be offered the new shares at a price slightly below the market price but they cannot be compelled to accept the offer. If it was a renounceable rights issue, the rights can be sold by the shareholders to others.

A 'Bonus Issue' is simply a capitalisation of profits. A company may, if authorised by its articles, credit its members with bonus shares as fully paid, instead of giving them a dividend in cash. Unlike a rights issue, shareholders do not have to pay anything for the additional shares. As there is no increase in the funds of the company, the effect of a bonus issue is to dilute the existing value of the issued shares. Accordingly shareholders' consent to capitalised profits must first be obtained before bonus shares can be issued.

(ii) The purpose of a 'Rights Issue' is to raise additional capital from the members for the company. The issued share capital in the company's Balance Sheet will therefore be increased by the total nominal value of the additional shares, and if the new shares were issued at a premium, the Share Premium Account will be increased by the difference between the nominal value of the new shares and the price at which they were issued. Current Assets will also be increased by the cash received for the shares.

The purpose of a bonus issue is to use existing company funds to pay for unissued shares being allotted to members. If paid out of profits, the profits are to be retained by the company and this may be an indirect way of raising additional capital. If paid out of capital, it may be a means of increasing members' shareholding in the company out of funds which cannot be otherwise used to make a distribution (e.g. the Share Premium Account, the Capital Redemption Reserve). In any event, the appropriate sum will be transferred from profit and loss account or from reserve account to share capital account in the balance sheet.

QUESTION 89 (a) How does a members' voluntary winding-up differ from a creditors' voluntary winding-up?
(b) In connection with the winding-up of a company under an order of the court:
　　1. what are the grounds on which such an order may be made?
　　2. by whom may a petition leading to such an order be lodged? and
　　3. what is the effect of the issue of a winding-up order?

ANSWER (a) A voluntary winding-up has to be initiated by a resolution by the members. A special resolution is usually required unless the winding-up is a creditors' voluntary winding-up in which case an extra-ordinary resolution is needed. In a members' voluntary winding-up a declaration of solvency must be made by the directors within five weeks before the resolution is passed;

the creditors are not involved in the winding-up; the liquidator is appointed by the members in general meeting and there is no committee of inspection. A creditors' voluntary winding-up only takes place when the company is insolvent. No declaration of solvency is required; whenever there is a meeting of members there must also be a corresponding meeting of creditors; the liquidator is, in effect, appointed by the creditors who may fix his remuneration and a committee of inspection may be appointed by the creditors, if they so wish, to act with the liquidator.

(b) The grounds for the compulsory winding-up of a company are set out in Section 122 of the Insolvency Act 1986 and they are as follows:

(i) Where the company has passed a special resolution to this effect. This ground is available only to members but is rarely used since members would normally prefer a voluntary liquidation to minimise court costs.

(ii) Where a company incorporated as a public company has failed within a year to obtain a trading certificate. This ground is available only to the Department of Trade and to contributories (i.e. past or present members), but with the latter they must take their shares from original allottees or by transmission from deceased members or must have held the shares for six out of the last 18 months.

(iii) Where the company has not commenced business for at least a year. This ground is available only to members and a petition based on it is at the discretion of the court.

(iv) Where the number of members falls below the statutory minimum of two. This ground is available only to a member and it is an outlet for his prima facie liability under section 31 where a company trades for more than six months with only one member left.

(v) Where the company is unable to pay its debts. Unless the company is unlimited, only a creditor can use this ground and he must show either that the company owes him at least £200 and has failed to pay the debt within 21 days of demand or that a judgement in favour of him has been returned unsatisfied wholly or in part, or that the company is unable to pay its debts having regard to its liabilities.

(vi) Where it is just and equitable to wind up the company. This ground is available to the Department of Trade and to members and it enables the court to subject the exercise of legal rights to equitable considerations.

In addition to the above general grounds, the Department of Trade may petition for a compulsory winding-up after receiving a report from inspectors appointed to investigate the company. The Official Receiver may also petition for a compulsory winding-up of a company already in voluntary liquidation if he is satisfied that the voluntary winding-up would lead to unsatisfactory results.

A winding-up order by the court has retrospective effect from the date the petition is presented. Accordingly, all legal actions against the company are halted from that date unless the court decides otherwise (S.126); any disposition of the company's property such as a payment of a debt is void unless the court decides otherwise (S.127); any seizure of assets is void (S.128); the powers of the directors cease from the date the winding-up order is granted, the employees are then dismissed and the company cannot continue to carry on business unless the liquidator decides it necessary (e.g. to dispose of the assets on favourable terms).

Chapter 7

Negotiable Instruments

QUESTION 90 Give an account of the essential characteristics of negotiable instruments and examine the rights of a 'holder in due course'. What is meant by 'notice of dishonour'? What are the legal requirements for a valid notice of dishonour? In what circumstances, if any, need such notice not be given?

I.C.S.A. 1979

ANSWER A negotiable instrument is a chose in action which is freely transferable and in respect of which a transferee in good faith can obtain a better title than his transferor.

The essential characteristics of a negotiable instrument are:
(a) title to the instrument must be capable of passing by mere delivery of it or by delivery plus indorsement;
(b) a bona fide holder for value must be able to take it free of any defect in the transferor's title;
(c) the holder of the instrument must be able to sue in his own name to enforce the rights under it;
(d) no notice of assignment need be given to the debtor or other party to it upon its transfer.

An instrument may be recognised as negotiable by mercantile custom or by statute and its negotiability may be restricted or destroyed altogether by the holder of the instrument. The most important negotiable instruments today are bills of exchange, cheques and promissory notes.

A holder in due course is one who takes a negotiable instrument complete and regular on the face of it before it is overdue without notice of any defect in the transferor's title and for value (S.29 Bills of Exchange Act 1882). His rights are contained in S.38(2). This section states that he will hold the bill free from any defect of title of prior parties, as well as from mere personal defences available to prior parties and he can enforce payment against all parties liable on the bill. Where an endorsement is forged rather than defective a subsequent holder cannot claim a good title in the forgery even if he is a holder in due course.

A notice of dishonour is a notice given by the holder of a bill to all prior parties if the bill is dishonoured by non-acceptance or by non-payment when the bill has been duly presented. Such a notice must be given immediately or within a reasonable time of dishonour if it is to be valid. A 'reasonable time' is the day after the dishonour if the parties live in the same postal district, or if they live in different postal districts then the notice should be sent off on the day after the dishonour of the bill. The notice of dishonour may be given orally or in writing so long as.it clearly identifies the bill. If the bill is a foreign bill and is dishonoured it must be noted and protested.

By section 50 notice of dishonour may be dispensed with in the following circumstances:

(i) where reasonable diligence is used but it is impossible to give notice to the person sought to be charged;

(ii) where the other party waives the notice;

(iii) as regards the drawer, where he and the drawee are the same person; or the drawee is a fictitious person or person who lacks capacity; or the drawer is the person to whom the bill is presented for payment or the drawer has countermanded payment or where the drawee or acceptor is as between himself and the drawer under no obligation to accept or pay the bill;

(iv) as regards the endorser, where the bill is an accommodation bill, or where the endorser is the person to whom the bill is presented for payment, or the drawee lacks capacity or is a fictitious person.

QUESTION 91 (a) 'In order to make the drawer and indorser liable on a bill of exchange it must be presented for payment.' Discuss.

(b) What is the legal effect of bills drawn in the following terms?

(i) 'Pay Arthur Brown one hundred pounds three days after the next General Election.'

(ii) 'Pay Charles Davis five hundred pounds on the day of the marriage of his daughter Ellen to George Harris.'

A.A.T. (I.A.S.) 1978

ANSWER (a) Presentation of a bill for payment is necessary in order to enforce it against the drawer and indorser. If the bill is not presented on the day it falls due, both the drawer and indorser are discharged. In **Yeoman Credit Ltd v. Gregory (1963)** a bill had been accepted 'payable at the N.P. Bank', but because the holder was informed by the acceptor's agent that there were no funds at the N.P. Bank and that presentation should be made at the M. Bank, the bill was presented on the correct day at the M. Bank which refused payment. On the following day, it was presented at the N.P. Bank, which also refused. It was held that as the bill had not been presented at the N.P. Bank on the correct day, the indorser was discharged from liability.

To constitute a valid presentment the following rules must be complied with:

(i) The bill must be presented by the holder or by someone authorised to act for him.

(ii) Presentment must be made at a reasonable hour on a business day, at the place specified in the bill; if no place is specified and no address appears on the bill, presentment must be made at the drawee's place of business if known, or if not, at his ordinary residence, or in the last resort at any place where the drawee can be found.

(iii) Presentment must be made to the person from whom payment is required or to someone acting on his behalf. If payment is made on presentment, the holder must hand over the bill to the payer.

(iv) Where a bill is payable on demand, presentment must be made within a reasonable time after its issue or within a reasonable time of its indorsement. If the bill is not payable on demand it must be presented on the day it falls due subject to a permitted three days' grace.

(v) Where agreement or usage authorises, presentment may be made through the post. Delay in making presentment will be excused if the delay is due to circumstances beyond the holder's control.

Presentment will not be necessary if it is waived either expressly or impliedly, or where, after the exercise of reasonable diligence, it cannot be effected; or where the drawee is a fictitious person. As regards the drawer, presentment is not required if the drawee or acceptor is not bound, as between himself and the drawer, to accept or pay the bill and the drawer has no reason to believe that the bill will be paid if presented. Similarly, as regards an indorser, presentment is not required if the bill was accepted or made for the accommodation of such indorser who has no reason to expect that the bill will be paid if presented.

(b) A bill of exchange is defined as an unconditional order in writing, addressed by one person to another signed by the person giving it, requiring the person to whom it is addressed to pay on demand or at a determinable future time, a sum certain in money to or to the order of a specific person or bearer. An instrument which does not comply with this definition is not a valid bill.

(i) Although the date of the next General Election is yet to be determined it is certain to take place because of the rules of British Constitutional Law. It is thus a determinable future event and so the bill payable to Arthur Brown three days after the occurrence of this event is a valid bill of exchange. In calculating the due date for payment of this bill the day from which the time begins to run is excluded but the day of payment is included and then 'three days grace' is allowed. Thus in effect, the bill will be payable six days after the General Election.

(ii) The marriage of Ellen to George Harris is not a certain event since the wedding may never in fact take place. Hence it is not a valid bill of exchange. The instrument is at best a mandate or request to pay Charles Davis £500 and cannot be negotiated in the usual way as a bill of exchange.

QUESTION 92 Write notes on the following:
(a) A cheque
(b) Qualified acceptance of a bill of exchange
(c) Transfer of a bill of exchange

A.C.C.A. 1977

ANSWER (a) A cheque is a bill of exchange drawn on a banker payable on demand. Since it is payable on demand, post-dated cheques are invalid although they may operate as an ordinary bill of exchange with the result that the banker will be able to debit the customer's account when the date for payment arrives and only if the customer has not in the meantime countermanded payment. A cheque differs from ordinary bills of exchange in that it is drawn on a banker and does not have to be presented to him for acceptance. Moreover, the provisions of the Bills of Exchange Act 1882 concerning crossings only apply to cheques not to other bills, and in certain circumstances the banker on whom a cheque is drawn is given statutory protection if he pays out on a forged indorsement, whereas there is no such protection for the drawee of a demand bill who is not a banker. Finally, a cheque crossed 'not negotiable' can be transferred although the transferor cannot give a better title to it than he himself has, but a bill of exchange marked 'not negotiable' on its face cannot be transferred **(Hibernian Bank Ltd v. Gysin & Hanson 1939)**.

(b) Acceptance of a bill of exchange is the signification by the drawee of his assent to the order of the drawer. A usual form would be for the person upon whom the bill is drawn to write

'Accepted' followed by his signature upon the face of the bill. This means that he accepts liability upon it. If acceptance is qualified the holder of the bill may treat the bill as dishonoured by non-acceptance and will have an immediate right of recourse against the drawer and indorsers subject to his having given them notice of dishonour. Acceptance is qualified if it is **partial,** that is, to pay part of the amount only; or **conditional,** that is, when it makes payment by the acceptor dependent upon the fulfilment of a condition stated in the acceptance; or local, that is, to pay only at a particular specified place; or qualified **as to time,** that is, to pay at a different date than that specified in the bill; or qualified **as to parties,** that is, where it is accepted only by some of the drawees.

Where the holder of a bill takes a qualified acceptance, then unless the acceptance was partial, the drawer or any indorser who, after receiving notice of the qualified acceptance, does not assent to it is discharged from his liability on the bill. In the case of partial acceptance, despite any dissent to such acceptance, the drawer or indorser will be liable up to the amount accepted during the currency of the bill, but in the event of the bill being dishonoured by failure to pay the partial acceptance, his liability will revert to the original amount.

(c) Transfer of a bill means passing on the bill from one person to another. If the transfer is capable of conveying a perfect title to the transferee who takes the bill in good faith and for value, regardless of any defects in the title of the transferor, this is called negotiation of a bill. Thus, 'negotiation' is a much more elaborate concept than transfer.

A bearer bill can be transferred by mere delivery; an order bill requires indorsement to pass the property in the bill, followed by delivery. Indorsement may be done by writing the word 'indorsed' (or 'endorsed') at the bank of the bill and signing it, but in practice, a simple signature of the transferor on the bill without additional words will suffice (S.32). An indorsement which is only partial does not operate as a negotiation of the bill but is simply an authority entitling the indorsee (or transferee) to receive that partial payment and to that extent he will have a lien on the bill. An indorsement may be **in blank,** i.e. no indorsee is specified and the bill becomes a bearer bill; or **special,** i.e. it specifies the person to whom or to whose order the bill is to be payable; or **restrictive,** i.e. prohibits further negotiation (e.g. 'pay C only'. C has a right to receive payment on the bill but he cannot transfer this right).

QUESTION 93 (a) What is the effect where a signature on a bill of exchange is forged or placed thereon without the authority of the person whose signature it purports to be.

(b) Advise Bena whether she has a good title to any of the following cheques transferred to her by Jeff:

(i) an uncrossed cheque payable to Raksha whose indorsement had been forged by Jeff;

(ii) a cheque crossed 'not negotiable' payable to Jeff and indorsed by him, which Jeff had obtained by fraud;

(iii) a cheque crossed 'account payee' payable to Jeff and indorsed by him.

Bena had no knowledge of the history of the cheques and gave value for them.

ANSWER (a) Where a signature on a bill of exchange is forged or placed thereon without the authority of the person whose signature it purports to be, the forged or unauthorised signature is wholly inoperative (S.24 Bills of Exchange Act 1882). By a forged signature is meant signing the name of another person with the intent to defraud.

The general rule as stated in section 24 is subject to two exceptions. First a signature which was unauthorised when it was signed can be subsequently ratified according to the ordinary rules of agency and is then as valid as a genuine signature. Secondly, although a forged signature cannot be ratified – since forgery is a crime, sometimes a signatory (who may be either previous to the forgery or subsequent to it) may be estopped from denying liability to a holder in due course. Thus, if the signature of the acceptor is forged, the drawer of the bill remains liable on it to a holder in due course (S.55) and if the signature of the drawer is forged a holder in due course can sue the acceptor on the bill (S.54). Similarly, an indorser of a bill by indorsing it, is estopped from denying to a holder in due course the genuineness and regularity in all respects of the drawer's signature and all previous indorsements (S.55(2)). It should be observed that estoppel does not permit a good title to pass after a forged signature is placed on the bill but simply allows certain rights as between the parties. For example, if a thief steals a bill belonging to *C*, forges *C*'s signature and negotiates it to *D*, a holder in due course and *D* endorses it over to *E*, *D* will not obtain a good title to the bill as he took it from the thief who had no title (not just a defect in title) but by signing it over to *E*, *D* is estopped from setting up the forgery of *C*'s signature.

As a bearer bill does not require indorsement, any indorsement on such a bill is completely superfluous. So forgery of any indorsement on such a bill will have no effect on the bill. In two cases, a bill which is prima facie an order bill will be treated as a bearer bill. If the drawer signs a bill in favour of a non-existent payee (i.e. a person who does not exist) the bill is treated as a bearer bill so that a forged indorsement will not prevent a holder in due course from obtaining a good title. In **Clutton v. Attenborough (1892),** a clerk fraudulently wrote out a cheque in favour of a non-existent payee whom he called *B* and persuaded his employers to sign it by falsely representing that *B* had done some work for the firm. The clerk forged *B*'s indorsement and negotiated the cheque to the defendant. The House of Lords held that the bill was a bearer bill and that the defendant as holder in due course obtained a good title. If the drawer signs a bill in favour of a fictitious payee (i.e. a real person whose name is entered in the bill as a pretence that that person was intended to receive payment) the bill becomes a bearer bill and any forged indorsement will be irrelevant. In **Bank of England v. Vagliano Bros. (1891),** a fraudulent clerk entered his employers' name as drawer of a cheque for the benefit of *C* & Co., customers of his employer. In fact the clerk did not intend that *C* & Co.. should receive payment. The clerk then forged the indorsement of *C* & Co. The court held that the bill was a bearer bill because the drawer (i.e. the clerk) did not intend *C* & Co. to receive payment with the result that the latter was a fictitious person.

(b) A cheque is by definition, a bill of exchange drawn on a banker payable on demand. An order cheque must be indorsed if it is to be negotiated.

(i) No rights can be transferred under a forged indorsement (S.24). Thus, Bena has no title to it although she gave value for the cheque and took it in good faith.

(ii) The effect of crossing the cheque 'not negotiable' is that the transferor cannot give a better title to it than he has, and, since he obtained the cheque by fraud, Bena will have no title to it and should return it to Raksha, the true owner.

(iii) The effect of crossing a cheque 'account payee' is to direct the collecting banker to credit the account of the payee. This is Jeff and so, although Bena is the indorsee of the cheque and entitled to it, she may find that the bank will refuse to collect it since it might be held to be negligent if it collected for anyone but the payee.

QUESTION 94 (a) Explain the rights and duties of a 'paying banker' and a 'collecting banker' in relation to cheques.
(b) How is a banker's authority to pay a cheque drawn on him by his customer terminated?

ANSWER (a) A 'paying banker' is the bank upon which the cheque is drawn and it is the duty of a paying banker to pay the cheques of his customer up to the amount of the customer's credit balance or an agreed overdraft. He is liable if he pays a cheque drawn on himself on which the drawer's signature is forged but the customer is bound to inform the banker immediately he becomes aware of any irregularity. The customer owes a duty to the banker to take care when drawing cheques and if, owing to a customer's negligence, a dishonest holder has been able to obtain a greater sum from the bank than that for which a cheque is drawn (no alteration of the cheque being apparent) the banker is not obliged to refund the difference he has paid. By section 60 of the Bills of Exchange Act 1882, a banker is protected if he pays a cheque drawn on himself in good faith and in the ordinary course of business although the **indorsement** has been forged. 'Ordinary course of business' means during banking hours or within a period not unreasonably disconnected from banking hours as in **Baines v. National Provincial Bank Ltd (1927)** where a cheque was presented and paid at 3.5pm when closing time was 3pm; and in the manner adopted generally by bankers. Thus, to pay a crossed cheque over the counter rather than paying it through a collecting banker would not be acting in the ordinary course of business and the paying banker will not be allowed to debit that amount from the customer's account. Section 60 provides protection to the banker whether the cheque is crossed or uncrossed and notwithstanding that the banker is negligent so long as he acted in good faith. Instances of lack of good faith would be where the banker knows than an indorsement has been forged or has been notified that a cheque payable to order was lost or stolen whilst still unindorsed by the payee but nevertheless pays the cheque when it is presented.

A banker is also protected if he pays a crossed cheque drawn on himself in good faith and without negligence and in accordance with the crossing (S.80 Bills of Exchange Act 1882). This protection is lost if the cheque is paid over the counter rather than into an account unless the cheque is specially crossed and is presented for payment over the counter by the bank specified in the crossing. Inland cheques paid into the account of the payee need no longer to be indorsed (Cheques Act 1957). Accordingly a paying banker who wrongfully pays a cheque through another banker can debit the drawer's account notwithstanding that the cheque bore no indorsement or an irregular indorsement (e.g. if there is a discrepancy between the name of the payee as it appears on the face of the cheque and an indorsement on the back) so long as the paying banker acted in good faith and in the ordinary course of business (S.1 Cheques Act 1957). Thus, if *A* draws a cheque on the N Bank in favour of Sam Ward who received the cheque and crosses it generally and the cheque is stolen by a thief who goes to the M Bank pretending to be Sam Ward and opens an account in that name, the N Bank will be protected if it pays the cheque in good faith and in the ordinary course of business when M Bank presents it for payment even though the cheque bore no indorsement. Uncrossed cheques paid over the counter are still required to be indorsed, so the paying banker will only obtain protection from Section 1 if the cheque is irregularly indorsed.

A 'collecting banker' is the bank which collects the proceeds of a cheque from the paying banker on behalf of a customer who has paid it in for credit of his account. He is protected if he receives payment for a **customer** in good faith and without negligence of a cheque to which the customer has no title or a defective title (S.4 Cheques Act 1957). The collecting banker is not treated as negligent simply because he fails to concern himself with the absence of or the irregularity in, the indorsement on the cheque of the customer if that customer is the payee of the cheque. However, the banker will be negligent if he failed to take up references when opening the customer's account **(Ladbroke & Co. v. Todd 1914).** The extent of the duty of care owed by a banker was discussed in **Lloyds Bank v. Chartered Bank of India, Australia & China (1929)** where it was stated that the duty of the banker to the true owner of a cheque was (a) to exercise the same care and forethought with regard to the cheque paid in by the customer as a reasonable man would bring to bear on similar business of his own; and (b) to provide a reasonable and competent staff to carry out that duty. Even if negligent, a collecting banker may obtain a good title to his customer's cheque as holder in due course and this may arise where he buys the cheque from the customer, or takes it to reduce the customer's overdraft or where the cheque was drawn by the customer before it was cleared.

Since the collecting banker is in contractual relations with his customer he would be liable for breach of contract if he wrongfully failed to collect the proceeds of a cheque.

(b) A banker's authority to pay a cheque drawn on him is terminated if the customer countermands payment before the cheque is paid, or the customer becomes insane, bankrupt or dies, or there is insufficient balance in the customer's account or if the customer's signature is irregular or is believed to be forged.

QUESTION 95 (a) What is an accommodation bill. If the holder knows that the acceptor is an accommodation party are his rights affected?

(b) *G* accepted a bill for the accommodation of *H* who endorsed it to *J* for value. *J* gave the bill to his daughter as a wedding present. The bill was dishonoured by *G*. What rights has *J*'s daughter:

    (i) if *J* knew that *G* was an accommodation party;

    (ii) if he did not know?

ANSWER (a) An accommodation bill is a bill which is accepted by an accommodation party to accommodate someone else without valuable consideration being given for it. Section 28 of the Bills of Exchange Act 1882 defines an accommodation party as some person who has signed a bill as drawer, acceptor, or indorser, without receiving value therefor, and for the purpose of lending his name to some other person. The accommodation party is a kind of guarantor and in practice is some well known person whose credit is good.

An accommodation party is liable on the bill to a holder for value; and it is immaterial whether, when the holder took the bill, he knew such party to be an accommodation party. By section 59 an accommodation bill is discharged if the bill is paid in due course by the person accommodated. If payment is made to the holder by the accommodating acceptor the bill is not discharged since he still has a right to claim an indemnity from the party whom he accommodated.

For example, if Carolle wishes to raise some capital and she persuades her wealthy friend, Lord C to accept a bill drawn on him in favour of Carolle payable '30 days after sight' and Lord C accepts the bill gratuitously solely to enable Carolle to raise the money by using his signature, Lord C becomes an accommodation party. Should Carolle negotiate the bill with X Bank, Lord C will be liable as acceptor to the X Bank. If Carolle subsequently pays the X Bank when the bill is presented for payment, the bill is discharged. If however, Lord C pays the X Bank, the bill is not discharged until Carolle indemnifies him.

(b) *G* is an accommodation party and *J*'s daughter is a holder for value because at some stage before she received the bill, value was given for it (i.e. by *J*). *J*'s daughter will have an action against all prior parties before value was given. *J*'s daughter may therefore sue both *G* and *H* and it makes no difference whether or not she or *J* knew that *G* was an accommodation party.

J's daughter cannot however sue *J* because as between the immediate parties (i.e. *J* and *J*'s daughter) the absence of consideration is always a defence to the indorser.

QUESTION 96 What are the liabilities of (a) the drawer and (b) an endorser of a bill of exchange? How does the liability of a transferor by delivery differ from that of an endorser?

ANSWER Both the liabilities of the drawer and endorser of a bill of exchange are dealt with by section 55 of the Bills of Exchange Act 1882. Section 55 (1) states that by drawing the bill the drawer of the bill undertakes that on presentation it will be accepted and paid according to its tenor and if it is dishonoured, he will pay the holder or any endorser who, because of its dishonour, has to pay it, provided that the necessary steps on dishonour are taken. Moreover, the drawer is precluded from denying to a holder in due course the existence and capacity of the payee. Section 55(2) states that by endorsing the bill the indorser undertakes that on presentation, it will be accepted and paid and if it is dishonoured, the indorser will compensate the holder or any subsequent indorser who is compelled to pay it provided the necessary steps of dishonour are taken. Moreover, the indorser is precluded from denying to a holder in due course the authenticity of all signatures prior to his endorsement; and to a subsequent endorsee, that the bill was valid and that he had a good title to it at the time of his endorsement.

Both a drawer and an indorser can limit or exclude their liability by adding words such as 'sans recours' to a bill (S.16). Moreover a person who endorses a bill in a representative capacity e.g. personal representatives, may indorse the bill in such terms as to negative personal liability (S.31) by using words such as 'so far as assets only'.

Where the holder of a bill payable to bearer negotiates it without endorsement he is called a 'transferor by delivery'. By section 58, he does not incur liability on the bill since he has not signed it. However by negotiating it he warrants to his immediate transferee that (a) the bill is what it purports to be, (b) he has a right to transfer it, and (c) at the time of the transfer he knows of no fact which renders it valueless.

This warranty will only operate against the transferor by delivery if the immediate transferee is a holder for value. A holder for value is anyone who holds a bill for which value was given at some time in the bill's history. It is not necessary for the holder to give value for the bill before he can become a holder for value. For example if *A* draws a bill of exchange in favour of *B* as a gift and *B* endorses it to his landlord, *C*, in payment of his rent and *C* endorses it to his daughter *D*, as a birthday present, *D* is a holder for value and can sue *A* and *B* if the bill is dishonoured. She cannot however sue *C* because as between immediate parties the absence of consideration is always a defence. A holder for value gets no better title than his predecessor.

QUESTION 97 (a) Discuss the nature of the duties owed by a banker to his customer in relation to cheques.
(b) Nationwide Bank Ltd, which had been mandated by Faith Company Ltd, to pay cheques when drawn by two directors, paid a cheque by one director only. Advise Faith Company Ltd whether Nationwide Bank Ltd can debit their account.

A.C.C.A. 1975

ANSWER (a) The nature of the duties owed by a banker to his customer is contractual based on the relationship between banker as debtor and the customer as creditor when the latter had a credit balance on his account. A banker however differs from an ordinary debtor in that he is only liable to repay the customer on payment being demanded. The relationship is also based on agency rules as when the banker makes payment or collects cheques on the customer's behalf.

The Banker's duties towards his customer are as follows:
(i) The Bank must honour its customer's cheques to the extent that he is in credit or to the extent of agreed overdraft. If the bank fails to do so it may be liable to be sued for damages, if either special damage is proved or a trader's credit is injured.
(ii) It must obey the mandate and may pay out of a customer's account only if that customer or his authorised agent

has signed the cheque. A bank has no right to debit a customer's account if the customer's signature was forged.

(iii) The bank must take reasonable care when paying a cheque. Where a customer is a company, cheques drawn for unauthorised purposes must not be honoured.

(iv) A bank is under a duty of secrecy in relation to the financial affairs of its customers. The bank may however disclose information about its client's financial affairs under a Court order, where there is a public duty to disclose, where the bank's own interests require disclosure or where the customer has consented to the disclosure.

(v) The bank must collect cheques paid in by the customer.

(vi) A bank must give reasonable notice before withdrawing overdraft facilities.

(b) A bank owes a contractual duty to take reasonable care in its conduct of the customer's business and it should only pay out of a customer's account if the customer or his authorised agent has signed the cheque. In **Ligget (Liverpool) Ltd v. Barclays Bank (1928)** where the facts were similar to those of the problem, it was held that the bank was not entitled to debit the company's account because the bank had honoured the cheques contrary to instructions.

Nationwide Bank Ltd, is advised that it cannot debit the account of Faith Company Ltd. The bank had failed to obey the mandate of its customer. However, Nationwide Bank Ltd would be able to debit Faith Company's account in respect of payments made to the company's creditors if the proceeds of the cheques paid contrary to the Company's mandate were used to pay the creditors.

QUESTION 98 *M* signed a cheque and crossed it 'not negotiable'. He then instructed *N*, his company accountant, to fill in a certain amount on the cheque and to fill in *O*'s name as payee. The accountant owed a personal debt to *P* so he filled in a different amount from that authorised and made the cheque payable to *P*. *P* cashed the cheque in settlement of *N*'s debt.

Advise *M*.

A.C.C.A. 1985

ANSWER This problem requires a discussion of the law governing inchoate (i.e., incomplete) bills. An inchoate bill is a negotiable instrument where some statutory requirement for the

159

instrument is missing. Section 20 of the Bills of Exchange Act 1882 provides that any person in possession of such an instrument has prima facie authority to fill in the missing particulars. Similarly, where the signature of a person is on a blank sheet of paper and the paper is delivered by the signor in order that it may be converted into a negotiable instrument, the act of delivery is prima facie authority to complete the paper as a negotiable instrument for any amount using the signature for that of the drawer, acceptor or indorser. For example, if Sam sells goods to Bob for £600 and Bob signs a sheet of paper accepting liability for that amount, Sam may fill in his own name as drawer and payee and sue Bob on the bill.

The signor is only liable if the instrument is completed within a reasonable time and according to his instructions. However, in favour of a holder in due course, there is an irrefutable presumption that the particulars filled in were in accordance with the signor's instructions, so that the signor will be liable to the holder in due course even if the instrument is completed contrary to instructions.

Apart from liability under section 20 the signor may also be liable under the doctrine of estoppel. In **Lloyds Bank Ltd v. Cooke (1907)** the defendant signed his name on a blank sheet of paper and gave it to his agent with authority to complete it as a promissory note for £250 payable to the plaintiff as security for an advance. The agent filled in a larger amount and obtained that amount from the plaintiff as an advance for his own purpose. The court held that although the plaintiff was not a holder in due course (because it was the original payee) the defendant was still liable for the amount stated in the note by virtue of the doctrine of estoppel since the plaintiff had altered its position in reliance on the note. However, this type of estoppel where a person alters his position without any other form of holding out is confined to the case of negotiable instruments. So in **Wilson and Meeson v. Pickering (1946)** where a blank cheque marked 'not negotiable' was handed to an agent to complete and the agent filled in a larger amount and in favour of his own personal creditor, the court held that estoppel could not apply.

From what has been said above and on the bases of the **Pickering** case, *M* is entitled to recover the amount paid to *P* from *P*. *M* can also sue *N* for breach of his fiduciary duty as an employee.

Chapter 8
Law of Tort

QUESTION 99 'The idea that there is a law of tort or torts derives from its definition.'

What do you understand by a tort and how does it differ from (i) a crime and (ii) a contract?

ANSWER Although the Law of Tort is extensively and largely judge-made the courts are not given a settled judicial definition and the matter has been left to learned authors. Hence Prof. Street comments: "Much ink has been spilt in unsuccessful attempts to define a tort."

Salmond defines a tort as "a civil wrong for which the remedy is a Common Law Action for unliquidated damages and which is not exclusively the breach of a contract or the breach of a trust or other merely equitable obligation."

Winfield states "Tortious liability arises from the breach of a duty primarily fixed at law: this duty is towards persons generally and its breaches redressible by an action for unliquidated damages."

James writes "Tort is an act or omission which is unauthorised by law and independently of contract infringes either an absolute or a qualified right or a public right giving rise to an action for damages at the suit of the injured party."

As all three definitions stress the procedural aspect, i.e. for damages, the following is offered as a more general definition:–
'A tort is a civil wrong independent of a breach of contract, quasi-contract and trust. Thus any harm to a person caused intentionally or negligently or in the case of strict liability creates a liability in tort unless the person causing the harm has some just cause or excuse for his act or omission. By the common law jurisdiction of the court, the person so harmed may bring an action for unliquidated damages (i.e. such damages as the court in its discretion is at liberty to award against the tortfeasor)'.

A crime is also not easy to define but can be described briefly as an offence which may be the subject of criminal proceedings instituted for the punishment of the offender. Thus the main difference between a crime and a tort turns on the distinct object which the law pursues. With a crime that object is punishment of the wrongdoer as a matter of public concern and proceedings are taken in the name of the Queen. With a tort the object is redress, the tortfeasor is not punished but is compelled to make compensation or restitution for his act to the injured party. To quote Salmond "Civil justice gives to the plaintiff; criminal justice gives to the defendant what he deserves."

This distinction between tort and a crime is comparatively modern as for a long period during early English history, there was no distinction and whether a crime is an offshoot from a tort or vice versa it is difficult to say. Even today, the two cannot be wholly divided into watertight compartments, e.g. some cases such as injury to the person and defamatory libel are both a criminal offence and a civil wrong.

No civil injury is to be classified as a tort if it is solely a breach of contract. The distinction today between tort and contract is that the duties in the former are primarily fixed by the law while in the latter they are fixed by the parties themselves. Further, in tort the duty is towards persons generally. In contract it is towards a specific person or persons. Nevertheless, the same facts may create alternative liability in tort or in contract. Thus Winfield says "A dentist who contracts to pull out my tooth is, of course, liable to me for a breach of contract if he injures me by an unskilled extraction. But he is also liable to me for the tort of negligence, for anyone who professes skill in a calling is bound by the law, agreement or no agreement, to show a reasonable amount of such skill **(Edwards v. Mallan 1908).** I cannot recover damages twice over, but I may well have alternative claims for damages under different heads of legal liability."

QUESTION 100 (a) What must be proved in order to establish a defendant's liability in the tort of negligence?
(b) Jeff and his wife Eileen are employed as storeman and typist respectively in Fennell Ltd. While Eileen is passing a stack of heavy metal components on her way to her office, Jeff leans across to give Eileen an affectionate pat on the back. In so doing, Jeff displaces some of the components which fall on Eileen causing a fractured leg.
Advise Eileen.

S.C.C.A. 1979

ANSWER (a) In order to establish liability in negligence a plaintiff must establish three propositions, namely, (i) the defendant owed him a duty of care, (ii) the defendant breached that duty and (iii) non-remote damage flowing from the breach.

Whether or not a duty of care exists in a particular situation is a question of law for the judge to decide. Though subject to criticism, the test most readily accepted is the 'neighbour' test laid down by Lord Atkin in **Donoghue v. Stevenson (1932)** "You must take reasonable care to avoid acts or omissions which you can reasonably foresee would be likely to injure your neighbour... (i.e.,) persons who are so closely and directly affected by my act that I ought reasonably to have them in contemplation... when I am directing my mind to the acts or omissions which are called in question".

Thus, there must be foreseeability of damage, proximity of relationship between the parties and "the situation should be one in which the court considers it fair, just and reasonable to impose a duty" (per Lord Bridge in **Caparo Industries plc v. Dickman and Others 1990**). In deciding whether there is proximity, the court will be guided by situations in which the existence, scope and limits of a duty of care had previously been held to exist rather than a single general principle that a duty of care always exists where a person could foresee harm to another by his act or omission to act.

In **Thorne v. University of London (1966)** the plaintiff, a Ph.D. failed Part 1 of his LL.B. examination and sued the University alleging negligence by its examiners. The Court of Appeal held that it had no jurisdiction as this was purely a domestic matter of the University. In general, the court is more ready to impose a duty of care to avoid causing injury to the person or property of others rather than for causing purely economic loss. Thus in **Carmarthenshire CC v. Lewis (1955)** a local authority was held to owe a duty of care not only to its children but also to third parties injured by them; and in **Clay v. Crump (1963)** an architect was held to owe a duty of care to builders who suffered physical injury as a result of the architect's negligent misstatement. But in **Spartan Steel & Alloys Ltd v. Martin & Co. Ltd (1973)** no duty of care was owed by the defendants to the plaintiffs who suffered loss of profits when their factory had to be closed down as a result of the defendants negligently damaging a cable supplying electricity to the plaintiffs' factory, since there was no damage to the factory itself.

There is no duty of care to a person who suffers nervous shock which is not accompanied by actual physical injury to him, unless such a person sees the negligent conduct and fears for his own safety or safety of a near relative (i.e., child or spouse) or he is a rescuer who acts under a moral obligation to save life in the aftermath of an accident **(Chadwick v. Br. Rlys Board 1967)** or he is the parent or spouse who learns of his child's or wife's injury immediately afterwards and suffers shock **(Mc Loughin v. O'Brien 1982).** In **Alcock and Others v. Chief Constable of South Yorkshire Police (1991)** the Court of Appeal held that a person who was not a parent or a spouse of the victims of the Hillsborough football ground disaster could not bring a claim against the police for damages for nervous shock and that even parents and spouses who had suffered nervous shock as a result of watching the disaster on television would fail the test of proximity. Nervous shock means mental injury or psychiatric illness and not simply grief and sorrow **(Brice v. Brown 1984).**

The test for deciding whether there is a breach of duty is whether a reasonable man guided upon those considerations which ordinarily regulate the conduct of human affairs would do what the defendant did or omitted to do. In **Latimer v. AEC Ltd (1953)** the defendants' factory was flooded by exceptionally heavy rain and the flood water had mixed with a heavy coolant making the floor slippery. Despite the spreading of three tons of sawdust and other precautions, part of the floor remained untreated and Latimer slipped on one such place and sustained injury. In considering whether the defendants were in breach of their duty of care towards their employee, the House of Lords said the question was "Has it been proved that the floor was so slippery that, remedial steps not being possible, a reasonably prudent employer would have closed down the factory rather than allow the employees to run the risks involved in continuing work?"

The defendant's breach must have caused the injury sustained by the plaintiff. If the injury would have resulted whether or not the defendant had broken the duty of care, then the defendant cannot be held liable. Thus in **Barrett v. Chelsea & Kensington Hospital (1969)** the deceased, a night porter and his colleagues were poisoned when arsenic was put in their tea by someone unknown. The defendant hospital sent the deceased home without giving him any proper attention. In an action by his widow for negligence by the hospital in not suspecting that the deceased's sickness was due to food poisoning, the defendant proved that even if food poisoning was discovered it would not have prevented the deceased's death in time. The court held that the hospital was not liable for his death.

Having established that the defendant's breach caused the damage, the defendant will only be liable for the damage if it can be shown that it was reasonably foreseeable that his breach of duty would lead to the type of damage which resulted **(The Wagon Mound (No.1) 1961).** Once this is established, it does not matter if the manner of its occurrence is unforeseeable or if the damage is aggravated by some physical peculiarity the plaintiff has (the egg-shell skull rule).

(b) An employer will be liable not only for his own negligence but, in certain cases, also for the negligence of his employees. Eileen may bring an action against Fennell Ltd for exposing her to unnecessary risks, and also for the negligence of Jeff.

Normally a person who alleges negligence must prove it unless the rule of Res Ipsa Loquitur (the matter speaks for itself) applies. This rule is concerned with the onus of proof and applies to particular circumstances in which the harm is presumed to have been caused by the negligence of the defendant, thus relieving the plaintiff from the onus of proving negligence. Such circumstances arise where an object (not being a live animal) is shown to be under the control and management of the defendant or his servants and the accident is such as in the ordinary course of things does not happen if those who have the management use proper care. In the absence of explanation by the defendant the very fact that the matter occurred is held to constitute reasonable evidence of negligence. So Eileen may rely on this rule but Fennell Ltd may say that the components were not packed negligently.

On vicarious liability for the negligence of Jeff, Fennell Ltd will have to prove that he was acting outside the scope of his employment, if they are to escape liability. Even if they are unable to do so, they may still be able to obtain an indemnity from Jeff for the damages they have to pay Eileen **(Lister v. Romford Ice & Cold Storage Ltd 1957).**

QUESTION 101 *X* has a factory in a built-up area for making toy models. A wire mesh fence divides the factory from the road. Sample models are exhibited by way of advertisement in the area between the fence and the factory building. *X* displays a prominent notice 'Keep out. Dog on patrol'. *K*, a five year old is attracted by the models, climbs the fence and is mauled by the dog. *R*, a passer-by, hearing *K*'s screams climbs the fence and goes to his rescue, but is in turn attacked and badly bitten and his clothing torn. Discuss *X*'s liability to *K* and *R*.

ANSWER There is, in general, no duty owed to a trespasser apart from the duty not to injure him intentionally or recklessly. However, in the case of a child trespasser, he is treated to special consideration because of his age. If an occupier habitually and knowingly acquiesces in the trespass of children on his land, then they cease to be trespassers by implied licence and are owed a common duty of care. Thus in **Cooke v. Midland Rly (1909)** where the defendants knew that children came to play on their turntable and did not do anything about it, e.g. like chasing them away, they were deemed to have given the children an implied licence. However, a child who is to succeed on this ground must show more than tolerance by the occupier **(Edwards v. Rly Executive 1952)**. A child who is a lawful visitor, does not become a trespasser merely because he moves to a place or on to an object outside the strict limits of the licence when that object is a trap or an allurement **(Glasgow Corp v. Taylor 1922).** Even if no licence is given by the occupier, provided he has on his land some danger and it is reasonably foreseeable that children may trespass on his land, he must take reasonable steps according to his economic position to protect those children from the danger (Occupier's Liability Act 1984). In the case of very young children almost anything might be a danger.

As there is no evidence of acquiescence by *X*, *K* is a trespasser. The sample toy models exhibited by way of advertisement in the area between the wire mesh fence and the factory building constitute an allurement and so it would have to be decided whether the fence was reasonable as to prevent a child from entering the premises. The court will look at the circumstances, e.g. the built-up area and the wire mesh fence and perhaps such considerations might be in *K*'s favour in which case *X* will be liable for the injury caused by his guard dog to *K*. The warning notice may not be of any help to *X* in view of *K*'s age.

R is a rescuer acting under a moral obligation when he went to *K*'s assistance. Since he was acting in an emergency to save life and the emergency was caused by *X*'s negligence in failing to control the dog which attacked *K*, *R* will also recover damages for the injuries he sustained **(Chadwick v. British Rly Board 1967).**

Quite apart from an action in negligence, *X* may be liable to *K* and *R* under the Animal Act 1970. S.2(2) states that where damage of any kind is caused by an animal which does not belong to a dangerous species, e.g. a dog, and the animal has such characteristic known to his keeper that it is likely unless restrained to cause damage of that kind or any damage that it may cause that is likely to be severe, the keeper of the animal will be liable for the damage. It will be a defence to *X* under the Act if he can show that the dog was kept on the premises for the protection of property and that keeping it there for that purpose was not unreasonable.

QUESTION 102 What do you understand by the tort 'Trespass to the person'? Explain the various forms it may take.

A.C.C.A. 1978

ANSWER Trespass to the person is the intentional harm done to the person or liberty of another without lawful justification. It may take one of three forms – assault, battery and false imprisonment; and is actionable without proof of damage.

Assault consists in intentionally creating in another person an apprehension of imminent physical contact. The application of force to the person of another without lawful justification is a battery. Usually both wrongs are committed in rapid succession i.e. the threat is carried out by the actual application of unlawful force, but one of these wrongs can be committed without the other. There will be an assault without a battery if the threat to inflict unlawful force is not in fact carried out; alternatively a battery may be perpetrated on a victim who does not expect it and so cannot complain of assault, as where he is struck from behind without warning. Mere words do not constitute an assault: **R. v. Mead & Bett (1823)** – the intent to do violence must be expressed in threatening an act; but words may render harmless what might otherwise be an assault, as where the defendant laid his hand on the sword and said: "If it were not assize-time, I would not take such language from you." As it was assize time, he was held not to have committed an assault **(Tubeville v. Savage 1669).** Pointing a loaded gun at a person is an assault. In **Blake v. Barnard (1840)** Lord Abinger C.B. held that "If the pistol was not loaded, it would not be an assault;" but in a criminal case in the same year **(R. v. St. George 1840)** Parke B. obiter had no doubt that it would be a common assault to point an unloaded weapon at a person at such a short distance that, if loaded, it might do injury. Of course if the person at whom it is levelled knows it to be unloaded, then he would not be put in fear, so there would be no assault.

In **Stephens v. Myers (1830)** the plaintiff was in the chair at a parish meeting. The defendant, who sat at the same table some six or seven places away from the plaintiff, became vociferous and by a large majority it was resolved that he be expelled. He said he would rather pull the plaintiff out of the chair than be ejected and he advanced with clenched fist upon the plaintiff, but was stopped by a third person sitting between. He was held liable for assault.

If however, the plaintiff has no reasonable belief that the defendant has present ability to effect his purpose, it is presumably not an assault, e.g. where *A*, who is in a train moving out of a station, shakes his fist at *B* who is on the platform.

Examples of battery include actually hitting another with a fist, an unwanted kiss, and taking from another some object which he holds or wears. Physical hurt is not necessary, for as Holt C.J. said in **Cole v. Turner (1704)** "The least touching of another in anger is a battery." But mere passive obstruction does not constitute force e.g. preventing entry.

The wrong of false imprisonment consists in the act of arresting or imprisoning any person without lawful justification or otherwise preventing him from exercising his right of leaving the place in which he is. The tort is not committed unless movement is restrained in all directions. It is not imprisonment to prevent a person going in some directions whilst he is left free to go as far as he pleases in others. In **Bird v. Jones (1845)** the defendants wrongfully enclosed part of the public footway on Hammersmith Bridge by putting seats in it for the use of spectators of a regatta on the river and charging for admission to the enclosure. The plaintiff insisted on passing along this part of the footpath, and climbed over the fence without paying the charge. The defendants refused to let him go forward, but he was told that he might go back into the carriageway and cross to the other side of the bridge if he wished. The court held there was no false imprisonment.

It is not necessary for the plaintiff to know of the restraint upon his liberty. Thus in **Meering v. Grahame White Aviation Co. Ltd (1920)** the plaintiff was being suspected of stealing a keg of varnish from the defendants, his employers, and they asked two of their police to take him to the company's office. The plaintiff went to the waiting room and the two policemen remained in the neighbourhood. In an action for false imprisonment the defence was that the plaintiff was perfectly free to go where he liked, that he knew it and that he did not desire to go away but the Court of Appeal held the defendants were liable because the plaintiff from the moment that he came under the influence of the police was no longer a free man.

QUESTION 103 (a) Explain, with examples, the difference between public nuisance and private nuisance.

(b) Your neighbour holds noisy parties on several evenings each week and these continue until the early hours of the morning. Discuss the factors that the court would take into account in deciding whether or not this constituted a nuisance. What remedies might you receive if a nuisance was deemed to exist?

ANSWER (a) Public nuisance is essentially a criminal offence rather than a tort. It consists of any act or omission which materially affects the reasonable comfort or convenience of life of a class of H.M. subjects. Examples of the type of act which would constitute a public nuisance at common law are: (i) quarrying causing dust and vibrations **(A.G. v. P.Y.A. Quarries Ltd 1957);** (ii) obstructing free passage of the highway or keeping a disorderly house. Public nuisance may also be created by statute with appropriate remedies laid down e.g. Public Health Act 1936, Noise Abatement Act 1960.

It is always a question of fact whether the number of people affected is large enough to imply public nuisance rather than private nuisance. The test is whether it is reasonable for one person to take proceedings or that a sufficiently large section of people are also affected, so that the community as a whole should act. The remedy for public nuisance is a relator action by the Attorney General often acting on behalf of the local authority concerned. The desired remedy in cases of public nuisance is an injunction.

A public nuisance becomes a tort and gives a right of action only where it causes the plaintiff special damage. Special damage means some peculiar loss above the ordinary inconvenience which the public usually suffer e.g., if the public nuisance consists of obstructing the highway no individual can sue, only the Attorney General. But if the plaintiff runs into the obstruction and injures himself he can sue.

Private nuisance is the interference by the owner or occupier of land with the use or enjoyment of another land which causes damage. Thus nuisance is a generic term and includes such forms as noise, smell, vibration, and pollution of air or water. Normally, private nuisance arises out of acts of the occupier of land as stated above but sometimes non-occupiers could be liable and a nuisance can originate from the highway. **(Halsey v. Esso Petroleum Ltd 1961).**

Since private nuisance is the interference with the enjoyment of land, the basic rule is that only the occupier of the land affected can sue. In particular, non-occupiers, licensees, lodgers and guests and other persons such as the occupier's friends and servants cannot sue **(Malone v. Laskey 1907).**

Private nuisance is not actionable without proof of damage. Two types of damages that are remediable are damage to the plaintiff's land or premises and interference with the enjoyment of property. But it is doubtful whether a plaintiff can recover in private nuisance for personal injuries.

(b) Many acts by a defendant on his land will inconvenience a plaintiff or even harm him but the defendant will not necessarily be committing a nuisance. It will only be a nuisance if he is making an unreasonable use of his land. No use of land is reasonable which causes substantial discomfort to other persons or is a source of damage to their property.

Thus the factors which the Court would take into account in deciding whether or not the holding of noisy parties by my neighbour until the early hours of the morning would constitute a nuisance would be based on the substantial discomfort of such noise to me judged against concepts of 'give and take' and 'live and let live'. It is a question of reasonable use of property. Holding noisy parties during week days until late at night cannot be deemed to be reasonable especially if the area is a residential area **(Andreae v. Selfridge & Co. Ltd 1938),** and if the noise was made wantonly or maliciously **(Christie v. Davey 1893).** To conclude, the factors that will be important will be the time and place of noise, the manner of committing it, whether it was done maliciously or in the reasonable exercise of rights, and the effect of its commission.

If the Court decides that the parties constitute a nuisance the remedies I may receive will be damages or an injunction.

QUESTION 104 Advise Sonny whether he is likely to succeed in an action in tort against each of the parties in the following cases, explaining the relevant principles of law involved:

(a) Desmond's son injures Sonny by careless driving while using Desmond's car to take a girl friend for a drive;

(b) Terry, a trade union official, defames Sonny;

(c) Sharman, whilst out shooting, takes all possible precautions and yet Sonny is injured by a bullet which ricochets off a tree;

(d) Sam wrongfully detains Sonny who thereby misses his bus. Sonny catches a later bus which crashes and Sonny is injured.

ANSWER (a) The owner of a motor car will be vicariously liable for the negligent driving of someone who is not his servant only if the driver was driving the car as agent of the owner and for the owner's business **(Ormrod v. Crossville Motor Services Ltd 1953).** Thus in **Rambarran v. Gurrucharran (1970)** where the owner of a motor car did not drive it himself but allowed one of his twelve children to use it for his own purpose and an accident occurred through the son's negligent driving, the court held that the owner was not liable.

So any action by Sonny against Desmond for his son's negligence is unlikely to succeed as the son was using the car for his own social venture. The son though, will be liable for his own negligence.

(b) Although a trade union may sue it cannot be sued in the tort of defamation even though the defamation was committed when there was no trade dispute (E.P.C.A. 1978).

This does not however prevent Sonny from bringing an action against Terry personally.

(c) Sonny may bring an action against Sharman for trespass to the person, but it is unlikely that he will succeed as the latter may plead inevitable accident. In **Stanley v. Powell (1891)** on similar facts an action was brought in negligence and trespass against the defendant but inevitable accident was successfully pleaded in both causes.

(d) Sonny may successfully bring an action against Sam for false imprisonment but Sam may plead remoteness of damage for Sonny's injuries.

QUESTION 105 (a) What are the essential features required in order to establish a defendant's liability in the tort of defamation?
(b) George, an accountant, read in the local newspaper "all accountants are rogues". George was furious and telephoned the Editor of the newspaper who responded over the phone by calling George "an interesting old fool and a busybody". Finally, a postcard arrived at George's office bearing a further message from the Editor "I consider you the worst rogue of them all". Advise George.

S.C.C.A. 1975

ANSWER (a) To establish a defendant's liability in the tort of defamation three matters must be established: (i) the words must be defamatory, (ii) the words must refer to the plaintiff, and (iii) the words must be published.

(i) **The words must be defamatory.** No action lies for mere vulgar abuse. A word which is used purely as abuse may be so classified even though it is capable of a defamatory meaning. It depends on the circumstances. For example, in **Field v. Davies (1955)** the defendant called the plaintiff, a married woman, 'a tramp'. The court held that it was mere abuse because it was so unsuited to be construed as otherwise by those who heard it, considering the obvious temper of the defendant at the time.

Generally, the question is 'does the statement tend to lower the plaintiff in the eyes of right thinking people in general?' A statement therefore which injures the plaintiff's reputation in the eyes of a very limited section of the community is not defamatory **(Byrne v. Deane 1937).** It may be defamatory to accuse a plaintiff who carries on a trade or profession of lack of professional judgement and efficiency even though no moral fault or personal default is suggested **(Drummard-Jackson v. Br. Medical Association 1970).** A statement may be defamatory by innuendo. This exists where the words have a latent and secondary meaning not obvious from the words themselves. Thus, in **Tolley v. Fry (1931)** to include a cartoon of a well-known amateur golfer in an advertisement for chocolate implied that he was prostituting his amateur status, by accepting payment for the use of his name and picture.

(ii) **The words must refer to the Plaintiff.** If the plaintiff is expressly mentioned by name there is no problem but a latent reference to him may be sufficient provided that the article itself contains some key or pointer that is reasonably capable of referring to him. The plaintiff can succeed even though the defendant does not intend to refer to him or even if he does not know of the plaintiff's existence, provided that the reader can reasonably infer that the words did refer to the plaintiff. In **Hulton v. Jones (1910)** the defendant published a humorous account describing immoral conduct of one Artemus Jones. The article was intended to be fictitious. Friends of the plaintiff thought the article referred to him. **Held** by House of Lords that the defendant was liable on those facts. If the defamatory words refer to a class which is large, then in general no member of that class can sue unless he can show that the defamation was particularly referable to him.

(iii) **The words must be published.** Publication is essential for the tort of defamation but 'publication' is a technical term. It means simply communication of the defamatory words to any individual except to the plaintiff or the defendant's spouse. The defendant is liable if he intended that the defamatory matter should be published to third parties or ought to have foreseen such publication. Thus in **Huth v. Huth (1915)** where a defamatory letter was sent in an unsealed envelope through the post and an inquisitive butler opened and read the letter the court held that there was no publication to him as it was not his duty to read his master's letters. Every defamatory statement repeated is deemed to be a fresh publication.

(b) The statement contained in the newspaper is prima facie defamatory of accountants and amounts to a class libel. With class libel no individual member of that class may sue unless the words point to a particular individual or the class is so small and ascertainable enabling each member of the class to sue **(Knuppfer v. London Express Newspapers Ltd 1944).** So George is unlikely to succeed on this ground. The statement by the editor over the phone that George was "an interesting old fool and busybody" is mere vulgar abuse and not defamatory. Moreover, it is doubtful whether there was any publication.

The statement contained in the postcard is prima facie defamatory of George as it refers to him in particular. With post cards and telegrams there is a legal presumption that they are published when sent through the post. So it is not necessary for George to prove that the defamatory words on the card were read by anyone.

QUESTION 106 (a) Distinguish between slander and libel.
(b) In casual conversation *S* said to *J* with reference to *R*, the headmaster at a local school "I suppose you know he loses his temper and swears at the boys". At a meeting of the local education authority of which *J* was a member, he repeated *S*'s statement which was incorporated in the minutes circulated to members. The authority made enquiries and found the allegation untrue. *R* wishes to sue. Advise him.

ANSWER (a) Defamation means the publication of a statement which tends to lower the plaintiff in the estimation of right-thinking members of society generally or which brings him into hatred, ridicule or contempt or which tends to make such people shun or avoid him. It comprises two separate torts – slander and libel. Slander is a defamatory statement published in transient form e.g. in speech or by gestures. Libel is a defamatory statement published in permanent form e.g. in writing or as in a picture or on stage. The test for deciding whether a defamatory statement is slander or libel is the way the words are used.

There are some difficult borderline cases some of which are settled by statute. For example, the Defamation Act 1952 provides that broadcasting for the general reception including radio and television is published in permanent form and the Theatres Act 1958 provides that defamatory words uttered in theatres should be treated as publication in a permanent form. In **Youssoupoff v. MGM (1934)** the Court of Appeal held that defamation in talking films was to be treated as libel.

Generally, the two torts are governed by the same rules but libel is not only a tort. It may be a criminal offence if the statement tends to provoke a breach of the peace. Slander as such is not a crime. Libel is always actionable per se. Damage is presumed. Slander is normally actionable only on proof of 'special damage'. Special damage means in this context, loss in money or something situated in money. Loss of reputation or the society of friends is not special damage but loss of hospitality is. However in the following cases which are considered as serious defamation, slander is actionable per se: (i) imputation that the plaintiff has committed a criminal offence which is punishable with imprisonment in the first instance and not merely with the non-payment of a fine; (ii) imputation that the plaintiff has suffered from contagious or infectious disease e.g. venereal disease or leprosy; (iii) by Slander of Women Act 1891 an imputation of unchastity or adultery to any woman or girl; (iv) imputation of unfitness, dishonesty or incompetence in any profession, trade or business carried on by the plaintiff at the time the slander was published.

(b) The statement made by *S* to *J* is defamatory of *R* and as such, *R* may bring an action for slander against *S*. There is no need for *R* to prove special damages. It is presumed because the defamatory statement is an imputation that *R* is unfit for his job as headmaster. *S*'s defence may be qualified privilege on statements made in the protection of an interest. However *S* must know that *J* was a member of the Council and *S* must have children going to the school. Malice may annul this defence.

When *J* repeated the slander at the meeting of the local education authority, he also committed the tort of defamation and a separate action may be brought by *R* against him. *J* may use the defence of qualified privilege on statements made in the performance of a duty.

When the statement was recorded in the minutes it became a libel and so an action for libel may be brought against the local education authority. The authority may plead qualified privilege but this defence will be lost if copies of the minutes were circulated to people outside the privilege class i.e. committee members.

QUESTION 107 In the context of the law of defamation, what is meant by 'publication'? What exceptions, if any, are there to the rule that a person who publishes a defamatory statement is responsible for it? To what extent, if at all, are publications by management to office staff protected by privilege?

I.C.S.A. 1979

ANSWER Publication is the act of making known the defamatory matter to some person other than the plaintiff himself or the defendant's spouse. It follows that communication to the plaintiff's spouse is publication **(Wenman v. Ash 1853).** A defamatory statement is published when dictated to a secretary but the secretary who returns the letter to her principal does not thereby publish it. There can be publication by omitting to remove defamatory matter on premises under the defendant's control even though written by another e.g. if a stranger writes defamatory words on the defendant's premises and the defendant knows the words are such then unless he wipes them off, he is guilty of libel.

The defendant is only liable if he intended that the defamatory matter should be published to third parties or ought to have foreseen such publication, but not otherwise. Thus in **Huth v. Huth (1915)** the defamatory matter was in an unsealed letter sent through the post and the letter was opened by an inquisitive butler. As it was not part of his duty to do this, there was no publication for which the defendant was responsible. The position is otherwise, if a letter not marked private is opened by the plaintiff's secretary or by Post Office officials in the course of their duty.

Where words are published innocently, a defendant may avoid liability to pay damages if he is willing to make an offer of amends (S.4 Defamation Act 1952). An offer of amends means an offer to publish a suitable correction and apology and to take reasonable steps to notify readers of the words alleged to be defamatory. Words are published innocently if either the publisher did not intend to publish the words of or concerning the plaintiff and did not know of circumstances by virtue of which they might be understood to refer to him; or the words were not defamatory on the face of them and the publisher did not know of circumstances by virtue of which they might be understood to be defamatory of the plaintiff.

Every defamatory statement repeated is a fresh publication. Thus in the case of a book there is a series of publication: author to publisher, then author and printer, then in publication of the book, author, printer and publisher, and finally the distributor when the book is sold. The distributor will not be liable for publication made by him if he proves that he was unaware of the libel contained in the book or journal and there was no reason for him to know that the matter was defamatory **(Sun Life Assurance Co. of Canada v. W.H. Smith & Son Ltd 1934).**

Publications by management to office staff are protected by qualified privilege if the publications were made in the discharge of a duty which may be legal, moral or social or if the publications were made in the protection of the management's own interest. In either case both the publisher and the recipient must have a common interest in the publications. In **Hunt v. G.N.R. (1891)** the defendants posted up a circular in such of their premises as would be frequented by their employees, stating (inter alia) that the plaintiff had been dismissed for neglect of his duty. The privilege of common interest was held to extend to the defendants.

QUESTION 108 Matter published in a newspaper is prima facie defamatory of *X*. The matter is contained in two separate reports of:–

(a) proceedings before the Law Society Disciplinary Committee and

(b) a criminal trial in Norway.

X sues the proprietor and the printers of the newspaper for libel.

Advise the defendants.

ANSWER If the matter published in the newspaper is true, the defendants may rely on the defence of justification. This is a complete defence for civil libel or slander irrespective of a defendant's motive for publishing the words. Justification is always regarded as a dangerous plea as the onus of proof is on the defendant and it may be hard to discharge. Moreover if this plea fails the judge may award higher damages.

Until 1968, it was dangerous for the defendant to report with approval conviction of the plaintiff on a criminal charge because the conviction was non-evidence in a civil action and the defendant may have to prove over again the guilt of the plaintiff. But now by Civil Evidence Act 1968 proof of a conviction is conclusive evidence of the person convicted of committing the offence in a subsequent action for libel by that person. The literal rule is not demanded in order to succeed in the defence of justification provided that the defendant's statement is in substance true. This principal will apply as long as the inaccuracy is not material; and where several allegations are made by the defendant, S.5 Defamation Act 1952 provides that the defence will not fail only because the defendant does not prove the truth of every charge.

If the matter in the newspaper is untrue, the newspaper proprietors may still be able to rely on absolute or qualified privilege. Absolute privilege is available, irrespective of malice, for reports of statements made in the course of and with reference to judicial proceedings in the U.K. provided the reports were fair accounts and contemporaneous with the proceedings (S.3 Law of Libel (Amendment) Act 1888). In **Addis v. Crocker (1961)** the court held that proceedings before the Disciplinary Committee of the Law Society were judicial in character.

If the report on the Law Society proceedings was not contemporaneous, the proprietor may still be able to rely on qualified privilege.

As regards the report of X's trial in Norway, the proprietor will be able to rely on qualified privilege if the subject matter of the report was of legitimate and proper interest to the English public as being matter much connected with the administration of justice in England **(Webb v. The Times Publishing Co. 1960)**.

In **Egger v. Viscount Chelmsford (1965)** the Court of Appeal held that a person who publishes a privileged statement by an agent will confer such privilege on the agent. Thus, the printers will also enjoy qualified privilege if sued by X.

Chapter 9

Law of Carriage and Insurance

QUESTION 109 (a) Distinguish between a 'common carrier' and a 'private carrier'.

(b) Define a bill of lading and explain its functions.

A.C.C.A. 1977

ANSWER (a) The law recognises two types of carriers – common and private. A common carrier is one who holds himself out to the public as being ready to carry their goods from place to place, either by land or water, for a fee. A common carrier is bound to carry all goods (or passengers) offered to him by persons willing to pay his hire unless he has no room in his vehicle or the goods offered are not of the kind he professes to carry or if the destination is not one to which he usually travels.

A common carrier is an insurer of the goods entrusted to him and is liable for their loss or damage in the absence of a special agreement or statutory exemption. However, he is not liable if the loss is due to an act of God, act of the Queen's enemy, negligence of the owner of the goods due to defective packing, or inherent vice. In **Nugent v. Smith (1876)** a mare which was being carried by a common carrier died as a result of exceptionally rough weather. It was held that the carriers were not liable because the mare's death was due to an act of God.

Although strict liability is imposed on a common carrier for the carriage of goods, he is only liable for injury to his passengers if negligent.

A private carrier is one who reserves the right to pick and choose his customers; and his liability is governed by the terms of the contract. Generally, a private carrier will not be liable for loss or damage to goods in the absence of negligence. In **Belfast Ropework Ltd v. Bushell (1918)** a hemp which a private carrier had contracted to carry was lost when his lorry caught fire without his negligence. It was held that he was not liable for the loss.

(b) A bill of lading is a document signed by the shipowner, his master or other agent, then handed to the shipper, stating that goods of a given description have been shipped on a certain vessel. It is used generally when goods shipped form only part of the intended cargo of the ship. It sets out the terms on which the goods have been delivered to and received by the shipowners. A bill of lading has three functions:

(i) It is a receipt given by a shipowner in acknowledgement of the shipment of goods specified in the bill and of the quality and condition of the goods when put on board. This acknowledgement is most important in view of the rule of law that the ship must deliver what she received as she received it unless relieved by the excepted perils.

(ii) It is a document of title to those goods by means of which the property may be transferred and upon which money may be advanced. It enables the holder to 'deliver' the goods while they are still in transit, by merely transferring the bill of lading. This function is particularly important in C.I.F. contracts.

(iii) It contains or evidences the terms of the contract of carriage under which the goods are to be carried and delivered by the shipper. Whether the bill of lading is a contract of carriage or is only evidence of such a contract will depend on the circumstances under which it is issued. Where the shipper is not a party to any charter (as in the case of parcel shipments on a liner or general ship), the bill of lading is not the contract itself for that was made before the bill was issued. It is, however, very good evidence of the terms agreed between the shipowner and the shipper **(Sewell v. Burdick 1884).** Once the bill of lading has passed into the hands of an indorsee or consignee it contains the terms of the contract of carriage and evidence may not be given which varies or contradicts it (S.1 Bills of Lading Act 1855).

QUESTION 110 In a contract for the carriage of goods by sea:–
(a) Who is liable to make a general average contribution?
(b) Under what conditions may such a contribution be claimed?
C.O.S. 1968

ANSWER (a) Where a ship and its cargo are exposed to a common danger and some part of the cargo or of the ship is intentionally sacrificed, or expenses are incurred to avert the danger, such loss will be subject to a general average contribution. This means that all interested parties who would benefit by the sacrifice are bound to contribute to the general average loss in proportion to their saved value.

There are three interests involved in a maritime venture:–

(i) Sacrifice of the cargo e.g. where the cargo is jettisoned. To give rise to a general average contribution, the cargo jettisoned must be stored in a proper place.

(ii) Sacrifice of ship or tackle e.g. where the ship's master deliberately runs the ship ashore when it is in danger of sinking, for the purpose of saving the cargo and possibly the ship.

(iii) Sacrifice of freight e.g. where the freight is payable on delivery, a jettison of goods involves not only sacrifice of the goods themselves but also a loss of the freight on them. Thus, the person to whom the freight would have been payable is entitled to claim a contribution from the owners of the interests saved.

A general average contribution is made by:

(a) the owner of the ship in respect of his ship and the freight payable either under the charter-party or under the bill of lading.

(b) the charterer in respect of the freight payable under the bills of lading.

(c) the owner of the cargo in respect of the cargo. A general average contribution may not be made by seamen out of their wages.

(b) In order to claim a general average contribution, the following conditions must be satisfied.

(i) There must be a danger common to the whole venture. If an interest was not in danger the owner of that interest cannot be called upon to contribute.

(ii) The sacrifice must be real and intentional. If the thing abandoned is already lost, there is no real sacrifice and so no claim for contribution will arise.

(iii) The sacrifice must be necessary. This will normally be decided by the master.

(iv) The peril must not have been caused through the fault of the person claiming contribution 'Fault' means actionable wrong. Thus where the contract of carriage makes certain exceptions to the liability which would otherwise fall on one of the parties, the party in whose favour the exceptions are made may still be entitled to claim a contribution.

(v) The property which was in danger must have been saved because of the sacrifice.

QUESTION 111 (a) What duty of disclosure, in a contract of insurance, rests on the assured. What is meant by an 'insurable interest'?

(b) Maurice's house, currently valued at £20,000 is insured with Reliable Insurance Co. for £10,000. The house has been damaged by fire to the extent of £9,000. Advise Maurice as to his rights against the insurance company.

What would your advice be if the policy contains a 'subject to average' clause?

A.C.C.A. 1977

ANSWER (a) An insurance contract, unlike most other contracts, requires a higher standard of good faith between the parties; and the law imposes a duty on the parties to disclose to each other matters which would influence the other whether or not to enter the contract. Explaining the nature of this duty, Scrutton L.J. in **Rozanes v. Bowen (1928)** said "As the underwriter knows nothing and the man who comes to him to ask him to insure knows everything, it is the duty of the assured, the man who desires to have a policy, to make a full disclosure to the underwriters without being asked of all the material circumstances, because the underwriters know nothing and the assured knows everything. This is expressed by saying that it is a contract of the utmost good faith – uberrimae fidei."

Thus every material fact must be disclosed and every fact is material if it can influence the judgement of a prudent insurer in deciding whether to accept the risk, and if so, at what premium. The duty to disclose continues up to the conclusion of the contract and covers any material alteration in the character of the risk which may take place between proposal and acceptance.

However, the assured only has to disclose facts which he knows and not facts which are within the knowledge of the insurers. Facts which would diminish the risk need not be disclosed **(Carter v. Boehm 1910),** nor are facts of which information is waived by the insurers.

Failure to disclose material facts would entitle the insurers to set aside the contract. The contract is not void but only voidable.

Every contract of insurance requires an insurable interest to support it otherwise it is invalid. The classical definition of 'insurable interest' was given by Lawrence J in **Lucena v. Craufurd (1806)** when he said "To be interested in the preservation of a thing, is to be so circumstanced with respect to it as to have benefit from its existence, prejudice from its destruction." In McGillivray on Insurance Law 'insurable interest' is defined as follows "Where the assured is so situated that the happening of the event on which the insurance money is to become payable would, as a proximate cause, involve the assured in the loss or diminution of any right recognised by law or in any legal liability, there is an insurable interest of that event to the extent of the possible loss or liability."

The Life Assurance Act 1774 which covers all types of insurances except insurance of ships and goods, requires an insurable interest at the time of the formation of the contract. The Marine Insurance Act 1906 requires an insurable interest at the time of the loss though not necessarily at the time of the contract. The insurance of goods are covered by the Gaming Act 1845 and it requires an insurable interest at the time of the contract, although an insurable interest is also required at the date of the loss in the case of an indemnity insurance.

(b) In the case of an indemnity insurance, the insured is entitled to claim the full cost of repairs in the event of a partial loss so long as it comes within the total amount covered by the policy. Where, however, the policy contains a 'subject to average' clause and the property is under-insured. the insurers are liable only for the proportion of the actual loss which the sum insured bears to the value of the property **(Acme Wood Flooring Co. v. Marten 1904).**

Maurice is advised that he is entitled to recover £9,000 from the insurance company even though he is under-insured as the sum is covered by the policy.

A 'subject to average' clause in the policy would have resulted in the insurance company being liable only for the proportion of the actual loss which the sum insured bears to the value of the property i.e. £4,500.

QUESTION 112 (a) In relation to contracts of insurance distinguish between (i) subrogation and (ii) contribution.
(b) Steven's house is valued at £15,000. He has insured it for £10,000 against fire with Wong Insurance Co. He has also insured it against fire with Shah Insurance Co. for £15.000. The house is damaged by fire to the extent of £5,000. Steven sues Wong Insurance Co. for an indemnity. Advise Wong Insurance Co. as to their rights and liabilities.

A.C.C.A. 1976

ANSWER (a) (i) **Subrogation.** It is the right of the insurers to take any legal action available to the insured person because of actions of a third party giving rise to a claim by the insured person against the insurers. It is taken in the name of the insured person. Subrogation applies to all insurance of indemnity but not to life insurance nor to personal accident insurance and the right does not arise unless and until the insurers have admitted the insured person's claim and have paid the sum payable under the policy. If money is received by the insured person from the third party, which in fact diminishes the loss, the insurers are entitled to the benefit of it even though it is paid as an act of grace or gift on the part of the buyer. However, where a payment is made to the insured person for the purpose of benefiting him personally, in respect of such loss as he may have sustained over and above that covered by the insurance, insurers are not entitled to the benefit of such payment **(Burnard v. Rodocanachi 1882).**

Subrogation has two main features. It prevents the insured person from making a profit and it gives the insurers the right to take any action in the insured's name and to stand in his place. The effect of subrogation was expressed in **Castellain v. Preston (1883)** by Brett L.J. "...as between the underwriter and the assured the underwriter is entitled to the advantage of every right of the assured whether such right consists in contract, fulfilled or unfulfilled, or in remedy for tort capable of being insisted on or already insisted on, or in any other right..."

(ii) **Contribution.** Where there are two or more insurances on any one risk, the principle of contribution applies as between the different insurers. Apart from any condition in the policy as to contribution any one insurer is bound to pay to the insured person the full amount for which he would be liable if his policy stood alone; but having paid he is entitled to an equitable contribution from his co-insurers. In order for the rights of contribution to arise, four conditions must be satisfied: (a) the insurances must have a common subject-matter though they may be on different plains (e.g., fire policy and motor policy); (b) the loss must be due to a peril which is covered by both policies; (c) the same interest must be covered by both policies; and (d) both policies must be identifiable.

From what has been said above, the basic differences between subrogation and contribution can be summarised as follows:

(i) Under subrogation, there need be only one policy, but under contribution there must be at least two policies on the same property.

(ii) Subrogation ensures that the insured will receive no more than an indemnity. Contribution ensures that insurers will not indirectly suffer injustice **inter se** because of that rule.

(iii) Under subrogation the claim must be brought in the insured's name, but under contribution the claim may be brought in the insurer's name.

(b) The problem is based on the doctrine of contribution. All the essential conditions necessary to give rise to a claim for contribution are present. The risk covered is common to both policies, the insurers have a common subject-matter and the policies cover the same interest.

Accordingly, Steven is entitled to recover the loss from Wong Insurance Co. but the latter, having paid, is entitled to an equitable contribution from Shah Insurance Co. in proportion to the amount insured. So Wong Insurance Co. could recover one-third of the amount paid to Steven.

Chapter 10

Succession and Trusts

QUESTION 113 Discuss the validity of the following wills:
(a) Louis wrote out his will and signed it in the presence of Terry (who is blind) and Tony (aged 14) both of whom then signed as witnesses.
(b) By his will George gave all his property to Andrew and Mark in equal shares. George's signature was witnessed by Andrew and Mark.
(c) Richard signed his will in the presence of two witnesses but one did not know that the document he was signing was a will and the other did not bother to watch the act of signing.
(d) Mike asked Sue and Bobby to witness his will indicating that it was in his pocket. He then revealed his signature on his will to Sue in an adjoining room but not to Bobby.

ANSWER (a) Although Tony, a minor, is competent to witness Louis' will Terry lacks capacity to act as a witness because he is blind **(Re Gibson)**. Since the Wills Act 1837 requires at least two witnesses to a will, Louis' will is invalid.
(b) S.15 Wills Act 1837 states that a witness or his spouse who takes a benefit under a will forfeits the benefit although his attestation will not be affected. Both Andrew and Mark being the sole witnesses to George's will, will forfeit their benefit and as there are no other beneficiaries under the will, it becomes abortive and George's estate will have to be distributed as on intestacy
(c) A witness need not know that the document he is signing is a will, nor is he required to actually see the testator signing. All that the Act states is that the witnesses should be present when the testator signs or acknowledges his signature. Presence means (i) mental presence i.e. the witnesses must know that the testator is there and signing; and (ii) physical presence i.e. the parties must be in line of sight. So Richard's will is valid.
(d) Mike's acknowledgement of his signature is defective because it was only made to Sue. He ought to have acknowledged it in the presence of both witnesses **(Re Groffman 1969).** The will is invalid.

QUESTION 114 *Y,* an antique dealer, died intestate in 1983. He was survived by the following: (a) a widow *W;* (b) a son *E;* (c) a stepson *F;* (d) an illegitimate daughter *G;* (e) two grandchildren *K* and *L,* both minors, who were the children of *E;* (f) two grandchildren *M* and *N,* both minors who were the children of his deceased son *P;* (g) a brother *Q;* and (h) father *R.*

The residue of *Y*'s estate consisted of:

(i) a house valued at £18,000 and which formed the matrimonial home apart from two rooms which served as a shop and office for *Y*'s business;

(ii) a valuable collection of antiques forming part of *Y*'s stock in trade;

(iii) a motor car bought for private use;

(iv) £50,000 in a deposit account in the bank.

Consider (a) whether W may claim the matrimonial home and the valuable collection of antiques as part of her entitlement to *Y*'s estate; and (b) how *Y*'s estate will be distributed.

ANSWER On the death of an intestate, his estate will be held on trust for sale by his personal representatives who have a discretion to appropriate any part of the estate in satisfaction of a person's share (S.41 AEA 1925). This discretion is subject to at least two restrictions. There is no discretion on the part of the personal representations if the surviving spouse exercises her right under the Second Schedule of Intestates Act 1925 to have the matrimonial home in which she was resident at the time of the deceased's death as part of her share in his estate. If an election is made the value at which the matrimonial home is to be appropriated to her is the value at the date of appropriation and not at death. The surviving spouse's right to elect is lost unless it is exercised within twelve months from the grant of representation to the deceased's estate. Moreover, if part of the matrimonial home was used for business purposes, an election cannot be made without the court's consent. The second restriction on the personal representatives' discretion is that they should not sell personal chattels unless there are special reasons e.g. the proceeds were required for administration purposes because no other assets were available. The surviving spouse is entitled to all personal chattels absolutely. However, in **Re Ogilby (1942)** the court said that chattels used for business purposes are not included in the definition of 'personal chattels'.

Thus *W* may claim the matrimonial home with the court's consent but she is not entitled to the valuable collection of antiques because they are not personal chattels.

The rules concerning the distribution of an intestate's estate are governed by the Administration of Estates Act 1925 as amended by the Family Provision (Intestate Succession) Order and subject to the Inheritance (Provisions for Family and Dependants) Act 1975. They state that where an intestate leaves a spouse and issue, the spouse will be entitled to (a) all personal chattels absolutely, (b) £75,000 plus interest @ 6% from death until payment and (c) a life interest in half of the residue. The issue takes the other half on statutory trust.

'Issue' includes illegitimate child (Family Law Reform Act 1969) and adopted child (Children Act 1975) but excludes stepchild. 'Statutory Trust' means the trust created by AEA 1925. Under this trust, a beneficiary's interest is contingent until he attains the age of 18 or marries under that age. Moreover, if an issue dies before the intestate, his own children will only take per stirpes the share of the issue if he had a vested interest.

From the foregoing, *Y*'s estate will have to be distributed as follows: *W* will get (i) the motor car (ii) £75,000 plus interest @ 6% from death until payment less the cost of the matrimonial home valued at the date of appropriation and (iii) a life interest in one-half of the residue. The other half of the residue will go to the issues or their children per stirpes in the following order: *E* gets $^1/_3$ share; *G* gets $^1/_3$ share, and *M* and *N* get $^1/_6$ share of *P*'s share assuming that *P* had a vested interest on his death. It should be noted that since *M* and *N* are still minors their share will not be paid over until they attain their majority. However, they are entitled to be paid the income from their share.

QUESTION 115 (a) Distinguish the following terms: (i) general legacy (ii) specific legacy and (iii) demonstrative legacy. Why is this distinction important?
(b) Jim has died leaving a will in which he gave his house, Blackacre, to his daughter Brenda. Brenda predeceased Jim leaving a son Syd who survived Jim. Explain the legal position.

Would your answer have been different if Brenda had made a will leaving all her property to her friend Pam?

ANSWER (a) (i) A **general legacy** is a gift of personal property and not distinguished from other property of the same kind (e.g., a horse). In practice, such a gift is often pecuniary in form.(e.g., £500).

(ii) A **specific legacy** is a gift of a specific asset, distinguished from all other property of the same kind (e.g. my horse Lassie).

In **Robertson v. Broadbent (1883),** Lord Selbore described it as something 'which a testator, identifying it by a sufficient description, and manifesting an intention that it should be enjoyed or taken in the state and condition indicated by that description, separates in favour of a particular legatee, from the general mass of his personal estate.'

(iii) A **demonstrative legacy** is a general legacy in the form of money payable out of a specific fund or property (e.g. £50 payable out of my Consols).

The distinction between these three types of legacies is important because general legacies must be used in full to pay off the testator's creditors before specific and demonstrative legacies can be used for this purpose. Specific legacies are subject to the doctrine of ademption i.e., if during the testator's lifetime, he disposes of the subject-matter, the beneficiary entitled to the specific legacy gets nothing. For the subject-matter not to adeem, the subject-matter existing at death must correspond with the description at the date the will is made. General legacies are not subject to ademption and in the case of demonstrative legacies, if the specific fund or property ceases to exist at the date of death the legacy is treated as a general legacy but is not subject to ademption. If there are insufficient assets to pay the legacies, general legacies have to abate so that specific and demonstrative legacies may be met. 'Abate' means 'reduce'. General legacies are reduced rateably before specific and demonstrative legacies which rank equally. A specific legacy is taken in the condition in which it existed at the date of death, unless a contrary intention is manifested by the testator. Thus, if the legacy is charged with the payment of debts (such as a house subject to a mortgage) the legatee takes it subject to payment of those debts. Finally, income derived from specific and demonstrative legacies after death and before payment of such legacies belongs to the legatee or devisee; but income derived from other assets of the estate belongs to the estate and will be distributed according to the will. If the will is silent, the income goes into residue.

(b) The general rule is that if a beneficiary under a will dies before the testator, his gift lapses and goes into residue, or if it was of residue it goes as on intestacy. Thus, if the general rule was to apply, the gift to Brenda would lapse as she pre-deceased Jim. However, the house given to Brenda is saved from the doctrine of lapse by S.19 of the Administration of Justice Act 1982. This section states that subject to a contrary intention, if property is given to a child or remoter descendant (e.g. grandchild) of the testator and the beneficiary predeceases the testator leaving issue alive at the testator's death, the gift does not lapse but passes on to the issue(s) of the intended beneficiary living at the testator's death.

Accordingly, the house will go to Syd. It makes no difference if Brenda had, by will, given all her property to Pam, because the house does not form part of Brenda's estate.

In executorship law, freehold property no longer bears its own tax unless the contrary is expressly stated. Thus, Syd, the specific devisee will not have to pay the tax on it.

QUESTION 116 Alkan Kemal, a resident of the United Kingdom, appointed Hussein Musa sole executor and trustee of his will and after bequeathing legacies to his faithful employees, directed Hussein Musa to hold the residue of his estate upon trust for his children.
(a) At what stage in the administration will Hussein Musa cease to hold the estate as personal representative and commence to hold it as trustee; and why is it important to know in which capacity he is holding the property.
(b) If Hussein Musa should die before completing all his duties, who will be entitled to continue his executorship or trusteeship.

ANSWER (a) The function of a personal representative is fundamentally different from that of a trustee. The former has to distribute the deceased's assets after realising them and paying his debts. The latter has to preserve the assets for the benefit of beneficiaries. Where a will appoints some people as personal representatives and others as trustees, the personal representatives after completing the administration will assent to the vesting of the trust property in favour of the trustees. Where the will appoints the same people as personal representatives and trustees and they are directed to hold part of the estate on trust, the personal representatives will become trustees when the administration is completed. It is always a question of fact at what stage the transition from administration to trusteeship takes place, although there is a presumption that when the personal representatives bring in their residuary accounts or exercise a power of appropriation the trusteeship begins. In **Attenborough v. Solomon (1913)** the executors completed the administration of the testator's estate one year after his death and thirteen years later one of them pledged some of his personal property. If the pledgor was still an executor his pledge would have been good because one executor alone could act in this way. However, the court said that the two executors had become trustees and their capacity had changed. Thus the transaction was void because both trustees did not assent to the pledge.

It is important to know whether Hussein Musa is acting in the capacity of an executor or that of a trustee because different laws apply in each case. Where only one personal representative is in existence he can still sell the deceased's land, whereas there must be at least two trustees of trust for sale of land unless the sole trustee is a trust corporation. One personal representative alone may dispose of pure personalty but all trustees must consent before such property could pass. A personal representative holds his office for life unless his grant of probate is for a limited period or he is released by the Court, but a trustee may retire from the trust at any time. Finally S.19(2) Limitation Act 1939 provides that an action by a beneficiary to recover trust property or in respect of a breach of trust cannot be brought after 6 years except in cases of fraud or retention of property by the trustees. However, S.20 of the Act provides a 12 year period for claims to personal estate against a personal representative and a 6 year period to recover arrears of interest on legacies.

(b) If Hussein Musa dies before completing administration of the deceased's estate, his office of executorship will pass through a chain of representation to his own providing executors (S.7 AEA 1925). Otherwise, the court will make a grant of administration de bonis non to anyone entitled to the grant in order to complete the deceased's unadministered estate. If Hussein Musa had completed administration but dies before completing all his duties of trusteeship, his office of trusteeship will pass on to his personal representatives.

QUESTION 117 Explain the meaning of the following: (i) Express trust (ii) Resulting trust (iii) Constructive trust and (iv) Charitable trust.

ANSWER (a) **Express trust.** 'Express' is ambiguous. It may mean a trust deliberately created by the settlor, rather than imposed by the court. It may also mean that the settlor has expressed his intention to create a trust as opposed to where his intention is only implied. An express trust may be declared inter vivos or made by will. Three specific types of express trust are secret trust, discretionary trust and protective trust.

(b) **Resulting trust.** Broadly speaking it arises when property is vested in trustees but the beneficial interest is not completely disposed of. Sometimes it is called an implied trust because occasionally it depends on the settlor's implied intention. In other cases it results back to the settlor much against his will. For example, if a person purchases property in the name of another then in the absence of a contrary intention and provided that the presumption of advancement does not arise, a resulting trust will arise in favour of the purchaser **(Re Vinogradoff).**

(c) **Constructive trust.** This is a trust imposed by the court regardless of the intention or wishes of the current owner of the legal estate in order to satisfy the needs of justice e.g. if a trustee makes some profit under the trusteeship, he must hold the profit as trustee for the beneficiaries.

(d) **Charitable trust.** For a trust to be charitable its purpose must fall within the spirit and preamble of the Charitable Uses Act 1601 for although this statute was repealed its preamble is still very much alive. In **Pemsel's Case 1891,** Lord MacNaghten classified trusts under four heads – (i) trusts for the relief of poverty (ii) trusts for the advancement of education (iii) trusts for the advancement of religion and (iv) trusts for other purposes beneficial to the community, not falling under any of the other three heads. Apart from falling within one of the four categories, there are two other requirements before a trust can be classified as a charitable trust. It must be exclusively charitable and, except for a trust for the relief of poverty, it must have a public element.

QUESTION 118 What are the essentials for a valid express trust? What is the legal effect if the trust lacks one of these essentials?

ANSWER In order to create a valid express trust, three requirements must be satisfied – the words must be certain, the subject-matter must be certain and the objects must be certain. These essentials are known as the 'three certainties'.

Certainty of Words. This means that there must be a clear intention on the part of the settlor to create a trust. Precatory words i.e. words of belief, hope, desire, confidence etc. were accepted at one time as being sufficient to create a trust, but the attitude of the court today is not to infer a trust in such cases. A clear intention is necessary. If the words are uncertain, the trust fails and the donee takes everything absolutely.

Certainty of Subject-matter. This means that both the trust property and the beneficial interest of the beneficiaries must be certain. The settlor must specify what property is subject to the trust. Thus to give 'some of my property' to trustees is an uncertainty. If the property is uncertain the whole trust fails and no property passes to anyone because it is unclear what the property is. The settlor must also determine how much property goes to each beneficiary or he must give the trustees a power (bare or trust power) to decide how the property is to be allocated. Where the beneficial interest is uncertain the trust does not necessarily fail. If the whole of the beneficial interest is given to one beneficiary subject to the right of other beneficiaries to an uncertain part of it, the court will ignore the directions of the uncertain part and the principal beneficiary will get everything **(Curtis v. Rippon).** Alternatively, the court may apply the maxim 'equality is equity' and divide the trust property in equal shares **(Doyley v. A.G.).** Failing this, the property will be held on resulting trust.

Certainty of objects. This means that the trust must be either for private individuals or for charitable purposes and these must be certain. In general, trusts for purposes other than charity are void. If the trust is a private express trust and its objects are uncertain, the trust fails and the property goes back on resulting trust for the settlor or if he is dead, his estate. If the trust is a charitable trust and its objects are uncertain, the property will be applied cy-pres i.e. it will go to some other charitable purpose 'as near as possible' resembling the original purpose.

QUESTION 119 By his will Jade left the residue of his estate on trust for his wife Linda for life and then to his three children absolutely. The residue of his estate consists of a house, a motor car, shares in ABC Ltd which has a paid up capital of half a million pounds, and £30,000 in a bank deposit. The trustees have power in the will to invest 'in any such trustee investments as they shall in their discretion select'. Advise the trustees of their legal position, and in particular whether they may invest in the following:
(a) shares in Limited Companies;
(b) deposits in building societies;
(c) second mortgage on freehold land;
(d) a leasehold house under a lease having 60 years unexpired.
    Would your answer be the same if the trust instrument did not contain an unrestricted power of investment clause?

ANSWER In carrying out the provisions of the trust under Jade's will the trustees must always bear in mind the two cardinal duties imposed on them namely, the duty to act with care and preserve the trust property by investing it prudently; and the duty to act impartially between beneficiaries and not to favour one at the expense of the others.

As the trust was made by will, involved successive interests and consisted of residuary personalty the **Rule in Howe v. Lord Dartmouth** will apply and the trustees will have to convert the motor car (a wasting asset) and the shares in ABC Ltd (unauthorised investments) from their existing forms into authorised investments. These assets should be sold not later than one year from death and if there is intermediate income e.g. dividends from the shares, Linda the tenant for life will be entitled to it. If the shares remain unsold within the year there will be an apportionment of the intermediate income between income and capital. Linda will be entitled to 5% interest per annum from the date of death of Jade until realisation, on the value of the shares one year from the date of death. Any surplus of income will go towards capital, any deficiency of income must be made up from future surpluses of income or if there are none, then from capital when the shares are sold.

The trustees must then invest all trust monies into authorised investments. They need not take recourse to the Trustee Investments Act 1961 since the trust instrument gives them unrestricted powers of investment. In **Re Harari (1949)** the instrument gave the trustees power to make 'such investments as the trustees may see fit'. Jenkins J. said that the clause meant power to make any investment the trustees desire. Hence the trustees may invest in shares in Limited companies and deposits in building societies. The trustees may invest in a leasehold house under a lease having 60 years unexpired only if the house will not be purchased for residence only. In **Re Tower (1947)** land was bought in order to give a home to a beneficiary. The court held this was not a valid exercise of a power to invest because no income was obtained. The trustees may not lawfully invest in a second mortgage on freehold land as only first legal mortgages are permitted at common law. A second mortgage has its drawbacks in that if the first mortgagee forecloses, the security will be lost unless there are funds available to pay him. Moreover if the first mortgagee goes into possession he may draw the whole of the income from the property.

It should be noted that although the trustees have an absolute discretion in choosing investments, this discretion must be exercised diligently and with care otherwise the trustees will be liable for any losses sustained by the investments. In **Learoyd v. Whiteley (1887)** Lord Watson said "It is the duty of a trustee to confine himself to the class of investments which are permitted by the trust and likewise to avoid all investments of that class which are attended with hazard".

If the trust instrument did not contain an unrestricted power of investment clause, the trustees would have had to obtain their powers to invest from the Trustee Investment Act. Since shares in limited companies are wider range investments requiring advice under the Act, the trustees would have had to divide the trust fund initially into two halves – a narrow range half and a wider range half. They would then have been able to purchase the shares from the wider range half provided the following conditions were satisfied (a) the shares were quoted on a recognised stock exchange and were fully paid up (b) the company had a total paid up capital of at least £1 million and (c) in each of the preceding five years it had paid a dividend on all its shares. Deposits in building societies are Narrow Range Part II investments requiring advice and they could be made from funds from either half. The Trustee Investments Act permits investments in mortgages on real securities (Narrow Range Part II) but not for the purchase of land (whether freehold or leasehold with an unexpired period of 60 years.) Like the common law only first legal mortgages are permitted. Thus, the trustees would not be able to invest in a second legal mortgage nor to purchase the leasehold house.

QUESTION 120 (a) Distinguish between a fully secret trust and a half secret trust. Why is this distinction important?
(b) In his will, Tom left property on trust to John. The secret beneficiary communicated to John is Mary.

What is the legal position if (i) John dies before Tom; or (ii) Mary dies before Tom? Would your answer be the same if the trust was a fully secret trust?

ANSWER (a) A fully secret trust arises where a testator leaves property to someone absolutely in his will but orally tells him that the gift is not for his own benefit but for someone else and the donee agrees to this. This agreement may be express or implied. If there is no communication before the testator's death, the trustee will take the property absolutely. If during the testator's lifetime only the fact of the trust and not the details of the beneficiaries have been communicated, the trustee must hold the property on trust for the testator's next of kin. In **Re Boyes**

(1884) the court said it would be sufficient communication of the details of the trust if the details were given to the trustees in a sealed envelope during the testator's lifetime even though the envelope was not to be opened until after the testator's death.

A half-secret trust arises where on the face of the will property is left on trust but the beneficiaries' identities are not known. Secret trusts sometimes conflict with S.9 of Wills Act 1837 which states that testamentary dispositions must be witnessed in writing and signed by the testator. However, as equity will not allow a statute to be used as an instrument to a fraud, it allows secret trusts.

It is important to distinguish between a fully secret trust and a half secret trust because, unlike fully secret trusts where the testator's intention need only be communicated before his death, with a half secret trust it must be communicated before or at the date of the will **(Blackwell v. Blackwell 1929).** Moreover, evidence of a half secret trust will not be admitted to contradict the terms of a will. In **Re Keen** property was given to two persons on trust to be disposed of 'as may be notified by me'. The court held that these words indicated a future notification and so evidence of prior notification was inadmissible.

(b) In **Cullen v. ATT. General for Ireland (1866),** Lord Westbury said that the title of a party claiming under a secret trust is a title dehors the will and cannot be correctly termed testamentary. This means that a secret trust is not part of a will but is quite independent of it. So in answering the problem, the rules governing wills must be ignored.

One of the rules of trusteeship is that a trust will not fail for lack of trustees to act. The court will, in the last resort appoint new trustees to carry out the provisions of the trust. If therefore, John the secret trustee under the half secret trust dies before the testator, a new trustee will be appointed unless the identities of the beneficiaries were known only to John in which case the gift under the half secret trust will fail. If the trust was a fully secret trust, the gift under trust would lapse, because no one but John would have known on the testator's death that a trust was intended. Should Mary, the secret beneficiary die before the testator, the property would go to the estate of Mary. In **Re Gardiner (1923)** one of the secret beneficiaries predeceased the testator and his P. R. tried to claim his share. The court held that he would succeed because the doctrine of lapse applied only to wills and not to trusts.

QUESTION 121 Supercabs Limited, which operates a fleet of taxis, engages Clutch as a driver. The company provides and maintains the taxi and pays for the petrol. Clutch promises to work only for the company. However, he does not receive a wage but instead is paid a commission on the earnings he collects. The journeys that he makes and the hours that he works are left entirely to his discretion.
(a) Discuss whether Clutch is an employee or an independent contractor.
(b) Explain why the existence of a contract of employment in this case might be of importance.

I.C.M.A. 1983

ANSWER Basically, an employee is a person working under a contract **of** service while an independent contractor is one working under a contract **for** service. In determining whether a contract of employment exists, the court has developed three main tests: the control test, the organisation test, and the multiple or mixed test. The fact that the worker is described as an 'employee' or 'independent contractor' is not conclusive **(Ferguson v. John Dawson & Partners Ltd 1976).**

The control test is the traditional one. It states that a person is employed under a contract of service if the employer controls not only what must be done but also how and when it must be done. If the employer does not control the manner in which the work is to be done, then the contract is one for services. The control test is very useful in identifying a simple contract of employment involving unskilled labour but not where the worker has a degree of independence as in Clutch's case, in determining the manner of doing the work. The organisation or integration test was expounded by Lord Denning in **Stevenson, Jordan Harrison Ltd v. Macdonald & Evans (1952)** when he said "under a contract of service a man is employed as part of the business and his work is done as an integral part of the business, whereas under a contract for services, his work although done for the business is not integrated into it but is only accessory to it". This test has its usefulness where the person employed is highly skilled. Thus, in **Cassidy v. Ministry of Health (1951)** the full-time

medical staff of a hospital were held to be employees even
though they had a certain degree of independence in doing their
work, with the result that the hospital was vicariously liable for
their negligence. If this test is used, Clutch will clearly be an
employee under a contract of service for although he decides his
hours of work and journeys, he seems to depend on Supercab
Limited for his living and so is an integral part of the business.
This is further strengthened by his undertaking not to work for
anyone else. However, the organisation test is not necessarily the
best test for determining the nature of a contract. It fails to take
into account cases where an employee is required to provide
some of his tools and where he is paid on a productivity basis.

The multiple or mixed test states that in order to determine
whether a contract of service exists several factors must be
considered, namely, the employer's power to select and dismiss,
the manner of payment of wages, the right to control, the method
of doing the work, and whether the worker has invested his tools
with a view to make a profit or risk a loss. This test allows the
court to determine the economic reality of the situation and it
was used in **Ready Mixed Concrete Ltd v. Ministry of Pensions
and National Insurance (1968)** where lorry drivers as a condition
of employment were required to purchase their employers'
lorries on hire purchase terms and, at their own costs, to maintain
them and were paid on a piece-work basis over and above
guaranteed minimum earnings. The court held that they were
independent contractors despite the fact that they were required
to wear the company's uniforms and had guaranteed earnings. If
this test was used it would appear that despite the fact that the
employer provides the tools (taxis) and meets their running costs,
Clutch could be considered an independent contractor since he
receives commission as opposed to wages and is able to determine
when to work and what journeys to make.

On balance, Clutch would appear to be an employee since
the existence of the restraint of trade agreement appears to be
directly opposite to the fundamental concept of self-employment
namely, the freedom to work for anyone. The conclusion would
be otherwise if it transpires that the employer pays his commission without the deduction of income tax and national insurance.

(b) The distinction between 'employee' and 'independent contractor' is of fundamental importance to the employer because
both common law and statute impose certain obligations on him
in cases where he has employed an 'employee'. The employer is

vicariously liable for the torts of his employee and only in exceptional cases for the torts of his independent contractor. Under statute law, the employer is required to give his employee written particulars of his main terms and conditions of employment not later than 13 weeks after the employment commences (Employment Protection Consolidation Act 1978); and his unfettered power of dismissal is statutorily restricted by the unfair dismissal and the redundancy provisions. If Clutch happens to be an employee, Supercabs Ltd will also have to make 'secondary' national insurance contributions on his behalf and to deduct tax by the PAYE system from any commission it intends to pay him. On the other hand, if he is an independent contractor Clutch will have to meet his own national insurance contributions by purchasing national insurance stamps at a flat weekly rate but he will receive his commission without deduction of tax although he has to declare his annual profits to the Inland Revenue.

QUESTION 122 What particulars is an employee entitled to be given when he starts employment? What are the legal consequences for failure to supply the necessary particulars?

ANSWER Unless the employee has a written contract, he is entitled to receive from his employer a written statement containing the main terms and conditions of employment not later than 13 weeks after the employment commences (Employment Protection Consolidation Act 1978). This statement must include the names of the parties, the date when the employment commenced, whether any period of past employment with his former employer is to be treated as part of the employee's continuous period of employment (this is important for e.g. redundancy and unfair dismissal), the rate or scale of remuneration or the method of calculating it, provisions as to sickness and sick pay, holidays and pension rights. Attached to this statement must be a note specifying any disciplinary rules the employer may wish to rely on and disciplinary and grievance procedures. The employee is also entitled to an itemised pay statement containing his gross and net wages, deductions made and the reasons for making them.

The written statement is not the contract of employment and it may be contradicted. In **Owens v. Multilux Ltd (1974)** the court said that the statement may be useful as evidence in subsequent legal proceedings between the parties but it cannot be regarded as conclusive. Nevertheless, in three circumstances it may be treated as the contract and not just evidence of it. The doctrine of estoppel may operate to prevent the parties from denying the accuracy of the statement **(Smith v. Blandford Gee Cementation Co. Ltd 1970).** Moreover if the employee signs a receipt for the written statement given to him by his employer then according to the C.A. in **Gascol Conversions Ltd v. Mercer (1974),** it is treated as a contractual document. Finally, if the written statement is supplied to him not by his employer but by an industrial tribunal, then it cannot be contradicted.

There is no legal sanction against the employer for failure to provide the written particulars to the employee. The employee will have to go to an industrial tribunal which will then determine what the particulars ought to be. Its findings will be conclusive. If the employee is not told what disciplinary and grievance procedures exist, then should the employer attempt to rely on any disciplinary power and dismiss the employee the dismissal may be held to be unfair.

QUESTION 123 Outline the statutory provisions passed since 1970 to prevent discrimination in employment.

ANSWER The anti-discrimination legislation passed since 1970 may be considered under three categories: (a) those aimed at preventing discrimination on grounds of sex; (b) those aimed at preventing discrimination on grounds of race; and (c) those aimed at preventing discrimination on grounds of trade union membership.

Under (a), the relevant statutes are the Equal Pay Act 1970, the Sex Discrimination Act 1975, the Employment Protection (Consolidation) Act 1978 and the Employment Act 1980. Under the Equal Pay Act 1970, an equality clause relating to pay, holidays, sick pay, and hours of work is implied in every contract of employment between a man and a woman doing broadly similar work or work given equal value under a job evaluation exercise carried out by an employer, and working for the same employer. The Act does not cover non-contractual terms, terms relating to death or retirement or any special treatment accorded to a woman in connection with pregnancy or childbirth; and it is a defence to an employer to show that the variation between the woman's and man's contract is genuinely due to a difference other than sex (for e.g., that the man was a long serving employee). The provisions of the Act may be enforced by an individual civil action in an industrial tribunal to implement the equality clause, or in appropriate cases, the amendment of collective agreements, employers' pay structures and wages regulation orders by the Central Arbitration Committee. Although the EPA 1970 is limited in application in that the comparison is between a man and a woman presently employed by the same employer, Article 119 of the Treaty of Rome which requires 'equal pay for identical work' between the sexes confers a similar right to every worker in the Common Market, and allows the comparison to be made with a predecessor i.e. the person whom the complainant replaced **(Macarthys v. Smith 1980).**

The Sex Discrimination Act 1975 makes it unlawful for an employer to discriminate on grounds of sex or marital status when deciding who will be given the job and in the terms and conditions of the job. It covers both contractual and non-contractual terms other than the payment of money; and it is a defence to the employer if he can show that the sex is a genuine occupational qualification for the job, for example, for reasons of physiology (as in employment of a model) or for reasons of decency or privacy (as in the case of a single-sex establishment such as a prison). The provisions of the Act may be enforced by an individual civil action in a tribunal for damages or by investigation of the complaint by the Equal Opportunities Commission with a view to get an injunction. Although the provisions of the EPA 1970 and the SDA 1975 do overlap, the Acts are completely exclusive of each other; and if a complainant has a good ground on which to make a complaint under the former, he cannot proceed also under the latter because, as Phillips J explained in **Peake v. Automative Products Ltd (1977)** "the remedies were different".

Section 60 of the Employment Protection (Consolidation) Act 1978 makes it an automatically unfair reason to dismiss a woman because of pregnancy or for reasons connected with it; and Part III of the Act gives a woman who has two years continuous service and who has been under a contract of employment up to the eleventh week of the week of confinement, a right to receive maternity pay from her employer provided she gives him at least 21 days written notice of the expected week of confinement. Maternity pay is payable for the first 6 weeks of absence and is nine-tenths of her wages. The woman also has a right to get back her job or a suitable alternative one if she returns to work not later than 29 weeks after child birth provided she had indicated to her employer in her pre-confinement notice or as soon as it was reasonably practicable to do so of her intention to return to work and provided she confirmed this in writing not later than 14 days if her employer asked for such confirmation after 49 days from confinement. Section 13 of the Employment Act 1980 gives a female employee a right to take reasonable time off work with pay for ante-natal care, regardless of her length of service with the employer.

Under (b), the Race Relations Act 1976 makes it unlawful for an employer to discriminate against a job applicant or employee on grounds of race, colour, nationality, ethnic or national origin. The Act does not cover employment in a private household and it is a defence to show that the race was a genuine occupational qualification for the job (e.g. photographic models, places of refreshments where persons of a particular racial group are required for reasons of authenticity, and jobs providing personal welfare services for a particular racial group). Like the Sex Discrimination Act, the Race Relations Act covers three types of discrimination: (i) direct discrimination e.g. refusing to employ the job applicant on grounds of his race; (ii) indirect discrimination e.g. imposing an unjustifiable condition or requirement for the job, knowing that the likelihood of the applicant and his race being able to satisfy the condition or requirement is significantly small; and (iii) discrimination by victimisation e.g., refusing to give the applicant a job because he had previously taken his former employer to a tribunal alleging a breach of the anti-discrimination statute. In **Panesar v. Nestlè Ltd (1980)** it was held that it was justifiable for a chocolate factory to refuse to employ a bearded Sikh on grounds of hygiene.

Under (c), Section 77 of the Employment Protection (Consolidation) Act 1978 makes it an inadmissible reason to dismiss an employee because he is a member of an independent trade union or because he takes part in its activities outside working hours. The importance of 'inadmissible reason' is that an action for unfair dismissal may be brought by the employee irrespective of his length of service with the employer. An employee dismissed for trade union membership may receive additional damages apart from the basic compensatory award normally granted in a tribunal. Section 23 of the Act gives an employee a right not to have discriminatory action short of dismissal taken against him by his employer because of his trade union membership. Section 27 gives an employee who is an official of a trade union recognised by the employer a right to take reasonable time off work with pay for his trade union duties, and section 28 gives employees who are members of such a union a similar right, although without pay.

QUESTION 124 Advise the various complainants who, at job interviews, have had their application for work turned down:

(a) Monti, an Italian, as waiter in a Chinese restaurant because he is not of Chinese origin.

(b) Daxa, an East African Indian, as a shorthand/typist to Woodford Ltd because she lives in the city centre and it is the policy of the company not to employ locals from the 'city centre'. Over 50 per cent of the city's inhabitants are coloured.

(c) Paula, as accountant with Pearce & Chase, because she is unmarried and over 30 years of age.

(d) Roy, as accounts clerk with Ascot Ltd, because he was convicted of petty theft eight years ago.

(e) John, as an economics lecturer, because he is a trade unionist.

ANSWER When recruiting and selecting applicants for work, an employer has to take into account the various anti-discrimination statutes.

(a) The Race Relations Act 1976 makes it unlawful for an employer to discriminate on grounds of colour, race, nationality, ethnic or national origin. However, it is a defence under the Act to show that the job required a particular race such as in the employment of Chinese waiters in a Chinese restaurant. So although Monti has been discriminated against on ground of nationality, the restaurant will not be liable.

(b) The facts of the problem are similar to those in **Hussein v. Saints Complete House Furnishers (1979)** where it was held that as 50 per cent of the population in the city centre was black or coloured whereas only 2 per cent outside the city centre was black or coloured, the company's policy of not employing inner city youths on its staff excluded a large number of black and coloured people in comparison with the proportion of white people to be affected. This was indirect discrimination under the Race Relations Act 1976. On the basis of the above authority, Daxa would be advised that she was unjustifiably indirectly discriminated against contrary to SS.1(I)(b) and 4(I)(a) of the Race Relations Act 1976.

(c) Paula will be unable to base her claim against Pearce & Chase on ground that she was single since the Sex Discrimination Act

1916 only covers discrimination on ground of sex or marital status. However, she may succeed in an action for indirect discrimination because of her sex. In **Price v. Civil Service Commission (1977)** the Employment Appeal Tribunal held that an imposition of an age limit of 28 could be discriminatory against women, a large proportion of whom are occupied with children at that age.

(d) Although the Rehabilitation of Offenders Act 1974 makes it unlawful for an employer to discriminate against an employee or job applicant on ground of a spent conviction, it has been held in **Torr v. Br. Railways Board (1977)** that an employer is under no duty to disregard spent convictions when engaging an employee to hold a position of trust. On the basis of the above authority, Roy may not be able to bring any action against Ascot Ltd.

(e) Under the Employment Protection (Consolidation) Act 1978 it is unlawful for an employer to take action against a person because of his trade union activities. However, it is not a violation of a person's trade union rights if he is refused employment because he is a trade unionist. In **City of Birmingham District Council v. Beyer (1976)** a job applicant alleged that he was refused employment because he was a well-known trade union activist. The tribunal dismissed his case on ground that he could not have been said to be carrying on trade union activities when he applied for the job; so his trade union rights were not infringed. Therefore, John may be unable to successfully bring an action against the employers.

QUESTION 125 (a) Distinguish the following terms: (i) summary dismissal, (ii) wrongful dismissal, and (iii) unfair dismissal. (b) Marise, a receptionist, is dismissed by her employers Fennell Computers Ltd because, it is alleged, she is often late for work. Marise denies this and accuses her employers of dismissing her because she attended a recent trade union meeting during working hours without permission. Advise her.

ANSWER (a) (i) Summary dismissal is on the spot dismissal or dismissal without notice. At common law summary dismissal will only be permitted if there are circumstances justifying it. In considering the circumstances which the law would consider as sufficient to justify such a dismissal, Lord Evershed M.R. in **Laws v. London Chronicle Ltd (1959)** said "The question must be whether the conduct complained of is such as to show the servant to have disregarded the essential conditions of the contract".

(ii) Wrongful dismissal is summary dismissal which cannot be justified by the employer. The employee is entitled to claim damages in a common law action for wrongful dismissal. The advantage of an action for wrongful dismissal is that the amount of damages the employee may recover is unlimited. Its chief drawback is that there can never be an action for wrongful dismissal if the employer had given notice of dismissal – however bad the reason for the dismissal.

(iii) Unfair dismissal is dismissal contrary to the Trade Union & Labour Relations Act 1974 as consolidated. In **W. Devis & Sons Ltd v. Atkins (1976)** Phillips J said "the expression 'unfair dismissal' is in no sense a common sense expression capable of being understood by the man in the street. In fact, under the Act, it is narrowly and to some extent arbitrarily defined. It is a form of words which could be translated as being equivalent to 'dismissal contrary to the statute' and to which the label 'unfair dismissal' has been given". Unfair dismissal enables an employee to bring an action in an industrial tribunal even though the employer had given notice of dismissal. Its chief drawback is that the amount of damages which can be recovered is limited.

(b) Marise may bring an action against Fennell Computers Ltd for unfair dismissal. She will have to prove that she was dismissed and the employers will then have to show that the dismissal was fair. They will probably rely on Marise's misconduct. However, the Code of Industrial Relations Practice generally requires an employer to issue warnings before resorting to dismissal. Such warnings may only be dispensed with in exceptional circumstances e.g. in the case of gross misconduct. Since Fennell Computers Ltd failed to issue the warnings, they will be deemed to have acted unreasonably.

If it is established that Marise was dismissed because she attended a trade union meeting she will be entitled to additional damages as the Employment Protection Consolidation Act 1978 requires an employer to give his employee reasonable time off without pay for trade union activities if the union is independent and recognised by the employer.

QUESTION 126 'Redundancy is now a matter of consultation and not just one of compensation'. Discuss.

ANSWER One of the aims of the Redundancy Payments Act 1965 (now consolidated by E.P.C.A. 1978) is to make financial provisions for a worker who loses his job on account of redundancy. Redundancy means that the employer has no need for the.worker's service because he has ceased or intends to cease carrying on business for the purposes of which the worker was employed or because the needs of that business for the worker to carry out work of that particular kind or in that particular place have ceased or are expected to cease or diminish.

The Act enables a worker who is dismissed, laid off or placed on short time by reason of redundancy to receive compensation which is to be assessed according to the length of the worker's service. Between the ages of 41 and 65 (women 60) the worker is entitled to $1\frac{1}{2}$ weeks' pay (max £120 per week) for each year of completed service up to a maximum of 20 years. In other age groups, similar provisions apply except that the weeks pay changes i.e. if the worker is aged between 22 and 40 it is one week's pay per year, and if he is aged between 18 and 21 it is $\frac{1}{2}$ week's pay per year. Since the Act is based on compensation the worker receives no redundancy payment if he is made redundant on reaching 65 years of age (women 60) as he would have had to retire anyway. If he is made redundant in the last year of his normal working life i.e. when he is over 64 (women 59) he loses $\frac{1}{12}$ of the payments for every month of that year he has worked.

The Employment Protection Act 1975, now requires an employer also to consult with representatives of any independent trade union which he recognises as soon as possible which is not less than 90 days before the dismissals take effect if 100 or more workers are being made redundant within a 90 day period, or 30 days if 10 or more workers are being laid off over a 30 day period. Even if only one worker is affected the union must be consulted. Consultation involves the employer telling the union the reasons for the proposal to dismiss the workers, the number and description of the workers affected, the total number of workers of that description employed at the establishment and the proposed method of selecting and carrying out the dismissals.

Failure to consult the trade union may result in an application being made by the union to an industrial tribunal for a protective award under which the workers will be kept in employment and paid for a period corresponding to the minimum time required for consultation. Consultation need not however, take place if there are special circumstances which rendered it not reasonably practicable for the employer to do so. In **Clarks of Hove Ltd v. Bakers' Union (1977)** the court said a company's insolvency could be a special circumstance.

QUESTION 127 *A* has worked for *B* & Co. for 10 years. He has a job in a dusty warehouse. As a result of bronchitis he has increasingly long periods off work, especially during the last two winters. He has now been off work for 6 weeks and is not yet better. *B* & Co. are finding that trade is falling off. They want to tell *A* that his job is no longer available for him.

Advise *B* & Co. as to *A*'s legal position.

I.C.S.A. 1975

ANSWER A contract of employment may be terminated by act of the parties or by operation of the law. With the former, legal consequences may follow, especially if the termination is due to dismissal. The E.P.C.A. 1978 defines dismissal as, inter alia, where the contract under which the employee is employed is terminated by the employer with or without notice. With the latter, the contract is automatically discharged and the parties are free from subsequent liabilities. Frustration automatically discharges a contract of employment and one of the events which may bring it about is sickness.

If *B* & Co. take steps to terminate *A*'s employment, then *A* may treat himself as being dismissed on grounds of redundancy and will prima facie be entitled to redundancy compensation from *B* & Co. He may also claim damages for unfair dismissal if he was unfairly selected for redundancy.

B & Co. may successfully resist *A*'s claim by showing that *A*'s contract of employment was not terminated by dismissal but rather by frustration **(Egg Stores Ltd v. Leibovic 1976). In Marshall v. Harland & Wolff Ltd (1972)** the court outlined the following factors as being relevant when considering whether sickness frustrates a contract – the terms of the contract including any provisions as to sickness pay; the length of time the employment is likely to last in the absence of sickness: the nature of the employment and the sickness, and the length of service already provided by the employee.

Quite apart from any contractual right *A* may have, *B* & Co. appear to be in breach of the Health and Safety at Work Act 1974. Under this Act an employer is under a duty to provide a healthy and safe working environment for his employees. *B* & Co. seem to have breached this obligation in that they permitted *A* to work in a dusty warehouse without any regard for his health and well being. If *B* & Co. are successfully prosecuted under this Act, *A* may use this conviction as evidence in an action for negligence against them for injury for his health.

QUESTION 128 'The Health and Safety at Work Act 1974 imposes obligations on persons involved at all stages of production'. Discuss.

ANSWER Unlike other health and safety statutes, the Health and Safety at Work Act imposes obligations not on premises but on people. It affects persons who by their work activities may endanger health and safety. Thus the Act is wide enough to cover persons engaged at all stages of production.

An employer owes a duty both to his employees and other persons who would be affected by his undertaking. To his employees he is under a general duty to take steps to secure their health, safety and welfare at work. This basic obligation towards employees may be satisfied by providing, for example, a safe system of work, adequate instructions to staff, adequate supervision by competent personnel and written information of his safety policy. Independent trade unions recognised by the employer may appoint safety representatives from among the employees and if the safety representatives so request, the employer must set up a joint safety committee which will review existing safety measures and recommend improvements where necessary. To non-employees such as members of the public, the employer must conduct his business in such a way as to ensure that such persons would not be exposed to risks to their health and safety.

An employee is under a duty while at work to take reasonable care for the health and safety to himself and to others who may be affected by his acts or omissions. Moreover, he must co-operate with his employer in carrying out the provisions of the Act.

The Act also imposes a duty on manufacturers, suppliers, installers, and designers of articles used at work. They must ensure that the articles are so designed and constructed as to be safe and without risks to health when properly used. Such articles must be tested before use and any research necessary to minimise risk must be undertaken. Moreover, adequate information about the use of the articles must be provided so that when the articles are put to use, they will not endanger health and safety.

Occupiers and owners of premises used for work activities must make sure that the premises are safe in all respects. This would include safe access to the premises and egress from them.

Factory Inspectors are appointed under the Act and are given wide powers to enforce its provisions. The inspectors can issue improvement and prohibition notices. They can also take an alleged breach to a magistrates court which has power to impose fines and even imprisonment on the offending party.

QUESTION 129 (a) What legal provisions exist to protect workers from injuries rising out of the use of dangerous machinery?

(b) Martin is employed by D.S. Mills Ltd. One day during working hours he went to see his friend, Norman, who worked in another department of the company, about a private matter. Martin dropped a packet of cigarettes and, as he bent over to pick it up, his clothing became caught in the machinery. Martin was seriously injured as also was Norman who tried to pull him clear.

Advise D.S. Mills Ltd.

I.C.M.A. 1980

ANSWER (a) The legal protection available to workers from injuries arising out of the use of dangerous machinery comes from the common law and legislation. Under common law, an employer is under a duty of care not to expose his employees to unnecessary risks. This duty extends to providing a safe system of work and adequate plant and machinery **(Barcock v. Brighton Corporation 1949).** If the employer breaches this duty, the employee may recover damages in an action for negligence under **Donoghue v. Stevenson (1932).** However, the standard of care set by common law is based on what reasonable employers would do at any given time and so it fails to meet new risks which often emerge in an industrialised society.

The main statutory protection comes from the Health and Safety at Work Act 1974 and the Factories Act 1961. By far the most important is the Health and Safety at Work Act. It imposes a duty on employers to ensure so far as is reasonably practicable the health, safety and welfare at work of employees at all places where work activities are carried on. Manufacturers, designers, suppliers and importers of machinery for use at work must ensure so far as is reasonably practicable that it is so designed and constructed as to be safe when used (S.6). Criminal sanction is imposed for breach of the 1974 Act. The Factories Act 1961 applies only to a factory i.e. a place where manual labour is performed in the manufacture, process or alteration of an article for a gain; and it imposes strict liability on the occupier of the factory. The fencing provisions contained in sections 12–17 require the occupier to fence his machinery. The prime mover (including flywheels) must be securely fenced (S.12). Transmission machinery must be securely fenced unless its position or construction renders it as safe as if it was fenced (S.13). All other dangerous parts of other machinery must also be securely fenced unless they are safe by reason of their position or construction (S.14). Fencing and other safeguards have to be substantial and constantly maintained and must be able to keep workers from contact with dangerous parts of the machinery. Criminal sanction is imposed for breach of the Factories Act but civil redress is also available if the fencing provisions are broken **(Groves v. Lord Wimborne 1898),** provided that the risk was foreseeable **(F.E. Callow Ltd v. Johnson 1971),** the type of injury was covered by the Act **(Nicholls v. Austin Ltd 1946),** and the damage was the result of the breach of duty. Thus if, as in **McWilliams v. W. Arrol Ltd (1962),** an employer fails to provide safety belts as required by statute and his employee falls to his death while erecting steel, the employer will not be liable for the death if it is proved that the employee would not have worn the safety belt was one provided.

(b) D.S. Mills Ltd is a place where work activities are carried on and it also appears to be a factory within the meaning of the Factories Act. Accordingly, both the Health and Safety at Work Act 1974 and the Factories Act 1961 will apply. The fact that Martin's clothing was caught in the machinery with the result that he was seriously injured, suggests that the dangerous parts of the machinery were unfenced and that the employer was in breach of its statutory duty under both Acts. D.S. Mills Ltd is liable to prosecution and a fine and the factory inspector may, under the 1974 Act, issue a prohibition notice directing the company's activities to cease unless safety measures are improved.

Both Martin and Norman may also obtain civil redress for the employer's breach of statutory duty under the 1961 Act. The employer is liable to Martin under the Act even though he was acting outside the scope of his employment at the time he was injured. In **Uddin v. Associated Portland Cement Manufacturers Ltd (1965),** a worker climbed a vertical steel ladder to a platform (where he had no right to be) and suffered an injury whilst leaning over a dangerous unfenced revolving shaft to catch a pigeon which was sitting behind the shaft. The employers were still held liable although the damages were substantially reduced for contributory negligence. Probably, as in Uddin case, the damages awarded to Martin will be considerably reduced by the court under the Law Reform (Contributory Negligence) Act

1945 if D.S. Mills Ltd raises the issue of Martin's contributory negligence.

Volenti non fit injuria is no defence to an action for breach of statutory duty **(I.C.I. v. Shatwell 1965)** so D.S. Mills Ltd cannot plead that Norman was a volunteer i.e. he came voluntarily to the danger in trying to pull Martin clear. Even if Martin was negligent and the employer was vicariously liable for his negligence, the defence of *volenti* would not have succeeded if used against Norman, because he was a rescuer acting under a moral obligation in an emergency **(Haynes v. Harwood 1935).** D.S. Mills Ltd as employer, is also under a statutory duty under the Employer's Liability (Compulsory Insurance) Act 1969 to insure against liability to its employees, Martin and Norman.

QUESTION 130 Smart and Jorpid are employed as labourers on a building site. They are instructed to wear safety helmets at all times, but they find it to be a nuisance to draw these from the site office and the helmets are cumbersome and uncomfortable. Smart therefore persuades Jorpid that it would be better to work without them. In the course of work, Smart throws a brick to Jorpid, shouting a warning as he does so. Jorpid is deaf, does not hear the shout or see the brick coming, and is struck on the head.
(a) What are the possible legal consequences?
(b) What further information about the incident should you request?

I.C.M.A. 1981

ANSWER (a) The Health and Safety at Work Act 1974 places employers under a general duty to ensure, so far as is reasonably practicable, the health, safety and welfare at work of their employees. This duty may be discharged by providing a safe system of work, adequate instructions to staff and proper supervision by competent personnel. Employers are also under a duty to take reasonable care for the health and safety to themselves and to their fellow employees who may be affected by their acts, and to co-operate with the employer in carrying out the provisions of the Act. It would appear from the given facts in the problem that both the employer and employees, Smart and Torpid, are in breach of their obligations under the Act and so are criminally liable. The employer for not ensuring that safety helmets are worn; and Smart and Jorpid for not wearing them.

An employer is also under a duty at common law to take reasonable care towards his employees and this includes providing reasonable safety equipment to be made reasonably accessible. If this duty is broken then the employee may be able to recover damages in a civil action for negligence. There are also special safety regulations for building sites under other statutes and if such regulations are broken the employer will incur both criminal and civil liability. There is a prima facie case against the employer for common law negligence and breach of statutory duty since the safety helmets were not readily accessible and are uncomfortable. If the employer argues, by way of defence, that Smart and Jorpid consented to the risks by not wearing safety helmets *(volenti non fit injuria)* this defence will fail as in **Smith v. Baker (1891)** where the action was for common law negligence, and **I.C.I. v. Shatwell (1965)** where the action was for breach of statutory duty. However, the defence of contributory negligence, if raised by the employer may succeed with the result that the damages recoverable by Jorpid will be considerably reduced under the Law Reform (Contributory Negligence) Act 1945.

Smart may also be liable for negligence against Jorpid because he owed him a duty of care and he appears to have breached this duty which resulted in injury to Jorpid. If Smart is found to be negligent, the employer will also be held vicariousiy liable because Smart was acting in the course of his employment and not on a frolic of his own (i.e. he was employed to move bricks and was doing so when the injury was suffered by his act). However, the employer is entitled to raise the defence of contributory negligence and may also obtain an indemnity from Smart for any damages he may have to pay Jorpid **(Lister v. Romford Ice & Cold Storage Ltd 1957).**

(b) Further information required about the incident is (i) the status of Smart and Jorpid. If, for instance, Smart was supervisor, then by telling Jorpid not to wear the helmet, he would be in breach of his statutory duty under the relevant building legislation. The employer will be **vicariously** liable for it but can plead the defence of *volenti non fit injuria* **(I.C.I. v. Shatwell),** (ii) the degree of accessibility of the helmets. If, as in **Finch v. Telegraph Construction & Maintenance Co. Ltd (1949),** the workers did not know where the safety equipment was kept, the employer's liability will be great. If however, they were easily accessible, then the employer's liability will be greatly reduced since his criminal and civil duties are only to take **reasonable** care; (iii) the attitude of workers in the industry towards safety helmets. If it was the practice of workers not to use the helmets even though they were provided and reasonably accessible, the employer will not incur any **civil** liability to Smart although the safety helmet was not reasonably accessible **(McWilliams v. Arrol Ltd)**; (iv) the employer's knowledge of Jorpid's handicap. If the employer knew of Jorpid's deafness then he owes him higher duties than he would owe an ordinary employee. In **Paris v. Stepney Borough Council (1951)** the employer was held liable to a fitter with one eye whom he knew to be handicapped, when he failed to take special precaution to protect him, since the fitter ran a greater risk of blindness than an employee with sight in both eyes. However in **James v. Hepworth & Grandage (1968),** where the employers were not aware that one of their employees was illiterate so that their notices to use safety equipment were ineffective as far as he was concerned, the court found them not negligent in failing to make special provisions for him.

QUESTION 131 *A* is rendered unconscious in a collision caused by *B*'s negligence. *A* is taken to *C* hospital where Doctor *D* decides that an immediate operation is necessary to save *A*'s life. Meanwhile the electricians in the local power station go on strike. The operating theatre is without light and Doctor *D* operates by torchlight. Because of inadequate light the operation fails and *A* dies.

Consider the liability, if any, of (i) *B;* (ii) *C* hospital; (iii) Doctor *D;* and (iv) the electricians.

ANSWER Under the Law Reform (Miscellaneous Provisions) Act 1934 as amended by S.3 of the Administration of Justice Act 1982, on the death of a person all causes of action vested in him, except a claim for bereavement, will vest in his personal representatives for the benefit of his estate. Damages that might be recovered by the estate where death comes after injury would include medical expenses and funeral expenses, and damages for loss of earnings up to the date of death (but not for loss of income in respect of any period after death).

An action for negligence may be brought by *A*'s personal representatives against *B* for *A*'s injuries. *B* might try to avoid liability by arguing remoteness of damage for A's death. However, it is now established in law that damages suffered by the plaintiff may have two causes. If one of them is caused by the defendant's negligence then the defendant would be liable. Thus, if the defendant negligently injures the plaintiff causing him certain damages, as *B* did to *A* in this case, the fact that a subsequent tort by another tortfeasor produces the same or greater damage, will not exculpate the defendant from liability for the damage he has caused **(Baker v. Willoughby 1969).** Doctor *D* will have to justify that the emergency was present and that his grounds were reasonable for believing that an immediate operation was necessary. Otherwise, he may be liable in trespass to the person of *A*.

An action in negligence may also be brought against *C* hospital as it would seem that the hospital did not have an emergency lighting system. If the court holds that *B* was not liable for *A*'s death, then the *C* hospital will be held liable for it. If on the other hand *B* was liable for *A*'s death, the *C* hospital would escape liability even though it was negligent in not having an emergency lighting system. In **Performance Cars Ltd v. Abraham (1962)** the defendant negligently collided with the plaintiff's Rolls Royce and the damage required a respray of the wing costing £75. Underneath the wing, at the time of the accident, the Rolls Royce needed a respray as a result of a previous accident which the defendant did not cause. The Court of Appeal held that the defendant was not liable as he had injured a car which was already injured. If the electricians were members of a trade union and the strike took place during a trade dispute between the electricians and their employer, then they are protected from certain tortious liabilities (S.13 TUIRA 1974 as amended by the EAs 1980,1982). Otherwise the electricians would be liable, perhaps in conspiracy, but like *B,* they might argue remoteness of damage for *A*'s death.

QUESTION 132 (a) In what circumstances, if any, is an employee entitled to remuneration during absence from work owing to sickness.
(b) Advise Lorraine, an actress whether she has any action against her employer, Wess Theatre Co., for its failure to provide her with work.

ANSWER (a) Whether or not an employee is entitled to receive remuneration during absence from work because of sickness will depend to large extent on the contractual intention of the parties. This intention may be express or implied. Section 1(4) of the Employment Protection (Consolidation) Act 1978 requires the employer to provide the employee with written particulars of any terms relating to sick pay, not later than 13 weeks after the employment commences. Where sick pay is payable, the usual provision is that the employee will receive full pay less sickness benefit for a period, after which he will receive half-pay for a further period, after which he will receive no pay. On the other hand, the particulars may simply state that no sick pay is payable. Sometimes, collective agreements provide for sick pay in which case the only question that arises is whether the agreement is effectively incorporated in the employee's contract to enable him to enforce such provisions as a contractual right.

Where there is no contractual provision as to sick pay, a distinction is frequently made between hourly-paid blue collar workers and salaried 'staff'. With the former, there is a presumption that they are not entitled to claim wages, through illness, if they do not work **(Browning v. Crumlin Valley Collieries Ltd 1962).** With the latter, there is a presumption in favour of sick pay unless the contrary is shown. In **Orman v. Saville Sportswear Ltd (1960)** where a production manager was absent after a heart attack, the court implied a term that during his illness, he was entitled to his basic wage of £30 per week together with the production bonus of £20 which he could reasonably have expected to earn had he worked. In **Orman Case,** Pilcher J. said "Where the written terms of the contract of service are silent as to what is to happen in regard to the employee's rights to be paid whilst he is absent from work due to sickness, the employer remains liable to continue paying so long as the contract is not determined by prior notice, except where a condition to the contrary can properly be inferred from all the facts and evidence in the case." In **Petrie v. Macfisheries Ltd (1940),** employers had placed a notice on the wall at the workplace to the effect that payment of wages to employees during sickness would be paid as a matter of grace and not right. The Court of Appeal held that this manifested an intention against payment of wages during illness. And in **O'Grady v. Sapor Ltd (1940)** where a commissionaire claimed his wages during a period when he was off work due to illness, the court held that there was an intention against the payment of wages during sickness because he had never been paid wages on previous occasions while absent through sickness.

(b) It is not settled whether an employer is under any legal obligation at common law to provide his employee with work. Thus, in **Turner v. Sawdon (1901)** the court said "It is within the province of the employer to say that he will go on paying wages, but that he is under no obligation to provide work". However, in **Langston v. A.U.E.W. (1974),** Lord Denning M.R. said obiter that "it is arguable that in these days a man has, by reason of an implication in the contract, a right to work". And, in **Breach v. Epsylon Industries Ltd (1976)** the court said it depends on the circumstances of each case, whether such an obligation exists on the employer. Nevertheless, it is settled that in at least three instances, an employer is under an obligation to provide work namely, in contracts with commission or piece-workers where the consideration is an agreed rate plus an implied obligation to provide a reasonable amount of work **(Turner v. Goldsmith 1891);** in contracts with skilled workers where the consideration is a salary and an implied obligation to provide a reasonable amount of work to maintain skills **(Langston v. A.U.E.W.);** and in contracts such as with theatrical performers where the consideration is a salary together with the opportunity of becoming better known **(Yetton v. Eastwoods Froy Ltd 1967).**

Accordingly, Webb Theatre Co., is under a duty to provide Lorraine with work of a type suitable to her according to her contract and so it will be liable in damages for breach of this duty. If Lorraine was not paid her salary she has a further right to a guarantee payment under Sections 12–28 of the Employment Protection (Consolidation) Act 1978 and if she has at least two years continuous service, she may treat herself as being dismissed for redundancy and so claim redundancy payments.

QUESTION 133 (a) In what circumstances is there entitlement to a redundancy payment?
(b) A factory is badly damaged by fire and it is expected that it will be four months before production is resumed. The employees are laid off but are told that they will be re-employed later when the factory re-opens. Are they entitled to redundancy payments?
I.C.M.A. 1982

ANSWER (a) The State Scheme for redundancy compensation is now governed by Part VI of the Employment Protection (Consolidation) Act 1978. Under this scheme, an employee who is made redundant and who satisfies certain conditions is entitled to redundancy compensation from his employer who in turn is entitled to a rebate of a portion of the compensation from the Department of Employment.

The employee must have been in continuous employment with his employer for at least two years and working for a minimum of twenty hours a week (or five years if working for less than twenty hours but at least eight hours a week). This continuous period of employment must be with one employer but in certain cases periods of employment with two or more employers may be taken into account for this purpose, for example, inter-group transfers of employees between a parent company and its subsidiaries, and the transfer of a business or trade as a going concern to another employer. The employee must have been dismissed, laid-off or placed on short time because of the cessation or diminution of work in the place where he was employed. 'Laid-off' means that the employee is not given any paid work during a normal working week; 'placed on short time' means that the employee is given less than half his normal work per week.

An employee who satisfies the above conditions may still be disqualified from receiving redundancy payment if the employer could have terminated his contract because of his misconduct. Thus if, as in **Simmons v. Hoover Ltd (1977),** an employee while on strike is dismissed for redundancy, he is disqualified from receiving his redundancy entitlement. However, if he goes on strike after given notice of redundancy, or returns to work after the strike is over and is then made redundant, he does not lose his compensation. An employee, otherwise entitled to a redundancy payment, is also disentitled to receive that payment if he unreasonably refuses an offer of suitable alternative employment by his employer. In **Fuller v. Stephanie Bowman Ltd (1977),** a female employee lost her compensation when she refused suitable alternative employment provided by her employer because the new office was situated over a sex shop in Soho, London. An employee who accepts alternative employment may, within four weeks of taking it up, claim his redundancy payment if the new employment turns out to be unsuitable.

Certain categories of employees are not protected by the Redundancy Payments Provisions. These include employees over the retiring age **(Nothman v. London Borough of Barnet 1979);** registered dockworkers and Crown employees; and employees covered by a collectively-agreed scheme exempted by order (S.96 EPCA 1978).

(b) Employees who are laid-off for four consecutive weeks or for any six weeks in a thirteen week period may treat themselves as being dismissed if there is no reasonable prospect of normal work resuming shortly (EPCA 1978). In **Gemmell v. Darngavil Brickworks Ltd (1966)** where the circumstances were similar to the facts of the question, employees were held entitled to a redundancy payment, even though they were only dismissed for three months whilst the factory was closed for repairs and though their jobs were to be made available again for them as soon as the factory re-opened.

Before terminating their contracts for redundancy, the employees should exercise their rights to claim guarantee payments from their employer (SS.12–18 EPCA 1978). They will then receive a maximum of five days pay in any period of three months.

QUESTION 134 (a) An employee of your company claims that he is being underpaid. What sources would you examine to ascertain the validity of his claim.
(b) Your company decides that it would be less costly to close the factory for a third week's annual holiday and to maintain production by working an extra three-quarters of an hour on each Monday evening throughout the remainder of the year. Advise on the legal considerations affecting the means by which this proposed change in the terms of employment could be introduced.

I.C.M.A. 1977

ANSWER (a) It is necessary as a first step to ascertain whether the employee is complaining about his net pay or his gross pay. If it is the former, then are the deductions made by the employer lawful, and if so, has the employee been given an itemised pay slip setting out the deductions and the reasons for them? If the employee is a manual labourer rather than a 'white-collar worker', then the Wages Act 1986 makes it unlawful for the employer to make deductions from the employee's wages except for food on the premises if specially agreed, rent for dwelling, medical attendance, education for children, and for fines, damage to goods and material provided certain formalities are complied with. Certain other statutes also provide for deductions (for e.g., PAYE and National Insurance contributions). Even if the deductions are lawful, the employee is entitled to an itemised pay slip setting out the deductions and the reasons for them (Employment Protection Consolidation Act 1978); and failure to provide one may result in damages being awarded to the employee by an industrial tribunal.

If the employee is complaining that his gross pay is too low, then the written particulars provided by the employer will have to be looked at, since it will include the rate or scale of remuneration or the method of calculating it. Any existing collective agreement between the union and the employer must be examined to see whether it provided for increased pay, and if so how the agreement was incorporated in the employee's contract to enable him to enforce it as a contractual right. If the employee was doing similar work or work given equal value under a job evaluation exercise undertaken by the employer and was paid less than a colleague of the opposite sex, then a claim may by brought in a tribunal to enforce the equality clause under the Equal Pay Act 1970. If the employee had taken over the job from his predecessor who was a member of the opposite sex and who was paid more, then an action for 'equal pay for equal work' may also be brought under Article 119 of the Treaty of Rome **(Macarthys v. Smith 1980).** In certain industries, wages councils are set up under the Wages Councils Act 1979, with power to make orders requiring minimum standards of wages for employees in those industries. If our employee is covered by a Wages Council Order requiring higher wages then he has a statutorily-implied contractual right to claim the remuneration underpaid subject to the statutes of limitation.

(b) Should the employer go for a third week annual holiday without a revised contract of employment for its workers the latter may claim guarantee payments under S.12 of the Employment Protection (Consolidation) Act 1978. This section gives employees with four weeks continuous service a right to a guaranteed day's pay (subject to a maximum limit) when they are not provided with work and if the failure to provide such work is not due to a trade dispute in the industry. This guarantee is paid for a maximum of five days in any period of three months.

The proposal to require the workers to work an extra three-quarters of an hour on each Monday evening also cannot be achieved without their consent. If the employer should attempt to enforce this proposal unilaterally, this will amount to a breach of contract and may amount to constructive dismissal with the result that the employer may be liable for unfair dismissal. Workers' contracts should therefore be re-negotiated and if there was a union recognised by the employer this could be achieved by collective agreement.

QUESTION 135 Your employer owns and operates a chain of garages. Advise him on the legal position with regard to the actions of the following employees:
(a) Albert, a mechanic, is carrying out repairs for payment in his spare time.

(b) Bernard, a supervisor, has invented a device that will reduce the cost of servicing cars and offers to sell it to his employer.

(c) Charles, a salesman, has taken a present from a customer who felt that he had been given a good price for his old car as part exchange for a new car.

(d) Doris, a secretary, asks for a reference for a new job for which she is applying.

I.C.M.A. 1981

ANSWER (a) An employee is under a duty of fidelity towards his employer. This duty requires the employee not only to provide faithful service to his employer but also to work only for the employer in the employer's time. In the absence of express agreement, the employee may accept part-time work in his spare-time. Whether the employee can go so far as to compete with his employer is another matter. In **Hivac Ltd v. Park Royal Scientific Instruments Ltd (1946)** Lord Greene M.R. said "It would be deplorable if it were laid down that a workman could, consistently with his duty to his employer, knowingly, deliberately and secretly set himself to do in his spare-time something which would inflict great harm on his employer's business." In **Hivac Ltd,** the employer whose skilled employees worked for him in the production of midget valves for hearing aids, was able to obtain an injunction preventing a rival employer from continuing to employ the said employees in their spare-time because of the possibility that confidential information might be disclosed to the rival employer. Accordingly, Albert may carry on his spare-time activities and this type of 'moonlighting' may not be in breach of duty of fidelity so long as it is disclosed to the employer and so long as Albert is not soliciting his employer's customers to take their custom to him. **(Wessex Dairies Ltd v. Smith 1935).**

(b) Employees employed to carry out research often have a term included in their contract that the ownership of inventions, patents and copyrights arising out of such research will vest in the employer. There is also a general common law rule based on the employee's duty of fidelity, that if the employee made the invention in connection with the proper fulfilment of his contractual obligations, he will not be permitted to exploit the invention for his own benefit **(British Syphon Co. Ltd v. Homewood 1956).** In **Homewood Case,** an employee was employed as a technical adviser. In his spare-time, he invented and patented a new device connected with syphons. Nevertheless, because of his position as

technical adviser the court held that the invention belonged to
the employer. The Patents Act 1977 Section 39 states that the
benefit of an invention belongs to the employer if the invention
was made in the course of duties, specially assigned to the
employee and the circumstances were such that the invention
might reasonably be expected to result from the carrying out of
his duties or if the invention was made in the course of the
employee's duties and at the time of making the invention the
employee had a special obligation to further the interests of the
employer's undertaking by reason of his duties and the particular
responsibilities arising from those duties.

From what has been said above, Bernard will have to assign
the invention to his employer if it was made at work, as it belongs
to the employer. However, he may be able to obtain compensation from the employer if he can satisfy the court, among other
things, that the invention is of 'outstanding benefit' to the
employer (Section 40 Patents Act 1977). If the invention was
made by Bernard outside work, then because he is only a
supervisor rather than technical adviser or research worker, the
invention belongs to him and he can sell it to his employer.

(c) An employee is like an agent in that he is in a position of trust
towards his employer. Accordingly, he must account to his
employer for all property received on behalf of him, for bribes
and for secret profits derived from the position which he holds
(Reading v. Att-Gen 1951). If Charles received the present before
the part-exchange, it might well be considered as a bribe in which
case the employer can rescind the transaction with the customer
and recover the bribe from either Charles or the customer.
Otherwise, it is only a secret profit in which case it belongs to the
employer.

(d) An employer is under no legal obligation to provide a
reference for his employees. So a reference for Doris is at the
discretion of the employer. If one is given and it turns out to be a
bad reference the employer cannot incur civil liability, if what
was said was true, either in the law of defamation or deceit. Even
if the reference contains untrue statements the employer may
still escape civil liability if he shows that the statements were
made in discharge of a moral obligation (as it would be if made to
a prospective employer) and without malice (i.e. improper
motive). The defence of qualified privilege will be available to
the employer.

QUESTION 136 The employees in the following circumstances are all dismissed. Explain whether or not a claim for unfair dismissal is likely to succeed:

(a) Arthur, where a 'closed shop' operates refuses to join a trade union.

(b) Brenda has become pregnant.

(c) Charles, a van driver, has been disqualified from driving for three months.

(d) David promises when he was engaged that he would make no claim in the future for unfair dismissal.

I.C.M.A. 1980

ANSWER (a) Under section 58 of the Employment Protection (Consolidation) Act 1978 as amended by Section 3 Employment Act 1982 a dismissal for refusal to join a trade union where a closed shop exists is automatically unfair unless the employer can prove that it was the practice at the workplace, in accordance with a union membership agreement, for employees of the same class as the dismissed employee to belong to a named trade union, the employee who was dismissed refused to join that union and that the union membership agreement had been approved by ballot by the vote of at least 80 per cent of those entitled to vote not more than five years before the closed shop sacking took place.

Arthur's claim in an industrial tribunal for unfair dismissal will succeed even if the employer comes within the provisions of section 58, so long as Arthur can show that he genuinely objected on grounds of conscience or other deeply held personal convictions to join the union; or that he was employed by the employer before the union membership agreement came into force and had not since joined the union.

The Employment Act 1982 allows the union to be joined as co-defendant with the employer and for it to be liable in damages if it had put pressure on the employer to dismiss unfairly. The Act also gives Arthur a right to ask the industrial tribunal for an interim order that his employment with his employer should continue until the outcome of the hearing.

(b) Under Section 60 E.P.C.A. 1978 dismissal of a woman simply because she is pregnant is automatically unfair unless the employer shows that the pregnancy made her incapable of doing the work adequately and that he had no suitable light duties for her to perform.

In order to bring an action for unfair dismissal, Brenda must have been in continuous employment with her employer for at least two years. If Brenda is fairly dismissed, she still retains her right to maternity pay. If unfairly dismissed for pregnancy, she may include her loss of maternity pay in her claim for compensation.

(c) Assuming that Charles has the necessary service to bring an action for unfair dismissal, his claim will not succeed if the employer shows that the dismissal was for lack of qualification and he had acted reasonably in dismissing him. It might well be held reasonable to dismiss Charles here, even though disqualification was only for three months.

(d) If David has a fixed term contract for at least two years, the E.P.C.A. 1978 allows him to agree in writing that he will not be entitled to compensation if he should be dismissed solely because the employer refuses to renew his contract when the term expires. In all others cases, any agreement to contract out of his rights will be void and the tribunal will hear a claim on merits and so long as it is brought within three months after dismissal.

QUESTION 137 It is sometimes said that trade unions are above the law because they are given legal immunities. Discuss this proposition in the light of current legislation and recent judicial decisions.

ANSWER At common law, a trade union and its members who take part in industrial action run the risk of incurring various tortious liability. For example, by calling a strike the tort of inducement to break a contract is committed. So in **Lumley v. Gye (1853),** where a person persuaded a dramatic singer to depart in breach of her contract the court held that he was liable for this tort. Similarly, if the union and its members agree to go on strike with a view to cause a loss or to injure another, they will be liable in conspiracy. 'Conspiracy' is based on an agreement by two or more persons to do a lawful act by unlawful means or to do an unlawful act, and it may be civil or criminal. In **Hutchinson v. Aitchison (1970)** workers who had pursued a vendetta against another worker were held liable for conspiracy when they procured his dismissal. Again, a mere threat to go on strike may result in the tort of intimidation. Thus in **Rookes v. Barnard (1964),** where shop stewards threatened to go on strike at Heathrow Airport, unless the Airport Authority dismissed its non-union workers, it was held that they were liable in damages to the employees concerned.

Section 13 of the Trade Union and Labour Relations Act 1974 gave total immunity to trade unions for personal tortious liability and limited immunity for the vicarious liability of its members for torts committed outside a trade dispute. Trade union members were also given statutory immunity for certain torts committed in the contemplation or in furtherance of a trade dispute. For these reasons it was said that trade unions were above the law.

The Employment Acts 1980 and 1982 have now radically altered this immunity. Section 15 of the 1982 Act makes a union liable in tort unless it was acting in the course of a trade dispute when the tort was committed. ' Trade dispute' covers differences between workers and their employer relating mainly to terms of employment, the allocation of work between workers, discipline, membership of a trade union and facilities for trade union officials including negotiating machinery. The immunity extends to trade disputes outside the U.K. only if their outcome would affect the working conditions of British workers. In **Express Newspapers Ltd v. Keys (1980),** the court held that a strike aimed at the Government's economic policies was not a trade dispute. However, where the strike involves two disputes, one a trade dispute, the immunity will still be given **(Duport Steels Ltd v. Sirs 1980).** Whether the union is liable for torts committed outside a trade dispute will depend on whether the act had been authorised or endorsed by a responsible person (e.g. the union president, secretary or an employed official). Acts of a responsible person cannot be repudiated by the union unless that person was prevented by the union rules from authorising or endorsing such acts. Except in the case of negligence, nuisance or breach of statutory duty resulting in personal injury to any person or breach of duty in relation to the use of property, the amount of damages in tort recoverable from the union is limited to the union's size. Moreover, the union's benefit and political funds are protected against the enforcement of judgements arising out of tortious liability.

Under the Employment Act 1980, statutory immunity available to trade union members no longer extends to secondary action taken by them i.e. actions against employers not directly involved in the dispute (S.17). From what has been said above, it can be seen that it is no longer accurate to say that trade unions are above the law.

QUESTION 138 Explain the use of (a) conciliation, (b) arbitration, and (c) mediation, as methods of settling industrial disputes. What statutory machinery is made available for these purposes?

ANSWER (a) 'Conciliation' is the reference of an industrial dispute to a neutral intermediary called a 'conciliator' to help the parties to reach a mutually acceptable solution to their problem. (b) Arbitration is the reference of an industrial dispute by both parties to a neutral intermediary called 'arbitrator' who will then give a decision (an award) on the matter. The decision has no legal force as such on the parties but is morally binding on them since they had initially agreed to let the arbitrator decide the matter. (c) Mediation is the hybrid of the two. Like conciliation, the mediator attempts to conciliate the difference between the parties in dispute, but it differs in that the mediator may himself make proposals which the parties may accept, reject or treat as a basis for further discussions. Mediation is only possible if both parties agree to it and to this extent it is similar to arbitration; however the terms of reference for mediation are in practice less rigid than those used for arbitration.

The statutory machinery available for conciliation and arbitration is now vested in the Advisory, Conciliation and Arbitration Service (ACAS). Under the Employment Protection Act 1975 which established this Service on a non-statutory basis, ACAS is charged with the general duty of providing the improvement of industrial relations, and in particular, of encouraging and extending collective bargaining, and where necessary reforming collective bargaining machinery. The conciliation function of ACAS may be exercised on request by one party to the dispute but ACAS must have regard to the desirability of encouraging the use of agreed procedure with the industry. Section 3 gives ACAS the power to refer a dispute to arbitration but only if all parties to the dispute agree to this, and only after all available domestic machinery and conciliation have been used up. Reference by ACAS may be made to a single arbitrator, or board of arbitrators, or to the Central Arbitration Committee (a permanent arbitration body maintained at the State's expense) depending on the gravity of the dispute.

To enable ACAS to carry out its general function, section 5 empowers it to hold investigation on matters relating to industrial relations and to provide advice on a wide range of advice set out in section 4 of the Act.

Chapter 12
Property

QUESTION 139 Compare the remedies of a legal mortgagee of land with those of an equitable mortgagee.

I.B. 1964

ANSWER Since a legal mortgagee has a legal estate in the mortgaged land, he has rights against the land itself apart from his personal right of action against the mortgagor.

Hence, he has a power to sell the property (S.101 L.P.A. 1925). The power of sale is only exercisable if (a) the mortgagor has defaulted in the payment of the money and a default notice is served on him and he has failed to comply with it within three months of its service; or (b) some interest is in arrears and unpaid for two months after becoming due; or (c) a breach other than non-payment is committed by the mortgagor.

The mortgagee may appoint a receiver to receive any income of the mortgaged land. This power arises when the mortgagee becomes entitled to exercise his power of sale.

The mortgagee may foreclose the property. This remedy arises when the mortgagor loses his right to redeem the mortgage; but it can only be exercised by consent of the Court.

The mortgagee may also enter into possession of the mortgaged land. However, if he does so certain duties are imposed on him e.g. he must collect rent at his own expense.

Finally the legal mortgagee may sue the mortgagor on the personal covenant to repay the loan.

As an equitable mortgagee has no legal estate, his position is much weaker than that of a legal mortgagee. He is not entitled to enter into possession of the mortgaged land unless such power is expressly reserved by the mortgage. Nor is he entitled to sell the mortgaged property or to appoint a receiver unless the equitable mortgage was under seal. Moreover he cannot convey a legal title to a purchaser unless he takes recourse to the Court.

An equitable mortgagee may, of course, sue the mortgagor for payment of the principal and interest.

QUESTION 140 What registration, if any, should (a) a legal mortgagee, and (b) an equitable mortgagee make in order to protect the mortgage in the case of (i) registered land, (ii) unregistered land.

I.B. 1978

ANSWER A legal mortgagee of registered land may take one of two forms – either by the creation of a charge on the land or by an absolute conveyance, with a proviso for reconveyance on payment of the principal with interest at the expiration of (usually) six months. The former is much more popular because of its simplicity and is effected by deed. The chargee is registered as the proprietor of the charge, and a charge certificate is then issued to him, the land certificate being deposited at the registry until the charge is cancelled. The registered charge takes effect as a charge by way of legal mortgage and its priority is determined by the date of registration. Only legal estates can be registered in this way and subsequent legal mortgages are similarly treated. The latter is rarely used for unless a mortgage of both registered and unregistered land is created, it has no advantage over the registered charge. A legal mortgagee, in this last case, is protected by a Mortgage Caution.

An equitable mortgage of registered land is created by depositing with the mortgagee the land or charge certificate. The deposit of such a certificate creates a lien which takes effect subject to overriding interests, registered interests and any entries then on the register. This lien is similar to a mortgage by deposit of title deed of unregistered land. In order to protect his mortgage, the equitable mortgagee should give written notice of his equitable mortgage of the legal estate of registered land to the Registrar who will enter on the Charges Register a notice which will operate as a caution. Priority of mortgages of equitable interests in registered land is obtained by lodging a priority inhibition (used in the case of absolute assignment) or a priority caution (in other cases) with the Registrar. The order of priority will be determined by the order in which these inhibitions and cautions are lodged.

A legal or equitable mortgage of unregistered land, accompanied by the deposit of the title deeds is incapable of registration. If it is not accompanied by title deeds it must be registered at the Land Charges Registry as a puisne mortgage (if legal) or as a general equitable charge (if equitable). Where a prospective mortgagee intends to register a charge at least fifteen days before the registration is to take effect, he must send in a Priority Notice to the Land Charges Registrar.

QUESTION 141 (a) Define or describe 'ownership' and 'possession'.

(b) Albert has contracted to sell his house to Douglas. Before the date fixed for the completion of the purchase, Albert decides to remove a picture hanging in the library. It is attached to the wall by plugs and screws. He also proposes to take away the conservatory which is attached to the side of the house and is built of bricks, with a metal framework and walls and roof made of toughened glass.

Is Albert entitled to remove these two items?

I.B. 1969

ANSWER (a) Ownership is the greatest right which a person can exercise over property. It is the legal right of a person to the use, enjoyment and disposition of any form of property or benefits arising from it. It is essentially a legal concept and its existence is normally determined by evidence of possession although possession is not decisive to determine ownership.

Ownership may be acquired in the following ways:-

(i) originally – where the property was not formerly owned, or the previous owner has abandoned it; or

(ii) by succession – on the death of the previous owner, under his will or under the rules of intestate succession; or

(iii) derivatively – either with the consent of the previous owner by gift or sale or by operation of law e.g. by bankruptcy or by adverse possession.

Possession is made up of two elements:– (i) physical control over the property; and (ii) the power to exclude others from it. There are two types of possession – possession in fact and possession in law. The former is equivalent to custody or detention. The latter requires a manifested intention not merely to exclude the world at large from interfering with the property but to do so on one's own account and in one's own name.

(b) Where a person buys land he is entitled not only to the land but also to fixtures. Fixtures are chattels which are so annexed to land or to a building on land that they lose their characteristics as chattels and becomes part of the land.

Whether a chattel has become a fixture is a question for the Court to decide. In general two matters must be satisfied before a chattel can become a fixture. It must actually be annexed to the land i.e. fastened or connected with the land or building; and the object of annexation must be for the convenient use of the land or building rather than for the chattel itself. In **Leigh v. Taylor (1902)** the owner of some valuable tapestry, laid strips of wood over the drawing room paper and fixed them to the walls, with two-inch nails. Canvas was stretched over these strips, and the tapestry was fastened by tacks to the strips. It was held that the tapestry had not become a fixture because, as Vaughan Williams LJ explained, 'everything which was done here can be accounted for as being absolutely necessary for the enjoyment of the tapestry'.

Albert is thus entitled to remove the picture but not the conservatory as the latter would appear to be a fixture.

QUESTION 142 Explain the protection afforded by the law of copyright. What remedies are available to a copyright owner in respect of an infringement of copyright ?

I.C.S.A. 1987

ANSWER Copyright is the right to protect the independent skill, labour and effort used by a person in producing certain work and to prevent others from copying or exploiting that work. Only work is protected, not ideas; and the work must be of a type covered by the Copyright, Designs and Patents Act 1988. Copyright protection is automatic. It takes effect as soon as the copyright work is created; there is no need for it to be published or to be registered. Protection lasts for 50 years from the owner's death.

The 1988 Act recognises the following types of works which are capable of having copyright protection: **authors' works** namely, literary, dramatic, musical and artistic works; **mechanical works** namely, sound recordings, films, broadcasts and cable programmes; and the typographical arrangement of published editions (e.g., the layout of the printed page containing the literary, dramatic or musical work). 'Literary work' is any work other than a dramatic or musical work, which is written, spoken or sung; and it must be recorded in print (e.g., in writing or on tape). 'Musical work' is music or tune and excludes the words accompanying the music; it must also be recorded in print.

Once work is entitled to copyright protection the owner of the copyright is entitled to prevent others from doing certain restricted acts and acts of secondary infringement. Restricted acts include copying the work, issuing copies to the public, broadcasting the work or including it in a cable programme service, and adapting the work. Acts of secondary infringement relate to dealings in infringed **copies** of the original work and include importing in the UK infringed copies (other than for private use), possessing in the course of a business or offering for sale or hire infringed copies or having in the course of business a device for making such copies.

There are various civil remedies available to the owner of a copyright for an infringement of copyright. He is entitled to monetary remedies such as damages where the infringement was not innocent (i.e., the defendant was aware or ought to have known that the work was copyright) or an account of profits. Additionally, he may ask for an injunction to prevent further infringements, and an order for the delivery up to him infringing copies or for their destruction. An order for the delivering up of infringing copies can only be made if the copyright owner made an application for such an order within six years from the date in which the infringing copy was made.

QUESTION 143 'Although the law provides protection for inventions by grant of patent, an inventor may still find that his invention is not fully protected."

Discuss.

ANSWER A patent is an exclusive right given by the State to a proprietor to exploit an invention and to stop others from doing so. This right lasts for 20 years. Patent protection is not automatic; it must be applied for by registering the invention. The main statute governing patents is the Patent Act 1977.

An invention can be registered under the 1977 Act only if it is new, involves an inventive step and is capable of industrial application. An invention is 'new' if it has never been disclosed to the public anywhere in the world. It 'involves an inventive step' if it is not obvious to any person skilled in that particular field, having regard to what that person is taken to know about the field. It is 'capable of industrial application' if it can be used in any kind of industry including agriculture.

Certain inventions are not patentable. They include discoveries, scientific theories or mathematical methods, and literary, dramatic and other work protected by copyright.

To obtain registration the specifications of the invention must be set out clearly in the claim. Thus, if a non-essential feature of the invention is included in the claim as part of the specifications there is no infringement if that feature is used by others. Also if an essential feature of the claim is missing or is vague the patent may be successfully challenged in court, resulting in it being revoked.

From the end of the fourth year beginning with the date of application, the patent must be renewed annually, so there is no infringement if the patentee fails to renew it and the patent is used during this period. In addition, there is no infringement if the unauthorised use of the invention is done for a private and non-commercial purpose or for experimental purpose, or in the preparation of a medicine for an individual in accordance with a doctor's prescription.

QUESTION 144 In relation to intellectual property law, discuss some of the main problems associated with protecting interests in any two of the following:
(a) fashion garments;
(b) spare parts, for example in the automotive industry;
(c) books and similar products which are liable to be photocopied.

I.C.S.A. 1989

ANSWER (a) Protection is necessary for the design of the garments. Design is the description of the appearance of a product and it may be protected by design right, copyright and rights in registered design. The main problem, therefore, is to decide which legal mechanism provides the necessary protection.

A new form of protection for designs, called 'design right' was introduced by the Copyright, Designs and Patents Act 1988. Design right applies to designs of three-dimensional features of products, and possibly to two dimensional features. However, surface decorations such as fabric patterns are expressly excluded from design right protection. Assuming that the particular design is covered by design right it will only be protected if the design is original, i.e., if it is not common place in the design field in question). There is no infringement of the design unless it is used for a commercial purpose. Design right protects the design for a period of 15 years commencing from the date of creation of the design.

The Copyright, Designs and Patents Act 1988 expressly excludes designs from copyright protection apart from surface decoration included as part of a design and where a design is for something which in itself is an artistic work (e.g., a sculpture). Thus, in the case of the fashion garments, dress making patterns and the like may be protected by copyright on the ground that they are artistic work. Design protected by copyright lasts for 25 years.

(b) The interest in spare parts can best be protected by relying on their design either through design right protection under the Copyright, Designs and Patents Act 1988 or rights in registered design under the Registered Designs Act 1949. The main problem with relying on design right protection is that while it covers designs of any aspect of the shape or configuration (whether internal or external) of the whole or part of an article other than surface decoration, it excludes features of design which enable an article to fit with another article so that either can perform a function and features which enable an article to form an integral part of another article. Thus, features of design of spare parts such as pipe fittings and valve guides for engines in the automotive industry are not protected by design right.

The Registered Designs Act 1949 as amended provides protection of designs of specific products or articles where the designs appeal to the eye and have never been published before in the UK. Both two and three dimensional features of articles are covered by the Act; but two dimensional features of articles entitled to copyright protection are not registrable. 'Article' includes part of an article where that part is made and sold separately, so the designs of spare parts are registrable.

The main problem with relying on registered design right protection is that if the appearance of a design is not material in a person's decision to buy or use it then the design cannot be registered. Thus, motor car exhaust systems and the like are not registrable. Registered design rights are protected only for a period of 5 years, but this period may be extended on application for four more periods of five years.

(c) To obtain copyright protection work must be original (i.e., it must originate from the author and not extracted from the skill and effort of others) and must be copied. Therefore if two persons use their own resources to create the same work independently there is no infringement. Also, a substantial part of the work must be copied, this depending on the quantity and quality of the work copied.

The Copyright, Designs and Patents Act provides various defences for breach of copyright. There is the defence of fair dealing such as where the copying was for private use or study or incidental inclusion as quotes for other work. Educational establishments are also permitted to make limited copies for educational use; so too are librarians.

QUESTION 145 Explain the scope of the tort of passing off as a method of protecting trade or professional reputation and goodwill.

I.C.S.A. 1990

ANSWER Passing-off is the unauthorised use of a mark (including name and get up) which is calculated to deceive and mislead the public into believing that goods or services offered for sale belong to the owner of the mark. The law seeks to discourage such unfair trade practices by allowing the owner of the mark to bring an action for damages and an injunction against the wrongdoer. In **Reckitt and Colman Products Ltd v. Borden Inc. (1990),** Lord Oliver described the law of passing off as follows: "no man can pass off his goods as those of another".

For a passing off action to succeed the plaintiff must satisfy three conditions. First, he must establish that because of the reputation attached to his goods or services there is a goodwill attached to the mark he uses in connection with those goods or services. Second, the defendant is representing to the public that the goods or services he (the defendant) is offering to sell belong to the plaintiff. Third, the representation has resulted or is likely to result in the plaintiff suffering damages.

In the **Borden** case, Borden attempted to sell lemon juice in lemon shaped containers, such get up being similar to the lemon shaped yellow plastic squeeze container which Colman had been using for years to sell its own lemon juice. The court granted an injunction to Colman since the lemon shaped containers had been associated in the minds of the purchasing public with the Colman's product and that by using a similar shaped container Borden was representing falsely that its own product was connected with Colman.

The court will allow injunctive proceedings only if the defendant is carrying on the same kind of trade as the plaintiff (as in **Bollinger v. Costa Brava Wine Co. 1960** where an injunction was granted to prevent a sparkling Spanish wine from being sold as 'Spanish Champagne' since 'champagne' was always conceived in the public mind to be produced in the Champagne region of France) or if the defendant is likely to attract business because the public will believe that he is in some way connected with the plaintiff (as in **Annabel's Berkley Square Ltd v. Shock 1972** where an injunction was given to prevent the defendant from starting an escort agency under 'Annebel's Escort Agency' since there was a sufficient likelihood that prospective members of the exclusive Annabel's club in Mayfair would assume that the two were connected).

The court will not restrain a defendant from carrying on a trade in his own name even if confusion is caused between his business and that of the plaintiff with the same name. Nor will the court intervene if the name used by the defendant is a descriptive term (i.e., of common use) and is not distinctive of the plaintiff's goods or services.

The law of passing off is confined to situations where a person is involved in a trading or commercial activity. Thus in **Kean v. McGivan (1982)** a Mr. Kean who had founded a small political party under the name 'Social Democratic Party' failed to obtain an injunction against Roy Jenkins, Shirley Williams and others from using that name for their own political party.

Table of Cases

Table of Cases

Table of Cases

Index